Sounding American

THE OXFORD MUSIC / MEDIA SERIES

Daniel Goldmark, Series Editor

oxford
music/media series

SOUNDING AMERICAN

Hollywood, Opera, and Jazz

Jennifer Fleeger

OXFORD
UNIVERSITY PRESS

Oxford University Press is a department of the University of Oxford.
It furthers the University's objective of excellence in research, scholarship,
and education by publishing worldwide.

Oxford   New York
Auckland   Cape Town   Dar es Salaam   Hong Kong   Karachi
Kuala Lumpur   Madrid   Melbourne   Mexico City   Nairobi
New Delhi   Shanghai   Taipei   Toronto

With offices in
Argentina   Austria   Brazil   Chile   Czech Republic   France   Greece
Guatemala   Hungary   Italy   Japan   Poland   Portugal   Singapore
South Korea   Switzerland   Thailand   Turkey   Ukraine   Vietnam

Published in the United States of America by
Oxford University Press
198 Madison Avenue, New York, NY 10016

Library of Congress Cataloging-in-Publication Data
Fleeger, Jennifer
Sounding American : Hollywood, opera, and jazz / Jennifer Fleeger.
pages ; cm
Includes bibliographical references and index.
ISBN 978-0-19-936648-4 (hardcover : alk. paper) — ISBN 978-0-19-936649-1
(pbk. : alk. paper)   1. Motion pictures and opera.   2. Opera in motion pictures.
3. Jazz in motion pictures.   4. Musical films – History and criticism.   I. Title.
PN1995.9.O64 F54 2014
791.43/6578—dc23
2013038313

9 8 7 6 5 4 3 2 1
Printed in the United States of America
on acid-free paper

To Hugo

CONTENTS

ACKNOWLEDGMENTS

This book has benefited from the conversation and guidance of many wonderful colleagues, teachers, and friends. At the University of Iowa, I was grateful for the mentorship, scholarship, and dedication of Rick Altman, Corey Creekmur, Rosalind Galt, Judith Pascoe, John Durham Peters, Lauren Rabinovitz, and Louis-Georges Schwartz. My writing crew provided continuous encouragement, helpful commentary, and delicious muffins: Gina Giotta, Kevin McDonald, Andrew Ritchey, Marianna Ritchey, Peter Schaefer, Margaret Schwartz, and Erica Stein. Ofer Eliaz has always been kind enough to read my writing and smart enough to know how to fix it. My colleagues at the Catholic University of America—Niki Akhavan, Jenny Horne, Steve McKenna, Abby Moser, Alex Russo, Anastasia Saverino, and Maura Ugarte—have all influenced my thinking and put up with my chatting. I am glad for the time I spent with all of them and for the friendships we share. I am also thankful for the support of Ursinus College and the scholars who have recently welcomed me into their community. This place has already been an inspiration. In addition, I have had many excellent discussions about pieces of this book with people at Music and the Moving Image and the Society for Cinema and Media Studies annual conferences, experiences that always invigorate my work and lift my spirits.

I am also incredibly thankful for the archives that housed much of the material I was able to see and hear for this project. The Motion Picture, Broadcasting, and Recorded Sound Division at the Library of Congress in Washington, DC, and the UCLA Film and Television Archive in Los Angeles allowed me to see prints of films that were unavailable elsewhere. The USC Warner Bros. Archives at the School of Cinema-Television, University of Southern California in Los Angeles, tolerated my peskiness for weeks as I combed through contracts, scores, photographs, and scripts. Finally, the Wisconsin Center for Film and Theater Research at the Wisconsin Historical Society in Madison provided prints of many of the opera shorts and scripts and documents related to other short films that were essential to completing this book. Trips to these archives were made possible by a Presidential Graduate Fellowship and a Robert Olney Sound Research Scholarship, both awarded by the University of Iowa.

At Oxford University Press, I have been lucky enough to work with the enthusiastic, brilliant, and extremely patient Norm Hirschy and the equally incredible Lisbeth Redfield. I am grateful to Dan Goldmark for his passion about film music and expert leadership of the Music/Media series. I also want to thank James Buhler, Krin Gabbard, and the anonymous readers selected by the press for their helpful and insightful comments on drafts of this manuscript. Their work helped to make this a much better project.

My husband, Joe, and my children, Irene and Hugo, are forever close to my heart.

Portions of Chapters 1 and 3 appeared under the title "How to Say Things with Songs: Al Jolson, Vitaphone Technology, and the Rhetoric of Warner Bros. in 1929," *Quarterly Review of Film and Video* vol. 27, no. 1 (2010): 27–43.

Sounding American

Introduction

When radio pioneer Lee De Forest released his short film *Opera Versus Jazz* in 1923, he tapped into the musical, technological, and cinematic currents that would come to define American film sound in the decade that followed. Ironically, his film didn't offer a very pleasant demonstration of either genre. The short's two stars, a husband-and-wife team of vaudevillians named Eva Puck and Sam White, perform a deliberately poor rendition of several Italian arias jazzed up with innuendo. The whole act culminates in a regrettable duet intended to show that music, like marriage, is built on compromise. As trite as it may seem, this aphorism proved to be the conversion era's guiding principle. In the 1920s, directors and executives negotiated differing points of view on the appropriate technical equipment, vocal quality, sonic perspective, and spoken dialect that ought to prevail on Hollywood soundtracks. Yet it was the style of the music that teemed with national significance and provoked the most heated debates beyond the California shores.

Opera Versus Jazz was one of a series of De Forest shorts made to demonstrate the advantages of sound technology to exhibitors and the public. Inventors like De Forest knew that music was the key to selling the American film industry on sound, just as it had been essential to the success of the phonograph and would be vital to the promotion of the radio. Not only would canned music reduce labor costs and increase sound quality for most film exhibitors, it would also bolster the studios' campaign for a standard performance practice. Thus De Forest was eager to use musical stars of the highest caliber. However, as Puck and White's act shows, he was fond of taking them down a peg as well. De Forest's films were to be artistic statements with mass appeal, a combination of attributes that would eventually become the key to promoting sound technology to the American public. Yet in 1923, few were ready to take the financial risk required to install De Forest's synchronous sound system. De Forest may not have standardized synchronous sound in 1923, but his musical selections were prophetic. Mixing styles and genres, the sound film seemed to quiver with the opportunity to say something new, even as it lacked a coherent set of aesthetic principles. As genres with very different compositional and performance styles, opera and jazz were readily incorporated into conversion-era rhetoric because they were already at the core of a national conversation about the uncertain future of American music.

In the pages of music journals and the popular press, composers, critics, journalists, and enthusiasts argued over what kind of music ought to be called "American." Prior to the 1920s, this discussion had largely been framed as a conflict between an older generation of American musicians who saw themselves as upholders of Puritan values and a new group of composers who suggested that American music might be better defined by blending multiple musical traditions.[1] Members of the latter group proposed the introduction of the jazz-opera, a new and definitively American musical style that would be epic in scope but jazz in tone. Though they may have been unclear about exactly what form it would take, they were adamant that the jazz-opera be performed in the nation's best opera venues and written by its most qualified composers. In spite of its nod toward a range of multicultural sources, the jazz-opera was conceived as an elite work that would not only provide the United States with its own tradition of concert music but also represent the nation to the world.

As anyone who has been to the opera recently can attest, this dream never came to fruition—at least, not in the way the composers of the 1920s imagined it would. The jazz-opera ran into significant obstacles before it could be established as a genre of its own. Not only was there little consensus on what jazz was or what it meant to Americans of different racial and ethnic backgrounds, there was also the problem of opera's European origins, questions over who could perform the music and in what context, and concerns over how to blend these diverse forms. Moreover, the dissonance between a segregated nation and an integrated music may have prohibited many listeners from taking the American jazz-opera seriously. In light of these difficulties, it isn't a surprise that most of the jazz-operas that were staged failed miserably. George Gershwin's one-act *Blue Monday* met with a general sense of disapproval, William Franke Harling's *Deep River* closed on Broadway quickly, and Duke Ellington's *Queenie Pie* was never professionally performed during his lifetime. However, the jazz-opera did find a home of sorts in the sound films of the conversion era. The instability of both the films themselves and the industry that produced them made Hollywood a particularly welcome place to experiment with a new American voice. Film directors and studio executives were seeking to record music that would distinguish the sound film from its silent predecessor. Jazz provided the sense of improvisation that recorded sound was lacking, while opera gave the new films the impression of coherence and complexity. Together, they defined the aural aesthetics of the emerging Hollywood film score, which its creators announced would be not only culturally significant but also as inventive as the sound technologies that allowed it to be heard. Thus the jazz-opera, an unrealized form on the stage, became an integral part of the American film soundtrack.

When the conversion to sound began in full force with the premiere of Warner Bros.' Vitaphone sound-on-disc system in 1926, it was evident how keen De Forest's instinct had been. The first Vitaphone feature, *Don Juan*, integrated opera and jazz modes into a score played by the New York Philharmonic. The shorts that preceded this and the feature films that followed in subsequent months were full of opera and jazz numbers. Moreover, cue sheets for the still-extant silent film accompaniments of the era mixed operatic and jazz references, short films produced by all the majors prominently featured singers of both genres, and feature film directors looked for ways to incorporate opera and jazz stages into their narratives. The combination of opera and jazz on the conversion-era soundtrack made good sense, not only because of some vague utopian musical vision shared by composers and filmmakers but for economic and artistic reasons as well. From a business standpoint, much of this music was either in the public domain or could be purchased cheaply, required little by way of reorchestration, and drew attention to the sound technologies the studios were trying to sell.[2] The melodies' familiarity lessened the uncanny characteristic of synchronous sound, and the musicians hired to perform them were first-rate. De Forest's focus on musical performances proved to be the approach that Warners would later take, investing in opera and jazz and setting the tone for fierce competition between sound systems that would dominate the conversion era.

Contrary to the popular myth that Warner Bros. released the *Jazz Singer* and immediately sent the other studios scrambling to create "talkies" for themselves, the conversion to sound was a relatively slow process that initially had little to do with the spoken word. Indeed, film history shows that the obsolescence of the intertitle was far from inevitable. Historians have pointed to the lack of dialogue in the first Warner Bros. sound films as evidence that its sound-on-disc technology was conceived as a substitute for live musicians rather than a mechanism for perfecting the talking picture.[3] The historical coincidence of the institutionalization of recorded film sound, the growing collections of sound shorts available from the major Hollywood studios, and the Great Depression meant that theaters needing to save money could do so by eliminating not just orchestral accompaniments but expensive and elaborate live preludes as well. The strategy appeared to have been effective. In August 1931, the *Monthly Labor Review* reported that half of all the musicians formerly employed in movie theaters across the United States had been dismissed.[4] Replacing them required a sound system that could make its listeners forget its mechanical origins.[5] Their ability to reproduce music became a major selling point for each studio's sound technology. Taking its cue from De Forest, who vigorously promoted his Phonofilm's musical capabilities in print advertisements, Warner Bros. highlighted the Vitaphone's essentially musical nature by comparing it to the phonograph. Following these efforts, when MGM, Paramount, and Fox all entered the conversion market with the Movietone sound-on-film system in 1928, they explained its superior quality by calling attention to the famous or uniquely talented musicians performing for its lens. Finally, latecomer RKO, founded in 1929 in order to provide a market for RCA's competing sound brand, the Photophone, emphasized its similarity to the radio, which had by this time gained intimate access to the finest musicians from both genres.

However, without live performers producing spontaneous sound, even the best instrumental recordings could seem detached from their human producers. The major studios may have initially focused their attention on feature films with instrumental scores and intermittent speaking sections, yet the short films that regularly received the admiration of critics and audiences relied heavily on vocal performances. Hollywood's newly converted studios quickly discovered how important an actor's voice would be in making or breaking his career. They reasoned that if the speaking voice could be powerful enough to summon high-paid vocal coaches to studio doors, then certainly the singing voice would pose a far greater risk and, potentially, offer a much larger payoff. Not only could the cultivation of the singing voice help the studios differentiate the style of their sound films, it could also provide an undeniable reference to the human body that reminded listeners of their past experiences in the cinema while pointing toward a unique artistic future.

In spite of the continuities in compositional style that we might trace across silent and sound cinema, it was vital that recorded film music differ dramatically from that which came before it, both in terms of its professionalism and because it was now required to prompt a particular encounter with the spectator. Certainly we can find all kinds of scores and performances in the annals of silent film history that compile a wide range of sources, use operatic voices, or employ jazz bands.[6] Yet because it was performed live, the quality could vary a great deal. Moreover, thanks to the perception of its co-presence, live music communicated differently than did recorded sound—but that is not to say it operated more effectively. Indeed, Steven Shaviro claims the *absence* of a frame of reference enhances the visceral experience of filmgoing: "Sounds and images are 'reactivated', multiplied and intensified, precisely by being cut off from their source or origin."[7] Thus the power of early sound films may have had less to do with their realism than with their strangeness. This is what Rob Spadoni refers to as the conversion era's uncanny effect: an uncomfortable awareness of the means of production arising from problems with synchronization, loudspeaker location and range, vocal delivery, and physical movements.[8] Although the recorded voice must have emanated from a live body at some point, it also reminded spectators both of the body on the screen that cannot really have been there for the film to exist, and of the bodies in the theater that must be there for the film to be heard. Like all audiences, conversion-era spectators were trying to piece together past and present into a moment that might be evaluated for its artistic quality and entertainment value. This is an active process. As Vivian Sobchack says: "The viewer . . . shares cinematic space with the film but must also negotiate it, contribute to and perform the constitution of its experiential significance."[9] Because it is capable of expressing intimate ideas and desires while separated from a human presence, the voice was an essential part of constructing a heightened artistic experience, one that the Hollywood studios hoped would prove tremendously profitable.

Many opera producers appear to have shared the studios' aspirations. Having arrived in Hollywood to train actors to sing, the self-proclaimed Metropolitan Opera "throat specialist" Mario Marafioti claimed: "Opera, as such, is dead. There will be only opera on the screen."[10] Marafioti was not alone in his conviction that the promise of sound technology might improve the artistic outcome of both music and cinema. The Russian critic and composer Leonid Sabaneev argued that opera could be saved only by mimicking the fast pace of cinematic storytelling. He urged artists to stretch the limits of film sound, asking them to "take the first step and create an opera that shall harmonize with the spirit and rhythm of the times."[11] Musicians may have wanted to hear a voice that registered the contemporary zeitgeist, but they were forced to contend with the limitations of emerging film sound technologies and the capabilities of inexperienced studio actors. Yet because it was constructed for a specific technological apparatus and managed by a select group of Hollywood moguls, the constraints being put on the cinematic singing voice were also its greatest asset, allowing the voice to develop a unique style particularly suited to the expression of both opera and jazz.

The voice is a guarantor of identity; as Steven Connor notes, "We *are* our faces as we *are* our voices, partly because we cannot hear or see them as others do."[12] The voice thus appears to deny mediation, to communicate without interference. What would it mean, then, for there to be a national voice, a voice that would articulate American identity? Whose voice would this be, how would it be heard, and by whom? Touting their ability to reach listeners in every town and city across the United States, the Hollywood studios would be well served by the appearance of a national voice that would uphold fundamental American musical ideals while speaking directly to the people. And they could do so better with a singing voice than a speaking one. Unlike actors transitioning from silent to sound roles, conversion-era singers had rarely appeared on film until this moment and were therefore not as burdened with on-screen personae culturally coded to match generic vocal types. The accent of the American cinematic singing voice could thus develop in tandem with Hollywood sound technologies. Moreover, conversion-era advertising emphasized the materiality of the voice over the lyrics it had been given to sing. Even though the kind of music being performed was important, it was not necessary that the studios generate it themselves. In fact, audiences would be able to focus on the sound of the voice more easily if the music it sang were familiar. In the 1920s, the opera and jazz numbers selected for Hollywood films were not only recognizable representatives of their respective genres, they were also heavily dependent on the voice.

Placed together in a movie theater far away from their independent jazz and opera contexts, however, these seemingly familiar styles were made strange by their encounter with the cinema. For competing Hollywood studios, opera and jazz now served as both conceptual frameworks and sonic fragments that could aid in the marketing of a new audiovisual experience. In such an environment, these genres' reliance on the voice became all the more significant. Opera, of course, requires a voice, and though jazz music *can* exist without one, jazz voices possess distinct qualities and perform unique stylistic feats. Combining them would mean negotiating how the voice would sound and what visceral reactions it would inspire. Moreover, the conversion-era's emphasis on synchronization meant that the voice would be called on to embody film technology. To make sense of these relations, Hollywood needed engaged and committed spectators capable of recognizing musical shorthand, yet open to interpreting what they heard in relation to the films they have seen. Jean Mitry notes that unless music is imported into the cinema with a structure of its own, once it is paired with an image "it must establish signifying reactions through contrast or unusual association."[13] This is one of the reasons the combination of opera and jazz was so appealing to Hollywood studios facing the introduction of sound. Having been unable to establish its compositional constraints before meeting the cinema, the jazz-opera on film could both look and sound new. The investment of the film viewer in this process lies in a desire for identity and empowerment. Like the critics arguing about the future of American music, spectators of Hollywood films were concerned about what the introduction of sound meant for the evening's entertainment and the nation's values. Singing voices on film asked listeners to take part in shaping the future by becoming actively engaged in musical listening.

JAZZ, OPERA, AND THE JAZZ-OPERA

"Jazz" and "opera" meant different things to audiences in the first decades of the twentieth century from what they mean to readers today, so any study of opera and jazz must take into account the shifting significance of these words and their relationship to evolving musical sounds. As Krin Gabbard famously notes, "jazz" in the 1920s usually referred to the style of any relatively fast popular tune.[14] This is largely because, as Winthrop Sargeant has shown, all sorts of songs would be transformed into jazz after being adopted by jazz bands.[15] Thus we must acknowledge that the images, sonorities, and bodies selected by Hollywood to represent "jazz" during this period might be all but unrecognizable to our modern associations of the style with a particular canon of performers, recordings, and rhythms. A similar procedure must be used to understand opera. Lawrence Levine shows how the division between highbrow and lowbrow art was far more convoluted for audiences in the nineteenth and early twentieth centuries than it is today.[16] Because of the rise of venues catering to different social classes, the availability of recordings, and the establishment of homegrown companies, "opera" in the 1920s was rather commonplace. Their social, ethnic, and racial differences cannot and should not be erased by this brief contextualization, but it is important to note that opera and jazz were both part of popular culture as it was made available to and influenced by Hollywood during its conversion to sound.

Opera and jazz were both "popular" music of sorts, and the format in which Americans listened to each was often similar. In the early twentieth century, operas were not always known in their entirety, but rather as highlights. *Opera* was a term frequently used to signify select Italian arias that had produced impressive record sales. Indeed, the phonograph and radio were vital in shaping Americans' understanding of opera. In the 1900s and 1910s, the immense popularity of recordings by singers such as Enrico Caruso and Geraldine Farrar helped make opera and the phonograph essential components of the middle-class home. The restrictions on record length, however, meant the arias they recorded were not only extracted from their sources but also often edited for length. It wasn't until Christmas Day in 1931 that the Metropolitan Opera began broadcasting live full-length operas, giving both context and commentary to what had essentially been, for many Americans, a series of popular songs. Indeed, on New Year's Day 1925, WEAF famously set the precedent for airing operatic highlights by having Irish tenor John McCormack and Met Opera star Lucrezia Bori sing a variety of selections to an estimated eight million listeners.[17] Since both singers had contracts with Victor, the program's producer, the radio concert also served as an ideal advertisement for their records. The McCormack-Bori concert was indicative of a larger trend: Shawn Vancour has shown that in the late 1920s radio producers were increasingly mixing abridged classical pieces with shorter popular melodies on variety programs. In fact, the same bands were often charged with playing classical pieces as well as jazz.[18] It is well known that both radio and phonograph were essential to the development of jazz, whose multiple influences were able to coalesce thanks to record companies and airwaves devoted to exploring its sound.[19] Hence ideas about what constituted opera and jazz, let alone what the jazz-opera itself might be, were dependent not just on established composers, performers, and musical institutions but also on the limitations of sound recording and reproduction, the interests of producers and inventors, and the American public's desire for musical commodities.

The perception of opera and jazz as genres of short popular tunes enabled these songs to fit snugly within the requirements of the conversion-era short film. Shorts produced during this period were typically seven to eleven minutes long, which reflected the length of a single film reel as well as the capacity of the sound disc. The aesthetics of the early Vitaphone films were also tied to the act of recording: the image track was shot with multiple cameras and edited to correspond to the sound record. Because these discs could not be easily edited in post-production, the quality of the sound took precedence over the creativity of the image. It is important to understand that, like many studios, Warner Bros. conceived of its conversion-era shorts as musical performances. In transcribing onto a film-strip or synchronized audio disc what would formerly have been performed live, studios and artists exploited the artistic aura of the performance space with cinematic techniques that called attention to vocal ability. Yet how they did so was by no means universal; nor were their effects. The major Hollywood studios had varied approaches to selecting, preserving, and presenting vocal performances that enhanced both product differentiation and unique modes of reception. This is especially evident in studio shorts. Typically containing two or three thematically unrelated numbers, each conversion-era musical short was a concert in miniature. The differences in their staging, editing, shot scale, stars, and musical selections demonstrated a profound disagreement over the relationship of technology, the arts, and the public. In spite of the fact that history has virtually ignored their existence, the prevalence and prominence of these short films in the late 1920s essentially shifted the debate over the value and meaning of opera and jazz from the stage to the screen.

Sounding American explains how opera and jazz worked together to archive performances for a nation conflicted about the meaning of these musical forms and the future of American film sound. To explore the complex interaction among opera, jazz, the screen, and the spectator, I combine film and musical analyses with an examination of advertisements and other primary documents, demonstrating how the meaning of each depends on the commercial and social context of both the music and the cinema between 1926 and 1932.[20] Literature on the conversion era thus far has tended either to explore industrial and stylistic shifts on a broad scale or to focus on technological change.[21] Both kinds of accounts have certainly been necessary, not only for establishing the historical context of the era and the role of technicians therein but also for defining sound studies as a worthwhile field of scholarship. In addition, there have been many excellent books published on film music in recent years, including specific studies of jazz or opera on screen.[22] However, short films have thus far remained a minor part of this research, and the importance of both opera and jazz to the development of the classical Hollywood film score has been neglected almost entirely. This book investigates formerly unexplored primary sources ranging from treatments and contracts to the films themselves in order to construct a new account of the period that explains the role played by opera and jazz in defining American film sound.

Much of the enthusiasm for the jazz-opera came from people invested in democratizing the musical experience while building on the aesthetic accomplishments of an elite musical culture. The Metropolitan Opera Company chairman, Otto Kahn, was a member of this camp. In 1924, he reportedly asked Irving Berlin, George Gershwin, and Jerome Kern to compose a jazz-opera to be performed in New York.[23] Kahn's invitation reflected fears about the future of opera's significance in light of the clash between the form and content of nineteenth-century music and the musical preferences and living conditions of the contemporary urban audience. Kahn and his colleagues were also concerned about the potential for negative political interpretations of canonical operas, the public's exposure to a wider range of musical styles, and the changes in format wrought by the radio and phonograph.[24] In both Europe and the United States, opera was asked to respond to shifting tastes by incorporating trends in both avant-garde and popular music, updating its narrative material, introducing modern technologies, and creating more innovative sets. Yet it was far from clear that an infusion of jazz would solve the problem of opera's creeping irrelevance.

The lack of clarity about the future of opera and the role of jazz in it may have been connected to a shift in the nation's demographics. The 1924 Johnson-Reed Act greatly restricted the flow of Eastern and Southern European immigrants to the United States. Some critics responded to the act with racist calls for coherent national expression, imagining in some roundabout fashion that the jazz-opera might bring about integration of black and white "native" Americans by barring more recent immigrants from operatic participation. As one critic asserted: "All the efforts to found a national system of opera upon Indian, Negro or Jazz themes or idioms have been markedly unsuccessful...now that indiscriminate immigration has there been stopped, perhaps its consolidation may prove to be more rapid and effective."[25] Others envisioned the jazz-opera as a means of assimilation. Both Paul Whiteman's 1924 Aeolian Hall symphonic jazz concert, which famously concluded with George Gershwin's *Rhapsody in Blue*, and his musical film *King of Jazz* (dir. John Murray Anderson, 1930) posited that jazz originated from the combined musical influences of all manner of immigrant communities (with the exception of African Americans). This notorious exclusion is a perfect example of Charles Hiroshi Garrett's claim that twentieth-century American sound resulted as much from the assertion of power and resistance as it did from creativity and connection.[26] Although there were many composers capable of writing a jazz-opera, the fact that they did not do so could be attributed to political pressure brought on by those resistant to African American expression.

Indeed, restrictions on American concert halls made it difficult to produce an African American jazz-opera. Harry Lawrence Freeman, the founder of the Negro Grand Opera Company, wrote *The Flapper* in 1928, but it premiered on Broadway rather than at the Met. Unsurprisingly, much of Freeman's oeuvre had either a nonexistent or an extremely limited run and was never recorded. There were also a number of pieces composed by black Americans that inspired the creation of an official jazz-opera but that preceded the official "birth" of jazz. Among them are William Marion Cook's *Uncle Tom's Cabin*, written for but never produced at the Chicago World's Columbian Exposition in 1893; Maurice Arnold Strothotte's *Merry Benedicts*, which played a few times in Brooklyn in 1896; and Scott Joplin's *Treemonisha*, completed in 1910 but unheard until 1972. Were there an available venue, we could imagine that Duke Ellington might have been prompted to finish *Queenie Pie*.

By contrast, white composers did occasionally meet with modest success in their attempts to merge opera with jazz. William Franke Harling opened *A Light from St. Agnes* with the Chicago Civic Opera in late 1925 to good reviews. Some critics thought of the piece as a jazz-opera,[27] but it was his next work, *Deep River*, that aimed at representing a "modern" American sound. Harling's ideas for the piece came up against widespread prejudice about what the appropriate subject matter for opera ought to be. For example, the American reviewer Herbert Peyser felt that "You can sing with serious intent about a motor car or a telephone just about as successfully as you could talk about them in blank verse or in rhymed Alexandrines."[28] To avoid this sort of critical reaction, Harling set *Deep River* in New Orleans in the 1830s (Figure I.1) and eschewed technological sounds, opting instead for

Figure I.1: The Imperial Theatre production of William Franke Harling's jazz-opera *Deep River*, October 1926. Photo taken by White Studios. © New York Public Library.

jazz instruments such as the banjo and saxophone. The opera's scandalous portrayals of drinking and voodoo may not have been a particularly flattering portrayal of African American life, but *Deep River* did incorporate jazz rhythms and tonalities. Yet for all the enthusiastic speculation, when *Deep River* was produced on Broadway it did not fare as well as anticipated: the typical theatergoer failed to appreciate its more sophisticated elements and the opera crowd wouldn't deign to attend.[29]

Gershwin's foray into jazz-opera was similarly disheartening. Although his *Blue Monday* received rather poor press at its premiere in 1922 as part of George White's *Scandals* revue, the composer's triumph with *Rhapsody in Blue* two years later created enough buzz about his jazz genre mixing to justify a revival. Subsequently produced as *135th Street* in 1925, *Blue Monday* was given a variety of labels, from the grandiose "real American opera" to the derisive "old hokum vaudeville skit."[30] This split is reflected in a 1945 Warner Bros. Gershwin biopic that shows reactions to a sleek production of *Blue Monday* ranging from fear and confusion on the part of elderly white spectators, who stammer, "Gershwin must have lost his mind," to admiration from conductor Paul Whiteman, who was inspired to educate the public so that they might better appreciate Gershwin's efforts.[31] Even if audiences didn't welcome Gershwin's one-act tragic-jazz-opera with open arms, the press coverage of this piece and speculation of a future "rag-time opera"[32] fueled interest in the composer's jazz-opera ventures. The two *Blue Monday* shows could be understood as precursors to the far more profitable *Porgy and Bess*. Although Gershwin called his 1935 *Porgy* a "folk-opera," its melodies resonated with the public as jazz. Many of the songs from *Porgy and Bess* found new life as popular tunes, and one, "Summertime," became the most recorded song in jazz history.

In spite of the jazz-opera's obvious pertinence to the American experience, the most successful jazz-opera of the era was written by an Austrian. Ernst Krenek's *Jonny spielt auf* premiered in Leipzig in February 1927 and instantly found favor with critics and audiences. *Jonny* spread quickly around Europe—it was the most performed opera on the continent during the late 1920s—and eventually traveled to New York, where it was opened at the Met in early 1929. In light of the history we've been tracing, *Jonny*'s relatively late arrival in the United States should not be surprising. As MacDonald Smith Moore notes, Europeans accepted the Americanness of jazz far sooner than did Americans themselves.[33] In the United States, the cultural value of jazz and its status as an American musical vernacular were the subjects of intense public debate. Composer Harling felt that "Jazz is the only real American music, and being a real American myself, I naturally want to compose American opera."[34] An editorial in the weekly

Musical America, however, claimed that jazz was American only because it descended from a capitalist culture of advertising centered in its cities.[35] There is no doubt that Harling and the editors of *Musical America* had very different definitions of jazz in mind when they made these reflections. This book suggests that the dueling conceptions of jazz as either a rarified artistic expression or a commercial product could be settled by its incorporation into the American cinema. A medium that is both art and commodity, film became the ideal site of performance for a conflicted musical style.

Thus, although American jazz-operas seemed doomed to failure, the late 1920s did offer the cinema as an alternative outlet for their presentation, though with some limitations. During the earliest years of the conversion, immobile cameras and microphones would have made it inconceivable to shoot a feature-length opera that incorporated the sophisticated aesthetics of the silent cinema. Short films, however, were understood as substitutes for live performances and were not likely to receive as much criticism for the lack of care they may give to the visual sphere. Short films were free to be sites of experimentation. Duke Ellington's films were typical in this regard. His *Black and Tan* (dir. Dudley Murphy, 1929) doubled narrative time, employed kaleidoscopic visual effects, and mixed genres—all within the space of two reels. The techniques that made this film interesting could have undermined the structure of a longer film and certainly would have been impossible to represent on the stage. Other short films followed suit. The most spectacular of these, *Yamekraw* (dir. Murray Roth, 1930) was a jazz-opera in miniature, boasting German expressionist backdrops that clashed with its rural Southern setting (Figure I.2). The extreme high and low camera angles, low-key lighting, and truncated shot length paradoxically naturalized the operatic voices in the film, which were interrupted by jazz melodies when the characters, played by an all-black cast, encountered the temptations of the city. *Yamekraw* proved that the combination of opera and jazz could work on film.

Alongside the possibility for experimentation that would attract film-makers to the form, there were several reasons opera and jazz could come together more fluidly in the short film than they had in other places. Much of the difficulty over staging the jazz-opera had to do with how American entertainment venues had become socially stratified. Though the cinema was by no means a bastion of class neutrality, the abundant and varied sites for film exhibition in the late 1920s made it possible to imagine unifying the values that had been respectively associated with either opera or jazz. Moreover, the frequent appearance of both opera and jazz on the live soundtracks for silent films persisted in opposition to their separate gestations in the opera house and nightclub. Emerging from within the mélange of

Figure I.2: A jazz-opera experiment on film. Frame grab from *Yamekraw* (1930).

melodic and harmonic ideas that typified audiences' experiences with silent films in the United States, a jazz-opera would not sound all that unique. In addition, Hollywood had developed a distinctive visual aesthetic. Unlike American opera, then, Hollywood cinema was not required to live in the shadow of European achievement. Finally, film camouflages its authors better than the stage. As Rick Altman has shown, sound cinema is something of a ventriloquist; careful synchronization distracts us from the loudspeakers actually projecting the sound and directs us to the lips moving on the screen.[36] Similarly, the composer's labor is hidden behind the singing screen voice, through which the illusion of spontaneity becomes excellent cover for the painstaking construction, and potential failure, of the jazz-opera.

In the argument over what the jazz-opera ought to be, critics and composers were conscious of the fact that each sound has a history, and that their manipulation of America's musical past would have important ramifications both at home and abroad. The jazz-opera may not have received a warm welcome on the American stage, but the issues that motivated its genesis would soon drive the development of the recorded film score. In the early 1920s American composers were plagued by the public's perception of an artistic crisis in their midst. Later in the decade, technicians, film actors, singers, and Hollywood studio executives had to figure out how film music would respond to the uncertainty posed by the limitations and possibilities of sound technology. One of these ambiguities lay in the rift between large urban theaters willing to convert and small-town cinemas where sound installation would have been economically disastrous. As Henry Jenkins points out, studios initially divided the American landscape into two parts that would correspond to their offerings; smaller theaters would be sold silent films with scores, while cities would be asked to buy recorded stage shows.[37] Eventually, as silent versions dwindled and talkies became the norm, these opposing techniques would be required to coalesce into an American film voice.

In addition to considering innovative and inoffensive ways of using the recording apparatus to their advantage in a medium that had not yet been fully standardized, film composers and arrangers had to deal with the vulnerability of the human voice. How to accomplish this task was debated in scientific and trade journals, at conferences, and, of course, within the films themselves. Thus there was more at stake in the competition among the Vitaphone, Movietone, and Photophone sound systems than the economic dominance of the film industry. The goals of individual Hollywood executives, cultural associations of the specific sound technologies, and values of the artists and technicians affiliated with each studio all affected the conflicting representations of music and musicians during the conversion to sound. Not only were the appropriation and combination of opera and jazz central to the negotiation of American artistic identity between 1926 and 1932, they would also determine the sound and structure of American film music for decades to come.

The first chapter of *Sounding American* examines the cultural connotations of opera and jazz during the conversion era primarily by analyzing the texts, reception, and advertising for the first successful synchronous sound system, Warners' Vitaphone. I read one of Warners' most frequently used pieces, Ruggiero Leoncavallo's opera *I Pagliacci*, as an urtext for the jazz-opera in order to tease out questions of form, genre, narrative, and timbre as they are incorporated by Hollywood cinema. As films that either directly incorporate *Pagliacci* or invoke its affect, *The Singing Fool* (1928) and the black-cast short film *Yamekraw* (1930) are ideal case studies to explore how opera and jazz could be combined to define the American voice. I locate the impetus for the cinematic jazz-opera within Warners' attempts to market the Vitaphone as both a novel experiment and the producer of a valuable cultural archive. As self-proclaimed arbiters of American taste, Warner Bros. produced a model of film music that treated the song as a unit unto itself and assured the public that the voices bringing it to life would never be lost again.

The middle two chapters study how the representation of opera and jazz were intimately linked to the depiction of racial, ethnic, and gendered bodies in Hollywood sound shorts. Chapter 2 discusses the sixty-five opera shorts released by Warner Bros. between 1926 and 1932 in relation to the conspicuously low number produced by the other major studios. Even though this "high-culture" experiment was primarily conducted by Warners, it nevertheless had an enormous impact on the way Hollywood as a whole envisioned the purpose of film music and prohibitions on the female voice. In order to convince spectators of the Vitaphone's sonic superiority, Warner Bros. leaned heavily on opera, hoping that audiences would compare the high-quality phonograph records with which they were familiar to the heavy sound discs used by the Vitaphone. Yet there is one significant way in which this plan fell short. Lying in wait beneath the furthest reaches of the operatic voice, the specter of the castrato haunts the visual style of Vitaphone opera films, reminding viewers that something is missing in this cinematic presentation. By examining the aria as an American operatic vernacular and showing how it evolved on film to showcase the talents of one particular tenor, Giovanni Martinelli, I expose the importance of the castrato's legacy for the American film voice.

Chapter 3 compares the function of jazz in the short films of Warner Bros., Paramount, and MGM, showing how each argued for the relevance and permanence of its sound system through its appropriation of the music. Each studio infused its representation of jazz with American ideals linked to the capabilities of the individual technology and the resources of the studio, even though filmmakers and musicians disagreed about what these values were, and indeed what jazz itself might be. These differences demonstrate the conversion era's confusion over how to make uniquely American films that were both popular and culturally significant. The improvisatory nature of jazz not only provided recorded sound with the impression of liveness lost during the conversion, it also became a remarkably prescient response to American cinema's cultural and economic instability during the early 1930s.

My final chapter examines the persistence of opera and jazz in the film score beyond the period of conversion. Film composers of the 1930s employed the musical strategies learned in the lush movie palace orchestras of the previous decade along with the techniques for representing opera and jazz that had become commonplace in Hollywood short films. Their reliance on opera and jazz, however, has been long overlooked. On the basis of the legacy of Max Steiner and his contemporaries, film musicologists have often asserted that classical Hollywood film music speaks in a Romantic voice akin to a nineteenth-century symphony. By analyzing the form and function of music in the first recorded and synchronized film score, *Don Juan* (1926), and a late entry, *Modern Times* (1936), I show that the frequent appearance of opera and jazz transforms the classical Hollywood film into an illustrated jazz-opera. Making comparisons to other films of the 1930s with more typical scores, I demonstrate that Hollywood feature film music struggles with the same questions about the sonic articulation of American identity that had been troubling musicians since the early 1920s. However, reading these films as jazz-operas allows us to imagine a new kind of active spectator, one encouraged to draw connections both within and outside of the text that are not entirely directed by the narrative trajectory of the film or its music.

As Lee De Forest's *Opera Versus Jazz* demonstrated as early as 1923, the two musical styles are not as incompatible as they may seem. Rather than being situated on opposite sides of an indissoluble barrier between high and low art, opera and jazz share a history as essential parts of American popular culture in the early twentieth century. This is the context in which Hollywood found itself grappling with the potential of sound technology. Combining opera and jazz proved to be an economic success, tapping into key sounds that interested investors and the public, and it also enabled the major studios to carve out an aesthetic identity for American film sound.

CHAPTER 1

Archiving America

Sound Technology and Musical Representation

While on contract to Warner Bros. in 1927, Michael Curtiz submitted a story to producer Darryl Zanuck that he suggested be titled "The Clown" or "Pagliacci." Zanuck asked Graham Baker to write a screenplay based on Curtiz's work, the result of which became *The Singing Fool*, the highest-grossing film of the 1920s and most of the following decade. Curtiz's contribution to the film was left out of the credits and does not appear in subsequent historical accounts of the film's production; nonetheless, the specter of his clown remains. Played by Al Jolson, Al Stone bears a strong resemblance to Curtiz's original Abie Rachman, the loving husband and father betrayed by his wife, devastated by the loss of his son, and forced to keep on singing in spite of it all. The film closes with a rendition of "Sonny Boy" by the jazz singer himself, and the story ends with Rachman staging a one-man version of Ruggiero Leoncavallo's opera *Pagliacci* for the nightclub crowd.

> The pianist plays the first chords of Pagliacci, and Abie starts to sing the sad song of the wounded heart of a clown, but sings it snappily, peppily, in fast-beating, dance-urging, body-twisting, leg-twisting, wicked, vicious, syncopated tempo....
>
> A blackfaced clown—a jazzy clown! "Hurrah...hurrah!" yell the people, enthused and exalted and hysterical...and jazz is throbbing in the veins...jazz is yelling in the air...the victorious syncopation of the wounded hearted Pagliacci....

"You see," says the manager happily to a man, "He is great....He wanted to sing Pagliacci...he imagined himself as Pagliacci...but THIS is the Pagliacci that he is...the Jazz-Pagliacci...."[1]

This chapter argues that Jazz-Pagliacci is not just a quirky invention by an overworked writer/director but is indicative of the way that Warner Bros. coupled opera and jazz to position sound cinema as the embodiment of national musical expression. Overcome with heartbreak in the midst of his operatic debut and unable to return to a life of pounding out popular tunes, Abie Rachman combines his emotional identity with his technical training to create a new medium. Breathing life into screen shadows, the American cinema infused new technology with old-world values: to bring about the kind of transformative encounter Curtiz describes, film needed both opera and jazz.

Jazz and opera are generally thought to represent two distinct traditions, or at the very least two stereotypes, one thoroughly American, the other manifestly European; one black, the other white; one originating with untrained street musicians, the other with highly skilled elites. The styles seem to lie on different sides of a great cultural divide. Yet, as Hollywood cinema found itself faced with new sonic requirements, jazz and opera were employed to signify beyond these strict associations. Contrary to the popular belief that opera and jazz were usually applied in an oppositional fashion, film music written during the conversion era established a complex matrix of representation that the studios used to articulate the value of their respective sound technologies. Close examination of period films, advertisements, and trade articles demonstrate the reliance of one form on the other in order for the film score to become what David Bordwell calls "a system of narration, endowed with some degree of self-consciousness, a range of knowledge, and a degree of communicativeness."[2] During the period of conversion, film sound had to rely on an audience aware of its pitfalls in order to communicate its potential.

The unfulfilled promise of the jazz-opera had been a dream for composers and entrepreneurs for most of the 1920s. The envisioned form's hyphenated identity imagined an Americanness built on immigrant experience, a style born in the United States but with roots that reach back to Europe. What, then, did the union of opera and jazz mean for the technologies of the conversion era and for Warner Bros. in particular? Both opera and jazz had been co-present with the nascence of cinema in vaudeville houses, nickelodeons, and picture palaces. An antecedent of jazz, ragtime had been featured on the vaudeville stage prior to 1900 in the form of minstrel shows and cakewalks, its popularity soaring with the prevalence of singers such as Ragtime Ben Harney in some of the larger houses. Abridged versions of operas, operettas, and other "high-class" entertainments also found their way onto the vaudeville circuit. As Andrew L. Erdman shows, vaudeville chains like that established by Benjamin Franklin Keith and Edward Albee had made it possible to imagine a distinctly American mass entertainment,[3] paving the way for national appreciation of both cinema and the jazz-opera.

A national appreciation of film music in first decade of the twentieth century, however, would have been difficult due to the fact that the soundtrack had not yet been standardized. Performed by local pianists and small orchestras, the same film might be accompanied by an opera hit in one nickelodeon and subjected to a ragtime melody in another. The colorfully hand-painted slides that illustrated popular theatrical sing-alongs during this period also featured the era's version of jazz. "Yiddle, on Your Fiddle, Play Some Ragtime" and other Irving Berlin tunes were sung by Americans in nickelodeons everywhere.[4] Opera and jazz made their way into accompaniment suggestions produced by studios and anthologies compiled by publishers and theater directors. These guides interspersed classical, operatic, popular, folk, and jazz melodies, at times blending genres in a single tune. For example, Rick Altman notes that one arrangement of a famous melody from Verdi's *Il trovatore* was made into a foxtrot.[5] One can only imagine the "creative" uses of some of the other pieces by less-talented musicians. As picture palaces sprang up around the country, so opera and jazz were produced by performers of a much higher caliber in acts that preceded the evening's recorded entertainment. Indeed, they were a part of film preludes throughout the conversion era. In 1932, the Italian soprano Luisa Tetrazzini appeared in the Boston Cinema and as part of the bill at the Paramount Cinema in New York, while Duke Ellington toured both cinemas and concert halls in the early 1930s.[6] Recorded sound would replace a variety of live voices. Addressing this diversity would become a way for the studios to articulate the differences in their products and the technologies that produced them.

In the late 1920s three distinct sound technologies competed to become the industry standard. As the first synchronous sound system to be implemented on a wide scale, Warners' sound-on-disc system, the Vitaphone, had an early advantage. It faced fierce competition starting in 1928, when MGM, Paramount, and Fox all decided to use a variable-density sound-on-film system known as Movietone. Although more easily synchronized, sound-on-film did not have the reputation for quality that the Vitaphone enjoyed. Later that year, RCA threw its hat in the ring with Photophone, a variable-area filmstrip used primarily by RKO. With a soundtrack now available, language became a problem for actors, audiences, and exhibitors; even as Hollywood produced multilingual versions for distribution overseas, accent and other vocal characteristics betrayed the racial, social, and ethnic identities of the bodies on the screen. The anxieties that surrounded the laying bare of the voice were addressed by origin myths that applied to individual actors, the studio system, and emerging film technologies and that justified the inclusion of certain sounds and the exclusion of others.

The reasons given for the selection of particular voices for sound cinema typically have something to do with the idea of authenticity. As Jacob Smith explains, proclamations regarding the authenticity of new media rely on unspoken conceptions of the body as a racial and gendered site of performance.[7] Because they are heavily laden with corporeal stereotypes (opera's "fat ladies" and jazz's unrestrained dancers being just two examples), opera and jazz were particularly appropriate choices to become the face of Hollywood's new sound systems. Studios exploited the familiar aspects of each musical style hoping to dazzle audiences with the veneer of the authentic performer, which in turn kept spectators from noticing the imaginative version of history drawn up by this revision of opera and jazz. By asking a body to stand in for the Vitaphone disc or Movietone or Photophone strip, Hollywood hoped to disguise the fact that sound and image are separate entities. Of course, as Mary Ann Doane explains, this is true regardless of what the actor says or how he moves.[8] Yet a *musical* body performs a double deception: the illusion of wholeness generated by the singing body and the perceived unity of the piece he performs remove the spectator's attention even further from the process of production.

This fantasy of unity was problematized during the conversion, however, because music was required to adapt to the demands of the cinema. Opera's unity is predicated on its combination of music, drama, and staging. A particular type of singing defines the opera and works in tandem with a compositional style and narrative construction to create the impression of a coherent work. In jazz, unity is dependent on an approach to performance involving play with a recognizable melodic line or harmonic structure. Of course, Winthrop Sargeant points out that there could be many possible ways to define "jazz"; looking at its social purpose would offer one set of characteristics, while an examination of its musical form would give us another.[9] Primary among the qualities that distinguish jazz from other forms, however, are its opposition to the scripted and rehearsed traditions of its European influences.[10] Emerging out of ragtime, jazz's polyrhythms unite the style against European dance traditions, while its blues origins establish harmonies that belong to African Americans. Although both opera and jazz could be performed by anyone with the appropriate skill, each nonetheless carries with it the markers of its racial and ethnic origins, factors that further solidify the notion of each as an authentic and unified style. In conversion-era Hollywood sound shorts, however, "opera" consisted of one or two arias, often originating from entirely distinct works, while "jazz" functioned to describe a collection of popular tunes written by different composers. In Sargeant's terms, the social function rather than the musical form of each style came to determine how it was defined by the cinema. Despite this general trend, the differences in the studios' representations of opera and jazz expose rifts in the system, demonstrating that conversion-era Hollywood did not maintain a single approach to unifying bodies and voices.

I tell the story of Hollywood's attempts to combine opera and jazz by examining the screen life of two musical pieces: the 1892 opera *I pagliacci* and *Yamekraw: A Negro Rhapsody* by James P. Johnson. Although these works seem to fall strictly under the headings of opera and jazz respectively, I show how each becomes a hybrid text through its encounter with film sound. To explore the relationship among jazz, opera, and sound technology, I consider the representation of the voice in the marketing of the Vitaphone and Movietone. However, the chapter concentrates largely on the Vitaphone, not only because it was the first successful synchronous sound system to produce musical shorts but also because Warners' aggressive approach to the music publishing industry demonstrated the studio's commitment to selling the song. In addition, Warners' promotion of the Vitaphone as a relative of the phonograph ensured that the public would associate sound-on-disc with musical listening in a way that was not true of the sound-on-film systems. As the nucleus of this investigation, *Pagliacci* and *Yamekraw* have not been selected at random. The pieces themselves are not only two of the period's richest musical inspirations, articulating concerns over race, the nature of performance, and the revelatory power of the voice; they also offer an overt thematic similarity, with both presenting stories of capricious lovers whose deception results in the creation of a new art form. The recurrence of these texts thus reveals an uneasiness about the relationship between art and lies that pervaded the conversion period and inspired the representational strategies of film sound technologies.

Since *Pagliacci* was included in several musical shorts, and *Yamekraw* provided the music and story for at least two others, it would be useful at this stage to address my focus on the short film. I claim that a major studio's style and values are more visible in its shorts than in its features. A classical Hollywood film is often easily tied to a studio when its subject and style fit the dominant trend. For example, in the late 1920s and early 1930s, MGM was famous for prestige productions built around star personalities,

Warner Bros. was known for its social consciousness, and Universal attached its name to inexpensive genre films. There were a number of reasons for this consistency, the first having to do with formal similarities. There is little work definitively addressing the structural or stylistic differences between short and feature films during the classical Hollywood era, but we can find something of an analogue in comparisons of the short story and the novel. In his formalist analysis, Boris M. Èjxenbaum identifies an important difference between the story and the novel in terms of narrative development: "The story must be constructed on the basis of some contradiction, incongruity, error, contrast, etc. But that is not enough. By its very essence, the story, just as the anecdote, amasses its whole weight toward the ending."[11] Because of its form, the short story emphasizes shock over understanding. This is what Roman Jakobson would label the "dominant" of the American short story, a term that he says "may be defined as the focusing component of a work of art: it rules, determines, and transforms the remaining components."[12] According to Èjxenbaum, the short story moves toward an unexpected ending that acts like a "dropped bomb" on all that came before it.[13] Its artistic value, then, is in its revelation of what lies underneath. It acts this way, Èjxenbaum says, because it has no space to present multiple and complex plot lines and no time for an extended dénouement. The limitations of the form are employed to produce a particular effect.

Of course, short films are not always narratives. Nevertheless, it is useful to compare their structure during the period of conversion to Èjxenbaum's description of the short story. The "contradiction" or "incongruity" in the short film should be fairly obvious: "telling" the "story" requires that the sound and image be divided, and the words and songs come from a loudspeaker and not the mouth of the face on the screen. Although the feature-length film might attempt to absorb spectators in an elaborate narrative, thus making them forget the impossibility of cinematic space, the short assures viewers of its congruity by putting synchronization on display.[14] As with the formalist distinction between novel and story outlined above, short films are more focused on event than character development. This structure lessens diegetic integrity and permits clearer recognition of the star as himself or herself. One has only to look at how popular musical stars carry their own names into supposedly fictional short films to see this is the case: Bessie Smith's character in *St. Louis Blues* (1929) was named "Bessie," and Bing Crosby was typically just "Bing."

Unlike the structure of the short story, however, the unexpected bang of a conversion-era short film is not necessarily found in its narrative conclusion. Instead, the surprise lingers at the limits of representation, the point where we suddenly become aware of the historical fact of the film's production. Ironically, this happens most frequently during the song. Though music provides an opportunity for the greatest display of synchronicity and the extratextual suggestion of unity, it also gives us the voice, the place where meaning might break apart. Voices can crack, shout, scream, scat, and otherwise dissolve signification such that the elaborate fiction of the set is suddenly exposed for what it is, and the star seen for her life outside this role. Thus the same voices that Hollywood used to conceal the absence of liveness can also reveal the conditions of recording. Because the song attunes spectators to the fragile relationship between this voice and its technological listener, their experience with conversion-era short films resembles their interactions with live performers. Even as they were told that the recording ought to be perfect, audiences at the end of the 1920s understood the limitations of sound technology.

This possibility for failure may originate either from the original scene of recording or from the site of projection. The recognition that these were two different moments heightens what Vivian Sobchack calls the "echo-focus" of "instrument-mediated perception," a process that forces the viewer to reflect on any act of seeing that has been assisted by technology.[15] The knowledge that music has been recorded similarly causes listeners to notice themselves listening and consequently to hear the mechanism at work in addition to the song it plays. Thus, conversion-era listening was apprehensive not only because it was framed by the studios' rhetoric of live experience but also because it was marked by an increased self-awareness of the spectator's inability to fully embrace the song's affect and assimilate to the cinematic scene. In a feature film, voices might be subsumed under a narrative function that could explain their faltering through story or character. In a short created primarily to feature the voice, however, such recourse becomes difficult. In Roman Jakobson's terms, then, the dominant of the conversion-era short film might just be the song, the aesthetic apotheosis of sound technology.

A further explanation for the homogeneity of studio shorts lies in the hierarchical organization of the Hollywood majors. After 1931 most studios employed production units, thus ensuring some consistency of participants in a group of films made in a single year.[16] Short subjects were often relegated to their own department within each studio. Even before this transition, when studios were organized more directly under a central producer, shorts were still often the property of a select team. For example, Roy Mack at Warner Bros. directed a large number of its shorts, using Edwin DuPar as his cinematographer. Herman Heller was the musical director of the Vitaphone Symphony Orchestra and was likely also responsible for the film direction on many of the studio's opera shorts.[17] Warners' shorts not made by Mack or Heller nonetheless exhibit a similar style, suggesting a mode of operation that extended beyond the decisions made by a single director. Moreover, since the firing of live musicians in theaters made the demand for shorts much higher, the industry experienced a rise in independent film production specializing in short subjects.[18] The majors were motivated either to usurp these efforts by purchasing distribution rights or to differentiate themselves from these upstarts and one another.

As Janet Staiger notes, the similarity of films across the industry can be attributed to industrial labor practices and the standardized use of products, yet we must nevertheless account for differences. She attributes studio differentiation to "controlled stylistic change" made possible by the variances in management.[19] I am hesitant to put all authorial control in the hands of businessmen, but I do believe that the values of the studio that manifest themselves in the rhetoric about sound technology are particularly evident in a studio's short film output. That each studio took a distinct approach to making opera and jazz shorts certainly reflects differences in their systems of labor and the separate workers and artists involved, but it also speaks to a set of underlying assumptions the studio had about the meaning and worth of opera and jazz. Film scholarship has often stressed the diversity of shorts during the conversion and in the decades that followed. Even though it is true there were many producers creating many genres of short films, we cannot ignore the fact that the major studios used shorts to articulate a set of ideals linked to the promotion of sound technologies and that these values were consistent across the body of work they released.

WHY *PAGLIACCI*? A STORY OF ORIGINS

I pagliacci is the salacious tale of Canio, a scorned lover who commits murder while on the stage playing the role of Pagliaccio, a clown who has been similarly spurned. The opera begins with a prologue addressed to the audience by Tonio, one of a troupe of actors who arrive in a small Italian village on a warm summer holiday to put on a show. Tonio is both narrator and character, capable of standing outside the text while seeming to influence the direction of the story. This muddying of the diegetic waters continues throughout the production as the actors' private lives are continuously exposed in front of a waiting crowd. It becomes immediately evident that all is not well in the relationship between Canio and his wife, Nedda, when Tonio attempts (unsuccessfully) to seduce her. His failure acknowledged,

Tonio hides and watches as Silvio, a local, has greater success. Armed with the knowledge of this secret affair, Tonio calls Canio to the scene, where, without exposing himself to the lovers, the clown tearfully performs the famous "Vesti la giubba" aria that brings down the curtain on the first act. Act II consists of a mise-en-abyme, wherein Canio, Nedda, Tonio, and Bebbe (the opera's Harlequin character) perform a comedy of infidelity that duplicates the "real" events presented in the first half. In front of the incredulous villagers, the "play" becomes "reality" as an enraged Canio kills both Nedda and Silvio, thus ending both the play-within-a-play and the opera itself.

Leoncavallo's short opera proved invaluable to early sound cinema in general and to Warner Bros. in particular. The role was Enrico Caruso's most beloved, and the Victor recording of "Vesti la giubba" his most popular. In addition to the familiarity of the aria and its attendant story, the history of the Pierrot character on which this opera draws and the form of the *commedia dell'arte* from which it emerges have some bearing on why references to it appeared so frequently in American films of the late 1920s. As Robert F. Storey points out, Pierrot began as the fool in the sixteenth-century Italian scenarios, moved through similar roles in France in the late seventeenth century, and made his way into twentieth-century literary manifestations. The Pierrot handed down through the Romantic period is a relatively isolated figure, with what Storey calls a "certain naïve sincerity" that enables him to comment on the action.[20] Pierrot's segregation was compacted on the stage by the difficulties posed by translation. As the character made his way around Italy, his spectators, who spoke a variety of dialects, had difficulty understanding him. To aid comprehension, productions began to accentuate the visual over the aural, eventually transforming Pierrot into a pantomime.

The audience played an even more active role in France, which was due to the early eighteenth-century prohibition against dialogue. There, Pierrot's story was staged as *pièces à écriteaux*, silent productions in which spoken text was represented on cue cards and sung not by the actors but by the audience, to the tune of popular melodies.[21] Essentially a sing-along with "intertitles," *Pagliacci*'s ancestry in the "mute" theater makes it excellent material for demonstrating the capabilities of the sound apparatus. By limiting itself to a representation of Pagliaccio's tearful "Vesti la giubba" rather than the entirety of the opera, early synchronous sound films were able to communicate with the audience while neglecting character development. Pagliaccio seemed real to film viewers not necessarily because they identified with his plight but because he occupied a familiar position as both a cultural archetype and a reminder of their experiences with live singing in the cinema.

In the thirty-four years between its initial performance and the Vitaphone premiere that featured Giovanni Martinelli's version of "Vesti la giubba," *Pagliacci* had not disappeared from public consciousness. Caruso's recordings of the aria remained hugely popular and the opera was (and still is) regularly matched in performance with the veristic favorite that inspired it, Pietro Mascagni's *Cavalleria rusticana*. In addition, *Pagliacci*, although a rather short work, was not limited to this pairing, or indeed even to a full-length presentation. In the 1910s, Leoncavallo himself toured with a shortened version of the already brief opera.[22] Thanks to Leoncavallo's reduction and the enormous sales of Caruso's recording, *Pagliacci* is remembered primarily for a single song sung by a tragic clown character, making it possible to project a host of conflicts onto his whitewashed façade.

Along with Mordaunt Hall of the *New York Times*, most reviewers gave far more attention to the presentation of opera in general, and Giovanni Martinelli's performance of "Vesti la giubba" in particular, than they did to other aspects of the Vitaphone premiere on August 6, 1926. According to Hall, "Nothing like it had ever been heard in a motion picture theater"[23] while the *Musical Courier* stated that "the most effective reproduction of the whole evening from a musical standpoint was Giovanni Martinelli, singing the familiar thing from *I Pagliacci*."[24] The *Chicago Daily Tribune* began its review with a discussion of Martinelli's costume and "exquisite music,"[25] and the *Motion Picture Bulletin of California* heralded the appearance of opera stars by singling out Martinelli, Marion Talley, and Anna Case while failing to mention any of the program's nonoperatic performers.[26] In addition to reprinting the entirety of Will Hays's opening address, which stressed the Vitaphone's cultural and educational value, a special issue of *Variety* outlined the goals and uses of sound-on-disc technology: "Vitaphone's Aims: To advance the presentation of motion pictures in theaters . . . by making available, on a broad scale, the music of the greatest symphony orchestras and vocal entertainment of the most popular stars of the operatic and theatrical fields."[27] The immediate critical reception of the Vitaphone indicates that rather than intruding on an already perfect silent screen, opera was perceived as being capable of elevating cinema to become a new art. That this art might reach the masses in a way not available to the producers of the live jazz-opera was articulated by Harry Warner's democratic vision: "There is a limited number of people who can go to the opera and pay seven or eight dollars to hear the great operatic artists of the world, but there are millions who cannot . . . the vitaphone [sic] makes that possible."[28]

Warner Bros. had initially sought to establish the stability of the Vitaphone *against* the impulsive inadequacies of jazz music. Rewriting its history decades after the fact, Warner Bros. executives recounted the failures of the Vitaphone's predecessors, which in this version were due in part to sound technology's prior association with jazz. According to a document compiled by the studio's legal department for the infamous 1948 antitrust case *United States vs. Paramount Pictures, Inc.*, Sam Warner inspired his brothers to implement Western Electric's device after seeing a demonstration of a synchronized film featuring a small jazz ensemble at the Bell Laboratories in New York.[29] The document goes on to note that even though this experiment was an improvement on previous attempts at the sound film, "the total result from the commercial and artistic point of view was entirely unsatisfactory."[30] Warner's interest may have been stirred by this rough jazz experiment, but his studio turned to opera to raise expectations for what sound technology could do. Indeed, the legal department's history often refers to Warners' efforts to compete with "deluxe motion picture houses" or "expensive" stage shows, scenes seemingly better suited to opera than jazz. According to this version of events, Warner Bros. did not innovate sound technology solely to bring culture to the masses, as it would often publicly claim[31] ; it used opera to prevent its property from being tainted by the poor production values often associated with jazz.

Even as it began to produce and profit from jazz shorts, Warner Bros. would strategically associate unrestrained racialized bodies with jazz in order to validate its commitment to opera. For example, in one *American Cinematographer* piece, Edwin DuPar, the cinematographer for many of Warners' early sound films, reverently described the difference between filming opera singers and shooting just about everything else. According to DuPar, the operatic context required that he heighten his attention to his surroundings, making himself aware of anything that could interrupt the voice. To illustrate the potential for difficulty, DuPar provided an account of a ruined take during the filming of Anna Case's performance of "Swanee River" in the Manhattan Opera House: "Everything was still and I had just received the signal to start.... Looking out the peek-hole, I saw that everyone was exceedingly excited. The cause, I learned, had been the screams of a colored janitress who claimed that she had seen the late Oscar Hammerstein walking across the balcony."[32] Noting that Anna Case, a soprano for the Metropolitan Opera Company, was recording "Swanee River" together with the Dixie Jubilee Singers would make it easy to interpret DuPar's story as a way to displace tensions about the pairing of white and black music. Conjuring Hammerstein's specter implies that the populist impresario would approve of Warners' mission, yet DuPar's exploitation of African American hysteria indicates that a blatantly integrationist approach could do damage to the studio's educational project. Despite

Warners' efforts to bring good music to the public, DuPar notes that not everyone knows how to "behave" at the opera.

Several other studios followed Warners' lead in producing opera shorts, and by 1928 Lee De Forest declared that the opera film experiment had lost its luster: "The public response to vaudeville presentations...indicates pretty clearly that even with such stars as Martinelli, Mischa Elman and Talley the interest seems to wane after ten or fourteen weeks of this sort of talking picture in any given theater."[33] Of course, as the inventor of Phonofilm, one of the "failed" sound devices Warners strove to outperform, De Forest would naturally be biased against the studio's efforts. Nevertheless, the tepid public reaction to the continued production of operatic shorts coincided with the adoption of Movietone as the industry standard and resulted in a shift in Warners' approach to Vitaphone sales. Warner Bros. had initially used *Pagliacci* as a way to legitimate its artistry. Once the appeal of opera films appeared to wane, Warners found new use for *Pagliacci* by combining it with jazz.

OF DISCS AND STRIPS: FILM SOUND COMPETITION AND THE ELECTRIC *PAGLIACCI*

How was Leoncavallo's opera translated to suit the cinema? The evolution of film sound technology in the first decades of the twentieth century has been well documented by a number of historians.[34] Instead of rehashing this work, I want to paint a picture of the market that greeted the cinematic adaptation of Curtiz's "Pagliacci" in 1928 by comparing Warners' strategy for selling film sound to those of the other majors. A conversion-era film such as *The Singing Fool* cannot be understood solely through an analysis of its aesthetic qualities or a factual recitation of its sales figures, but must consider its means of production. Of course, this is not a new assertion. Bordwell, Thompson, and Staiger have documented the depth of this connection by examining stylistic trends and industrial decisions.[35] However thorough their investigation may be, it nonetheless reads the whole of Hollywood as an economic and ideological industry. We ought to recognize the contribution of distinct sound technologies to the construction of studio identity. In other words, it matters to both the immediate reception and the historical record that *The Singing Fool* was produced by Warner Bros. rather than Fox and that it was designed for disc rather than film sound. The specificities of Hollywood's marketing decisions, moreover, are intricately linked to the signification of jazz and opera, which came together to articulate the value of sound cinema as the 1920s drew to a close.

If Douglas Gomery calls the transition to sound a period of cooperation and organization rather than turmoil and disarray, it makes sense that the industry's approach to advertising would be calculated as well.[36] Indeed, contemporary trade publications instructed theaters in how to call attention to sound as an attraction in itself. As the number of sound films increased, articles in the *Exhibitors Herald-World* (*EHW*) stressed the financial drawbacks of not foregrounding technological change. Despite these warnings, many managers continued to advertise their sound screenings as they would silent films. *EHW* responded: "Several who proceeded on that theory learned to their sorrow that many of their prospective customers didn't know whether Vitaphone was a means of reproducing synchronized sound or the second cousin to a vitamin."[37] *EHW* further suggested that to be successful, exhibitors must rely on a specific set of terms: "At no time did any of these exhibitors fail to use the words 'SEE AND HEAR' as a means of impressing on the minds of the public just what this new form of entertainment meant."[38] Managers also urged one another not to give priority to either system: "I give Vitaphone and Movietone...equal prominence with my picture in the newspaper ads and advance notices, 24-sheets, street-car cars, lobby frames, trailers, throw-aways, etc."[39] If theaters were more interested in defining the cinematic encounter than differentiating sound technologies, how were the studios meant to distinguish themselves?

Although the slogan "see and hear" was employed in the service of all sound cinema, it was not implied that audiences were seeing and hearing the same thing in every case. In an ad for *The Desert Song* (1929), the text "You *See and Hear* Vitaphone only in Warner Bros. and First National Pictures" fits neatly into a single staff framed between a treble clef and a double bar line, seemingly substituting for musical notation (Figure 1.1). This new context positions "Vitaphone" not only as something in motion but also as something musical; the streaks through its letters are now understood as a materialization of the otherwise missing staff. Furthermore, rather than being merely a means of communicating a musical message, the Vitaphone *becomes* the message that the music exists to transmit. The ad sings the praises of technology rather than giving us a song to hear. The repetition of this logo in connection with multiple films reinforces a familiar association between the Vitaphone and phonography and suggests that any sighting of the Vitaphone must be inherently musical.

Figure 1.1: "Musical" Vitaphone Logo.
Photoplay Magazine, July 1929.

Where the expression "see and hear" appears in Fox's Movietone campaign, it asks readers pay attention to a specific film. The studio repeatedly tells the spectator to "see and hear *Speakeasy*" or "hear and see *Thru Different Eyes*" or declares, "until you've seen and heard *In Old Arizona* you can't appreciate to what heights the technique of the talking motion picture has been advanced by Fox Movietone."[40] Even though it adopted the same sound technology as both Fox and MGM, Paramount's ads use "see and hear" to refer to the spectacle of its productions. With suggestions like "Paramount, the greatest name in motion pictures, now presents its greatest entertainments—the Super Shows of the New Show World. See and hear them all!" and "See and hear *The Whole Show on the Screen—by Paramount*" the studio advertises an entire program and a mode of viewing constructed by its brand rather than either an individual film or a specific sound technology.[41] With their unique deployments of the "see and hear" imperative, the studios demonstrated the differences in their conceptualization of the relationship among technology, audiences, and film texts.

Although each of these advertising campaigns used its own referent to explain the value of combining image and voice, all three distracted audiences from the absence of live music and proposed instead that it was silent film that had been operating with a gaping hole at its core. For Warner Bros., the referent was technology. The studio released publicity photos of the Vitaphone, a device that literally pieced image and sound back together again, drawing attention to the space that had thus far existed between live musical bodies and their recorded analogues. In pointing to individual films, Fox attempted to revise preconceived notions about the cinema as a silent art. These ads suggested that until that moment, audiences had no idea what they were missing by not hearing the voice. Finally, Paramount relied on the notion of a program inherited from vaudeville. By referring to the "whole show," the studio implied that every act would supplement the others, creating a chain of diversion that would make it undesirable to see and hear what was no longer there.

In light of the similarity to the phonograph, Warner Bros. could have marketed its device to emphasize either historic significance or ordinariness. Getting the audience to accept the Vitaphone as a technology of monumental importance meant that Warners would have to do more than stress its novelty. Rather than situate the Vitaphone within a history of attempts to construct synchronous sound, Warner Bros. initially placed it within a particular narrative about the phonograph, one that worked in tandem with its operatic origin story. Steve Wurtzler points out that many of the first to sign contracts with Warners had already made their names known through Victor's prestigious Red Seal record line. By foregrounding quality and talent as the merits of its system, Warners skillfully avoided a technological comparison with sound-on-film and was able to call sound-on-disc an artistic triumph in line with that achieved by Victor.[42] However, this tactic eventually became impossible to maintain. By 1930 the studio still failed to publicly recognize that the industry of the sound film had other players. Its advertising spread in the *Film Daily Yearbook* of that year begins with the claim: "As the acknowledged leaders in the production of the new Vitaphone art, Warner Bros. are proud to have been the instrument through which Talking Pictures...have been introduced and brought to their fullest flower."[43] Of course, the text fails to mention that Warners was the only major studio still using the "new Vitaphone art," or recognize that there might be any more progress to be made in the production of new sound films. In the end, Warners' association with the cultural status of the Victor phonograph was no longer enough to drive the production of sound films. The studio needed to appeal not just to the musical elite but also to everyone else.

It may appear that the creation of an American jazz-opera would not be in line with Warners' mission. For example, the program book for *Don Juan* (1926) articulated a global rather than national approach by giving a history of Warner Bros. that linked its innovations to world peace: "Vitaphone, by its world wide transmission of the best in music—truly the universal language—will be a tremendous factor in promoting good will by and between people of all nations."[44] Harry Warner himself echoed this hyperbole: "We honestly believe the vitaphone [sic] is going to do more good for humanity than anything else ever invented."[45] For Warner Bros., then, making music was initially not a nativist enterprise. So what was "American" about Warners' soundtrack? The same questions about assimilation and representation that led George Gershwin, Duke Ellington, and others to "invent" the jazz-opera sent the Warners in the direction of *Pagliacci*. Certainly Warner Bros. wanted to show that American film sound would be both accessible and respectable, thus making a popular opera a rational choice. Moreover, *Pagliacci* is essentially the tragic story of a clown's failure to assimilate to the rigors of the stage, a tale begging to be retold in the context of the cinema. The use of *Pagliacci*, an Italian opera, to articulate American identity through the appearance of Al Jolson, a Jewish jazz singer, therefore, should not be all that surprising.

If Michael Curtiz had simply wanted to convey the severity of his character's shattered heart, he could have looked to literary or musical sources other than *Pagliacci*. Certainly there are texts better suited for a film that would have needed to be produced in both silent and sound versions in order to guarantee market saturation.[46] It seems Warner Bros. may have agreed. Rather than adapt Curtiz's story with *Pagliacci* intact, the studio removed all references to the opera from its eventual product, leaving the figure of the clown and his struggle as the only remnants of Curtiz's inspiration. Erasing opera from what would become the highest-grossing film of the decade helped transform the Vitaphone into an instrument of popular culture. By ignoring Curtiz's direct citations, Warner Bros. failed to acknowledge either that the "Vesti la giubba" melody appeared in the film or that it had originated as part of an opera. Unfortunately for the studio, its neglect led to copyright problems. *Pagliacci* not only found its way into the recorded score of *The Singing Fool*, it played a prominent role in at least five other Vitaphone shorts in addition to the widely screened 1926 Martinelli film already mentioned.[47] The opera's publisher, Sonzogno, wanted $1,000 from the studio to compensate for the reproduction of eight bars of "Vesti la giubba" whistled by the Arnaut Brothers in their short film and the sixteen bars of the melody used in *The Singing Fool*.[48] Warners countered that their score was a mere paraphrase and initially refused to pay. Anyone familiar with the opera and listening to the scene in question, however, would easily spot the insincerity of the studio's claim. Warner Bros. had licensed the use of seventy-nine other pieces in *The Singing Fool*.[49] Moreover, at one point Warners must have acknowledged the story's operatic origins, since earlier that year the *New York Daily News* reported that Jolson would be starring in a film version of *Pagliacci*.[50] Perhaps *Pagliacci* had seeped so deeply into the consciousness of studio executives that they themselves could no longer hear it.

This refusal to admit to using *Pagliacci* certainly had something to do with preserving Warners' bottom line, but it also may have been related to the studio's deployment of the phonograph in getting audiences to understand how the Vitaphone worked.[51] Studios and trade publications alluded to phonography to explain sound-on-disc technology and used photography as a reference for sound-on-film systems such as De Forest's Phonofilm, Fox's Movietone, or RKO's Photophone. This distinction is crucial to understanding Warners' approach to music. Steve Wurtzler shows how advertising for Victor and Columbia had emphasized the phonograph's ability to accurately transcribe events.[52] However, in introducing the phonograph to the American marketplace, promoters, vaudevillians, and urban parlor managers used the device to create new performances, building events in which the phonograph was the star.[53] The phonograph, then, has been simultaneously understood as a way to document artistic performances and as a spectacle in itself. Like the phonograph, the Vitaphone stakes a claim to fidelity but in the end rejects realism in favor of good entertainment.[54] By contrast, De Forest argued that his Phonofilm was superior to other synchronous sound systems in part on the basis of its more "natural" sound.[55] Yet in spite of De Forest's efforts in the early 1920s, sound-on-film came to prominence *after* the widespread introduction of Warners' sound-on-disc system, forcing audiences to make a comparison. Unlike the Vitaphone, which was elaborately attached to the images that accompanied it, the Phonofilm and other sound-on-film technologies placed image and sound together on a single strip. This ontological difference is an important one, for it insists that every Vitaphone screening be a performance, while sound-on-film might maintain a closer relationship to the events it documents by making their input streams inseparable.[56] If we were to excuse Warner Bros. for its failure to register *Pagliacci*'s presence in *The Singing Fool*, then we might do so on the grounds that it believed its own promotional rhetoric about Al Jolson's improvisatory ability. Perhaps Jolson channeled the melody through the sheer power of his performance without the knowledge of the studio's music department.

In the same way that *The Singing Fool* eventually substituted the phonograph in Curtiz's story for the body of Al Jolson, early reviews of the Vitaphone seemed to revel in anthropomorphic analogy. For example, the *Daily Tribune* described *Don Juan*'s Chicago premiere: "Every word formed by the lips of Will Hays falls as formed from—well, the lips of the Vitaphone."[57] Hays himself repeated this substitution of the body for the machine when he wrote about film technology in his 1929 monograph on the history of the cinema: "There are men and women of every race and of every tongue, moving slowly forward, seeking something, seeking, searching, yearning, asking for a place to dream.... The motion picture is the epitome of civilization and the quintessence of what we mean by "America."[58] Hays's short book simultaneously labels film a universal language and a distinctly American art, modifying Harry Warner's assertion of the Vitaphone's global approach: "Is it not possible that this very quality of harmonized diversities enabled America to express itself to the world by the creation and development of the world's most universal method of expression—the motion picture?"[59] In this formulation, immigrants make the cinema both universal and American. Echoing the rhetoric of the jazz-opera, the cinema is a force of assimilation, not just because it can integrate spectators or inventors into the American way of life but also because its mode of communication is a function of the technology itself.

It was important that the Vitaphone be different enough from the failed sound-on-film experiments of the 1910s and 1920s to merit a new vocabulary and yet similar enough to the technologies of both film and phonography to be accepted by the general public. These two approaches were mirrored by the repertoire chosen for the instrument. By emphasizing opera (the other "universal language"), Warner Bros. alluded to an established cultural hierarchy, and by including jazz (an American idiom) the studio assured the public that the Vitaphone could capture spontaneity. The ontology of the Vitaphone supported such a democratic paradigm. Unlike the phonograph, on which sound spirals inward, condensing the meaning of noise into a single point (that is also a hole), the Vitaphone stylus moves from the inner circle to the outer edge, evoking the image of an entity that has brought these sounds together and is now releasing them to the world. The scientific descriptions of the Vitaphone in the trade papers, then, did more than increase the public's understanding of the technology; they defined sound cinema as a process in which audiences would be asked to play an active part. Even as the studio and the press delighted in detailing how the Vitaphone worked, they nevertheless infused it with a kind of mysticism, first by differentiating it from phonography and then by choosing a particular voice to represent the sound of Warner Bros.

To make a sound film presentation seem more like a performance, Warners employed a campaign to defamiliarize the cinema itself, a project assisted by its promotion of the biggest star on the Great White Way and the nation's best known "jazz singer," Al Jolson. Following the positive reception of his 1926 short *A Plantation Act*, 1927 feature *The Jazz Singer*, and 1928 hit *The Singing Fool*, Jolson became the symbol for Warners' rise in the industry and synonymous with the Vitaphone. Jolson was, of course, a Jewish blackface singer who performed with heartfelt sincerity while wearing a disguise (Figure 1.2). His performances were thus clearly marked as such, but they have also been read as portrayals of American identity. For example, Michael Rogin argues that Jews became white by pretending to be black; blackface assisted assimilation by alluding to racial anxieties that were impossible to address directly.[60] Ted Merwin underscores performances of Jewishness in order to note that Jewish participation in the entertainment industry was more about acculturation than assimilation. Jewish characters typically strove to belong to the middle class, but were at the same time dedicated to maintaining Jewish identity.[61] In thinking about Jolson as the stand-in for the Vitaphone, we have to take into account these overlapping discussions of his ethnicity. Jolson's roles may have often been performed in blackface, and were thus intense distillations of sweeping racial stereotypes, but his place on the Warner Bros. roster was recognizably Jewish, and his ethnic identity wove its way into his films. Moreover, Warners has been memorialized as the little studio that could, inventing sound from the brink of disaster. Jolson was the perfect figure to emphasize the studio's marginal status in Hollywood at the beginning

Figure 1.2: Jazz-Pagliacci.
Frame grab from *The Singing Fool* (1928).

of the sound film experiment and demonstrate the Vitaphone's ability to create real American music.

The "jazz" of Jolson's style is equally important in determining his candidacy for the preeminent sound-on-disc body. Scholars such as Joel Dinerstein have identified jazz with an aesthetic of modernism epitomized by machines. Jazz captures the sounds of the environment around it, which, in the 1920s, was a world of industry.[62] Because it often connotes technology, jazz music was an ideal choice to highlight the newness of the Vitaphone sound-on-disc system. In most contemporary circles, jazz was synonymous with popular music, a fact that could be explained through either its cultural connotations or its musical structure.[63] From 1914 onward at least half of all Tin Pan Alley songs relied on the sort of blues' melodic and harmonic techniques later inherited by jazz.[64] Certainly, *The Jazz Singer* positions jazz as the music of the younger generation, an American sound pitted against the Old World rituals of aging immigrants. The "jazz" that Jolson sings is popular music, yet like much of the jazz presented in Warner Bros. shorts it carries the weight of history, directly referencing its rural roots with an uncomfortable nostalgia.[65] In his homage to minstrelsy, Jolson's blackened body returns the real to the technological, making the Vitaphone more than an engine for film projection.

As Michael Rogin contends, blackface pays sad tribute to the past in a modernist performance that belongs to the future.[66] Jazz may have incorporated the rhythms of repetitive labor, yet it also provided freedom for African American expression and bodily movement. Of course, Jolson was not black; nor did his melodramatic movements resemble the carefree attitude projected by the dances performed in Harlem nightclubs. Thus even though Jolson gestures in the direction of authentic American music, he is a constant reminder that in the late 1920s the definition of *jazz* was far from concrete.

MICHAEL CURTIZ'S PHONOGRAPH

Michael Curtiz's original story for *The Singing Fool* with which this chapter began employs *Pagliacci* as a cultural lens through which to interpret Abie Rachman's betrayal by his wife, Molly. The story's association of the opera with both Jewish and Italian immigrants pits the emotional excess of Pagliaccio against the rational cruelty practiced by urban women. In an early scene, Abie happily tucks his son into bed while an old Italian man living above the family plays *Pagliacci* on the phonograph. On hearing the record, Molly violently urges Abie to silence the music, a gesture that causes great discomfort to their little boy. Later in the story, Abie hears the opera again as he discovers the truth about his wayward wife. As the strains of the melody float into the apartment, Abie transforms himself into a grotesque Pagliaccio by constructing a costume out of ordinary household items. Usually a doting husband, Abie lashes out at Molly and is promptly ridiculed: "What's the matter? What's that silly costume for? Oh, I see...The great comedian—Mr. Pagliacci himself!" Molly's harsh words return Abie to his deferential role and trigger a series of desperate pleas for her love. Finally unable to keep his own identity separate from that of the infamous clown, Abie falls into a feverish sleep during which he finds himself amidst a sea of violins and somersaulting clowns as the score of Pagliacci falls into his hands. Curtiz makes the point clear—this is Abie's "realization that he is the real Pagliacci—the clown with a broken heart."[67] From that moment until the end of Curtiz's story, we hear the opera only when Abie performs it; the character no longer needs the phonograph in order to identify with the clown.

Pagliacci's placement in Curtiz's story calls attention to the phonograph in order to cement a particular reading of Abie Rachman's condition. Try as they might to turn off the music, the moments when Molly and Abie hear *Pagliacci* are out of their control; the record and the man playing it remain unseen. The symbolic weight of the opera and the mobilization of off-screen sound make it appear that Curtiz had been considering how to best maximize the potential of the new technology. Indeed, what better way to introduce the Vitaphone to the public than to place it in opposition to an older, simpler method of hearing music? Both the record player in Curtiz's imagined film and the sound-on-disc technology that would produce it are invisible, but the quality of the final product would be demonstrably better than the "battered old phonograph"[68] drifting though the speakers. The story positions the Vitaphone as the heir to phonography, a successor that both knows its history and looks forward to the future.[69] The phonograph thus becomes an amalgamated body of sorts, capable of uniting musical styles and disparate vocal performances. Reviving the phonograph's capacity for unity in an age where images can be seen and heard, Curtiz demonstrates the Vitaphone's potential by setting up the opera record as the straw man against which Jolson's impulsive Jazz-Pagliacci will be brought to life.

Not only has the phonograph within the story seen better days, the owner of the operatic recording is an Italian immigrant of a former generation, irrelevant to the plot except as a symbol. Yet he serves an enormously important role in selling the Vitaphone as a tool of assimilation. Filtered through the implied space of the old Italian's apartment, the record reminds us of a world that appreciated opera as popular entertainment and had not yet embraced the modern (and, the story hints, vulgar) music produced by Abie and Molly at the Bowery Cabaret. At the same time, the opera as performed by Abie demonstrates how ethnic works might be adapted to represent the values of all immigrants, indeed, of all Americans.[70] At first, the story had confined emotional expression to the domestic sphere. After his conversion, however, Abie can publicly share his feelings of sorrow and betrayal, albeit in disguise. Abie Rachman's Jazz-Pagliacci, Curtiz suggests, is a compromise made for a generation of assimilated Americans. Bringing the story in line with American cultural values meant disposing of some of the opera's racier elements. Rather than having an outraged Abie murder his wife and her lover as Canio had done, Curtiz's story constructs a productive ending in which American music is born from tragedy. Hardly the triumphant conclusion to Ernst Krenek's *Jonny spielt auf*, the end of Curtiz's *Pagliacci* asserts that the origins of the jazz-opera lie in betrayal and decay: like opera, jazz rises from the ashes of an unspeakable crime.

By the time *The Singing Fool* went into production, the conceit of the phonograph proved no longer necessary. Instead, the film sneaks in "Vesti la giubba" at a particularly melodramatic moment, transforming it from an isolated number into part of a larger expressive movement. As Jolson prepares for his last performance, he blackens up while facing a mirror, which remains fully visible to the viewer in an over-the-shoulder medium shot that contains both the "real" Jolson and his stage persona as reflected by the image. At this point the score indicates a two-bar statement of the aria's theme by the French horns followed by a shot of Jolson turning to face the camera.[71] As Jolson stares pitifully outward, the horn iteration neglects to reach up to finish the phrase on a major second interval and instead falls chromatically, accompanied by a diminished chord. By refusing the listener the satisfaction of a familiar cadence, this arrangement emphasizes the fact that this clown, like *Pagliacci*, will remain unable to achieve his characteristic smile: the real Jolson and his double will become one. Rather than ending with a conglomeration of jazz and opera as Curtiz had, however, *The Singing Fool* concludes with Jolson singing "Sonny Boy" one last time, and seemingly declares the triumph of jazz over opera. Yet eliminating the voice from the film's incorporation of *Pagliacci* demonstrates the ambivalence of the producers about the meaning of the change. Instead of making the story "jazzier," the film has succeeded in deflecting attention from the violence of Jolson's blackface by condensing the history of both the opera and the minstrel show into a story about a single American family. As such, the brutality revealed by the voice in Curtiz's admittedly shocking version has been camouflaged by a score that hid its source material so well that not even Warners' executives could find it. By placing the "Vesti la giubba" theme into the score and away from the control of the main character, *The Singing Fool* makes it possible for listeners of all backgrounds to identify with the Jewish Jolson through the audible figure of the clown.

JAZZ TAKES THE LEAD

The concealment of *Pagliacci* within the soundtrack of *The Singing Fool* was an early manifestation of a shift in Warners' strategy to popularize the Vitaphone by minimizing its association with opera, which was officially kicked off with a big advertising campaign in 1929. Although Jolson's second feature was the undisputed success of the 1928–29 season, challenges posed to the Vitaphone by the Movietone and Photophone systems began to take their toll on the reception of Warners' product. Douglas Gomery outlines some of the reasons for the Vitaphone's waning popularity by pointing to problems experienced by distributors and exhibitors with regard to the weight, cost, shelf life, and synchronization of Vitaphone technology.[72] Reviews of Warner Bros. films in *Harrison's Reports* in August 1929 more often than not cite some grievance with regard to sound recording or reproduction while the audio quality of the films produced by other studios goes unnoticed.[73] In spite of published critiques of the Vitaphone and the unlicensed, poor-quality disc systems abounding in independent houses,[74] Donald Crafton speculates that the shift away from sound-on-disc technology would be better explained by economics than aesthetics. Constructing dual soundtracks added expense for producers and distributors. Censorship also threatened to play a role in eliminating disc production, for it was impossible for exhibitors to cut a line of dialogue from a ten-minute disc, whereas sound-on-film promised the ability to edit image and sound simultaneously.[75] With the writing seemingly on the wall, Warner Bros. needed new ways to convince the public that its technology was both cost-effective and culturally relevant.

To emphasize the newness of the Vitaphone, Warners' 1929 campaign shied away from its earlier invocation of the phonograph's capacity for creating an enduring record of worthy performances. There was a logical reason for this shift. As Eric W. Rothenbuhler and John Durham Peters explain, before the invention of wax recording the notion of "live" music was an impossible thought: any musical encounter was always experienced "live."[76] Thus even as it purportedly enables voices to exist forever, the phonograph always carries with it the concept of death. How, then, could Warner Bros. continue stressing the concept of "liveness" to sell a technology that defined itself in radical opposition to "live" performance? As it had done with the body and voice of Al Jolson in *The Jazz Singer*, Warners' ad strategy for the Vitaphone reintroduced the possibility of liveness to recorded music through the signifiers of jazz. Although the number of jazz films produced for the Vitaphone was on the rise, the nature of the instrument as a *producer* of jazz was emphasized in print by connecting it to the urban and technological. As such, the studio would seem to rely on Joel Dinerstein's definition of jazz as the expression of life in the age of industry, conjuring up a mechanical American urban milieu.[77] After all, Le Corbusier once called the New York skyline "hot jazz in stone and steel."[78] By reminding viewers of the rhythms of modern life and the speed at which it moves, Warners suggests that the city might inspire its films and thus distinguish itself from competitors who had by this time established a different set of representational prerogatives.

Publicity for the Vitaphone accentuates its innovativeness by associating it with technologies of transportation, and in the process suggests that Warner Bros. enigmatically carries whoever talks and sings in front of the camera directly into the theater. For these advertisements, it is not just that the singer seems to be physically present that is important; how the Vitaphone gets him there is equally valuable. One ad makes this connection clear by featuring an airplane, a train, and a zeppelin all racing away from a major city as a headline announces that the Vitaphone is a "Marvel of this Marvelous Age."[79] Unlike its prior attempts to place sound-on-disc squarely within a history of phonographic content, here Warners frames the evolution of sound technology within the context of other scientific developments in order to assert its continued relevance. Another ad features a couple rounding the corner from their small-town home and arriving on a street braced by several bright theaters. The text announces: "Broadway has burst Manhattan's boundaries.... No longer must you travel to New York to see the greatest stage attractions. Just—Step around the corner...and you're on Broadway!"[80]

Warners' 1929 campaign draws attention to sound technology in a way that denies its phonographic origins. Indeed, Steve Wurtzler describes how Victor stressed the phonograph's ability to "collapse the distances between entertainment centers and geographically dispersed listeners."[81] By underscoring the *movement* between spaces rather than eliminating the importance of distance itself, the new Warner Bros. ads compared the Vitaphone's modernity to the relative antiquity of the phonograph. The positioning of the Vitaphone name in advertisements for individual films underlines this notion of transmission by animating the word itself. At the top of a July 1929 ad for *The Desert Song*,[82] for example, "Vitaphone" is given streaking effects that both allude to the fact that the device is in motion and specify how it moves; the lines that cut through the word look like grooves in a record (Figure 1.3). Advertisements like these imply that even though

Figure 1.3: Advertisement for *The Desert Song.*
Photoplay Magazine, July 1929.

the Vitaphone merely rotates, its process of creating music nevertheless exceeds the laws of physics that keep bodies bound to a single location.

Warners' conflation of music, technology, and industry in its print advertisements, however, seemed to have little impact on the reception of its shorts or the representation of music within its films. Throughout the conversion-era pages of the *New York Times*, for example, reviewer Mordaunt Hall often devoted more ink to discussing Warners' shorts than he did to its feature-length films and steadily praised the studio for introducing opera stars to the public. In one early review, Hall compares opera to popular music. Not surprisingly, the former comes out ahead: "Was it not far better to hear the strident tones of Giovanni Martinelli, singing the 'Vesti la giubba' aria from 'I Pagliacci' than to hear a dubious entertainer rendering to the full of his ability that well-known classic, 'Yes, We have No Bananas'?"[83] Years later, Warner Bros. bested Hall by producing an operatic version of this very song in a sketch for *Mammy* (1930). Dressed in blackface, Jolson and company spoof the tune by singing its words to the melodies of various familiar arias. It is important that the song serving as Hall's comparison is not just any popular tune, but one that had been repeatedly called on to describe the urban immigrant experience. A Tin Pan Alley song initially illustrating the humor of a Greek shop owner's misunderstanding of the English language, "Bananas" had been reworked in countless situations, transforming the Greek into an Italian, German, or nameless immigrant of virtually any other nationality. The song had been performed by the "king of jazz" himself, Paul Whiteman, in 1924 and categorized as a jazz tune by others.[84] The skit in Jolson's film, however, bears no resemblance to the representation of opera and jazz that Warners was promoting elsewhere. Singing to the camera while on stage in the presence of an audience, this blackface Jolson has none of the emotional sincerity displayed in his *Singing Fool* character. Instead of being an integral part of a feature film, the scene reads like an early Vitaphone short. As such, the parody seems to suggest Warners' self-awareness about the distance between its musical representation and its marketing campaign.

The studio's reflexivity was epitomized by its foregrounding of the sound apparatus, both within the films themselves and with respect to their promotion. Taking the lead from Warners, exhibitors began to associate Jolson with the phonograph itself, recontextualizing phonography as a producer of jazz. One example of this shift comes from Tuscaloosa, Alabama. In order to draw crowds to his presentation of *The Singing Fool*, W. D. Kyle, Jr., the manager of the Ritz Theater in that town, mounted a cutout of Al Jolson's face above the marquee, situated a loudspeaker behind the mouth, and had "Jolson" "perform" the songs from the film. As Kyle explained, "it looked and sounded like the huge head was singing."[85] Another manager, in Buffalo, New York, started the promotion with an organist playing a medley of Jolson's familiar songs, accompanied by photos of the singer and his lyrics. As "Sonny Boy" began, the organist would stop and "Jolson himself" would continue in his own voice, amplified from a phonograph located in the projection booth.[86] Though they were intended as teasers for the "real" Jolson available via the cinema, these experiments nonetheless conflate the actor, phonograph, and Vitaphone in moments of jazz performance. Putting the unmistakable Al Jolson at the center of its ad campaign, Warner Bros. hoped to stave off the tide of bad publicity that threatened to sink the future of its formerly peerless sound technology. However, even this strategy proved problematic, as Jolson's distinctive sound could not be a permanent substitute for the real African American voices that created jazz.

YAMEKRAW: JAZZ-OPERA ON SCREEN

Directed by Murray Roth, who had been responsible for a number of other Warner Bros. jazz shorts during the conversion, *Yamekraw* (1930) is a twelve-minute film based on James P. Johnson's symphonic jazz composition of the same name. Johnson wrote the piece in 1927 as a response to Gershwin's *Rhapsody in Blue*. Johnson's *Yamekraw* was compared to Dvořák's "New World" Symphony because it incorporated preexisting songs and spirituals with key elements of the composer's primary style, which in Johnson's case was jazz, in order to make a musical statement about America.[87] Like much of Gershwin's music, *Yamekraw* not only integrates traditionally white and black musical characteristics; it also reveals an anxiety about the place of jazz in American popular culture. Gershwin's *Rhapsody* attempted to sophisticate jazz; Johnson's work aimed to provide insights into African American life in an idiom that New York City's elite might understand. Certainly his work can be placed within the larger context of the Harlem Renaissance. Johnson was a Harlem stride pianist who composed pieces such as *Harlem Symphony* and *Manhattan Street Scene* that commented explicitly on life in Harlem.[88] In *Yamekraw*, modernist musical sounds tell a story about African American Southern history, a combination that not only echoed the artistic choices made by some of Johnson's colleagues working in other mediums but also made the piece ideal for adaptation by Warner Bros. *Yamekraw* was an educational project, nostalgic narrative, and artistic statement that, in spite of its seemingly eccentric imagery, was neatly aligned with Warners' approach to representing both opera and jazz.

Promotion for the premiere of Johnson's composition at Carnegie Hall in 1928 centered on performer Fats Waller's "authentic" jazz background and made strides toward revising the whitewashed version of jazz history presented by Whiteman at the Aeolian Hall four years earlier. The *Chicago Defender*'s review of the premiere contains nothing but praise, and ends with a directive for African American composers: "Let us show Gershwin that we are the originators of syncopation, can write jazz operas, which will very soon be as popular as the old standard operas."[89] Yet *Yamekraw* is not an "opera"—or is it? Although Johnson did not refer to his instrumental piece in this way, by adding the voice and a visual element the 1930 cinematic version of Johnson's work comes much closer to realizing the American jazz-opera than anything Hollywood had produced before it, and certainly more than *The Singing Fool*, which had done its best to erase its operatic influence. In spite of its length, the compositional mode, visual style, and narrative trajectory of Warners' *Yamekraw* tailors operatic tendencies to the African American condition and contains them within larger jazz sonorities. If the music itself held the spark of "jazz-operas" waiting to be written, the film hinted at the potential for a uniquely American artistic form.

While situating Johnson's original *Yamekraw* within the development of concert jazz, the jazz historian John Howland labels Warners' adaptation of the work a "quasi-folk opera."[90] The addition of *quasi* is important here, for it signifies that something is amiss in this celebration of African American life. The film simultaneously moves away from a realistic picture of black experience by paying homage to German Expressionism and returns the piece to its religious roots by adding lyrics reminiscent of a black spiritual (Figure 1.4). Other than the substitution of voices for various brass instruments (which is no small matter), the film's alterations to the original score are minimal.[91] Yet these changes are important in presenting the short as a condensation of cultural forms that elevates folk culture to American art.

Yamekraw opens with a credit sequence that defines the title: "A negro rhapsody which expresses the moods and the emotional ideal of negro life, Yamekraw is a settlement on the outskirts of Savannah, Georgia." Yamekraw may be based on a real place, but any understanding of *this* Yamekraw as a literal location is wiped away by the film's initial moments. The first shot reveals what is clearly a two-dimensional cabin in silhouette, while the following images are filmed in a canted frame: a woman rocking her baby, a smiling older man in overalls and a straw hat, and a boy eating a generous slice of watermelon. The lighting and contrast of this opening, however, skew its stereotypical Southern imagery. Such shots aim to commemorate the past, yet the style in which they are presented articulates

Figure 1.4: A Spiritual Chorus.
Frame grab from *Yamekraw* (1930).

explicitly modern attitudes: the Vitaphone Release Index's entry even boastingly calls *Yamekraw*'s scenery "futuristic."[92] Howland claims that the visual choices made for the film successfully revamp Johnson's piece for a white audience. Certainly, the familiar and unthreatening imagery could make white viewers more comfortable with black music. Yet the strangeness of the cinematography and mise-en-scène seem to imply a greater project. I argue that *Yamekraw* attempts to insert an authentic, unnamed, and collective jazz voice in Jolson's place, an effort that, ironically, could be achieved only through asynchronicity.

Unlike the majority of Warners' operatic and jazz shorts, *Yamekraw* flaunts its lack of synchronicity. The body of the film consists of eighty-four shots—about four times as many as would be found in a typical performance short from the same period. The characters lip-synch their vocal parts, but it is plain that the image track has been edited after the fact to match the rhythm of the music. Moreover, the camera angles do little to draw attention to moving lips, instead emphasizing the set design and refusing to situate the viewer in a comprehensible space. Such a sound-image relationship seems more akin to Soviet filmmakers' infamous calls for a contrapuntal soundtrack than it does to Warners' recreations of the theatrical experience.[93] Indeed, *Yamekraw*'s soundtrack negates the assumptions of its fragile plot. Incorporating many of the offensive tropes found in film narratives about African Americans, Warners' *Yamekraw* is a motiveless tale of a young man who leaves his family in Georgia to try his prospects in the city, falls for a loose woman, realizes the degrading nature of the fast life, and remorsefully returns to the idyllic rural South. The film's lack of sound fidelity makes this stereotypical story ludicrous: the disregard for matching bodies to voices suggests that any nameless black character can be substituted for any other. Had *Yamekraw* been shot and edited in line with Warners' other opera and jazz films, we would be presented with a very different idea about American sound, one that offered *Yamekraw* as representative of black performance to be filed among the studio's multiple recordings of groups such as the Nicholas Brothers and, perhaps, easily dismissed. Instead, the film makes a statement about the artistry of contemporary black music that contradicts the limited role Warners usually allotted to black performers.

Though it was purportedly made to showcase Johnson's music, in many ways *Yamekraw* is reminiscent of a much later style of opera film. Invoking André Bazin's discussion of theatrical adaptations, we might suggest that opera films can "speak side by side" with their predecessors, "in front of and behind the stage."[94] Films that do this, among them Ingmar Bergman's *Magic Flute* (1975) and Hans-Jürgen Syberberg's *Parsifal* (1982), put on versions of operas that intersect with the capabilities of the camera and convey the core dramatic conflict in a cinematic dialect. Following this logic, the jazz-opera film would necessarily be ambivalent about African American participation in an industrial Hollywood production. It would neither idealize the black experience nor realistically illustrate its hardships. It would recognize the origins of jazz while attending to the artificiality of the opera stage. It would be exempt from the rules governing continuity editing and sonic matching. It would heighten the impact of character struggles and geographic settings rather than making them more extravagant.[95] In other words, it would look and sound very much like *Yamekraw*.

What exactly is *Yamekraw* saying about jazz? Is it fair to consider a film with such overtly oppressive racial and gender politics "progressive?" The plot pits the values of the rural nuclear family against the dangers of city women, an old story that would seem to echo the picture of jazz painted by many other Hollywood films. In its city sequence, *Yamekraw* takes our nameless male character to a nightclub, where he finds a seductive woman dancing in close-up. Yet when he enters the club, the music we hear fails to match the live band we see. Instead of dance music, the soundtrack offers voices singing about Yamekraw in a spiritual motif taken from the first half of the film; it grinds to a halt as the woman takes to the floor, in spite of there being no observable change in the dancers' and musicians' behavior around her. It would be easy to read such a moment as a critique of jazz, awarding the sensual urban female character the ability to kill the pastoral purity of Yamekraw. Indeed, the city here signifies something quite different than it did in Warners' ad campaign for the newness of the Vitaphone: rather than technological progress, we have sin and sex. However, the film's appropriation of Johnson's piece forces us to understand the scene differently. Even though the plot is divided between urban and rural spaces, Johnson's music constantly blends the elements typically associated with each. This move familiarizes jazz by grounding its tonalities in old American values rather than relegating it to an exotic urban space. Yet it also makes the music of the old South sound very unlike the version audiences had become accustomed to hearing when Al Jolson sang. The film responds to the 1920s' question of how composers ought to go about creating definitively American music by pairing an overtly stylized image with a soundtrack that prided itself on its authenticity.

The visual treatment of Johnson's work echoes the weighty symbolic value given to the mise-en-scène in many of Warners' opera shorts. For example, shadowy stripes cast by a mysterious source cloud a close-up of the central couple, members of a choir stranded in a hole wave their arms at the camera above, and crooked windows and a jagged barber shop pole (Figure 1.5) define the nameless two-dimensional city reminiscent of the carnivalesque milieu in *The Cabinet of Dr. Caligari* (dir. Robert Wiene, 1920). These sorts of shots, like the operatic arias culled from much longer works and preserved by the Vitaphone, hint at a deeper story rather than develop the plot. On first viewing, therefore, it is very difficult to tell not only where these scenes are in relation to one another but also what exactly is "happening" in this film. *Variety*'s review echoes this sentiment: "It's a short that started out to be made along lines that brought German art to pictures, but in carrying out these ideas entertainment value has been neglected to a certain extent."[96] John Howland argues that Warners' interpretation of Johnson's music ought to be understood as an expression of "Hollywood artificiality and excess" rather than art.[97] Certainly, the film isn't subtle. However, reading *Yamekraw* alongside the studio's opera shorts and taking into account the quality of its soundtrack requires that we see the film in a different context.

In addition to *Yamekraw*'s audacious mise-en-scène, the film integrates incredibly high- and low-angle shots in such a way that it becomes impossible to determine the spatial position of the viewer. This technique suggests the possibility of a mass spectator, which could be reminiscent of the

Figure 1.5: A Jazzy Barber.
Frame grab from *Yamekraw* (1930).

multiple points of perception in an opera hall. Because of restrictions governing camera movement during the conversion era, the short is able to maintain its dizzying editing effects only because it has been filmed without sound, a surprising choice given the Vitaphone's history of visualizing the voice at its source. The film's disjointedness becomes even stranger when we realize that *Yamekraw* was filmed in the first half of 1930, the period when Warner Bros. decided it would fully transition to a sound-on-film system of recording, which meant the sound editing would not have been quite so onerous should the studio have wanted to record on set. The decision to use playback not only further enables the film's flamboyant style; it also preserves the unity of Johnson's piece while allowing the image track to meander, providing snippets of African American life as if teasing a melody from an otherwise stable key. The obvious lack of audiovisual matching, moreover, parallels the mobile listener conjured by the rhapsody, who is asked to identify with the experiences of a wide population over a relatively lengthy period of time. Asynchronicity here lets us hear "opera," expressed by a collection of African American performers, through the idiom of jazz. Moreover, the film's style attempts to overcome the episodic structure of the musical piece, which was derisively noted by many at the time of its debut.[98] Instead of stringing together visual fragments to match Johnson's musical sketches, the film constructs a minimal narrative around the settlement, a story that begins and ends at the cabin. In its opera shorts, Warners assumed that its listeners already knew the music, or at the very least that they would be able to locate the signifiers of quality provided by the studio and understand they *ought* to recognize it. By doing the same thing with *Yamekraw*, refusing to tie the music to the image in an easily comprehensible way, Warner Bros. took both jazz and its listeners seriously. Thus Sobchack's "echo-focus" returns with full effect: *Yamekraw* made spectators aware of the act of listening, and consequently of the work that they had to do in order to weave together the threads of this film and make sense of the role serious art could play in the cinema.

Of course, the relationship between opera and jazz as presented by Warner Bros. and "serious art" as we understand it today is by no means explicit. Thus the assertion that the studio treated jazz in *Yamekraw* as it did opera in its other shorts must be understood within the context of what the studio *thought* it was doing to preserve and provide music for Americans rather than from an a priori definition of what art ought to be. In both of these cases, music with high cultural roots (Johnson's *Yamekraw* premiered at Carnegie Hall while *Pagliacci* toured in houses across Europe) was snipped and simplified to play in far more pedestrian locations. Yet in another sense, Warners actually elevated the cultural status of these musical works by positioning them within the educational mission of the studio. *Pagliacci* became a teaching tool to help future generations understand opera; Johnson's music was no longer a little performed response to Gershwin's more famous composition but became a statement about the capabilities of African American artistry that was heard across the nation. More importantly, the cinematic version of each work significantly transformed the nature of the voice. Both Curtiz's story for *The Singing Fool* and Warners' version of *Yamekraw* are efforts to combine opera and jazz, yet while the former excised opera from its history, the latter forced the spectator to face the consequences of segregated artistic production through the addition of African American voices. The temporal vagueness of *Yamekraw*'s set suggests that the plantation could have existed in the midnineteenth century, yet the presence of jazz and the city make the film about the present. The musical arrangers could have limited the voice's role to the rural scenes, at least suggesting that such oppression existed only in the past. By letting the voices of Yamekraw seep into the city scenes, the film suggests that jazz is the progeny of oppression and must always be understood within a broader cultural context.

In *Yamekraw*, the improvisational qualities that have often been identified as essential to jazz are subordinated to lyrics that speak about a historical place and time in which African Americans remain bound to a particular
way of life. The words sung by the young woman before her husband leaves
for the city illustrate this role: "I've got a feeling that keeps me at the home,
and when I get there I never want to roam.... I'm trying, crying, dying just
to get there someday. To Dixieland, it is so grand, you understand." The film
doesn't give us space to ask exactly what is so "grand" about the woman's
tiny cabin inhabited by countless children who work all day in the fields,
particularly because the music at this point ends on a C-sharp major chord
(an unusual cadence outside of the tonal regularities of A major in which
the rest of the tune is written) before making a transition that's so uneasy
the music almost seems to stop.[99] Johnson's orchestral version scales back
at this point, allowing us contemplate the strangeness of the completed
theme; the film produces an image of a baby crying, refocusing our attention on the action (like the child, we're supposed to be upset at the man's
departure from such an idyllic spot) rather than letting us think too much
about the meaning of the musical phrase. There are many moments in
Warners' *Yamekraw* that suggest the film is struggling between the tendency to let the music express ambiguity about the past and the desire to
define it for the audience along the lines of a contemporary film genre. In
all such cases, the black voice is audibly operatic, emphasizing the impossible cohesion attempted by a film that seeks to deploy African American
agency in the name of a regressive image of the South, reminding us of the
theft that lies at the center of this music. Indeed, as it did with *Pagliacci*,
Warner Bros. seems to have initially forgotten to credit the music's origins,
and consequently found itself embroiled in yet another lawsuit.[100]

In many ways, *Yamekraw*'s images of jazz resemble other conversion-era
attempts to represent the music visually, such as the emphasis on shadow
and pathos in the conclusion of RKO's 1929 *Black and Tan* or the references to everyday life in Paramount's later *Symphony in Black* (1935).[101] As
it was with these films, jazz in *Yamekraw* is enveloped into an epic struggle
of opposition and death (the end of *Yamekraw* is marked by the passing
of the older generation, as indicated by the lyrics if not made obvious by
the image track). Yet even though *Black and Tan* contains jazz music within
a larger and fully comprehensive narrative arc, *Yamekraw* persists in its
Expressionism as well as its continuous musical arrangement. Thus it functions more as an opera might, with moments of "recitative" (albeit deliv-
ered instrumentally) followed by an aria (performed vocally). It is easy to
hear how the arranger (NBC conductor and violinist Hugo Mariani) managed to assign voices to particular melodic moments. For example, the

horn or saxophone solos, close in range and timbre to the human voice, are often selected for this transposition. The larger orchestral interludes are occasionally represented by a gospel choir, which at times appears on the screen. Most importantly, Johnson's rhapsody, like Gershwin's, employs the piano as a focal point. In Johnson's version, it is clear that the piano is used to rearticulate the widely varied forms of expression introduced by other instruments: whether blues, jazz, or gospel, the piano represents the "voice" of a people, and its relationship to the rest of the text is almost like a call and response. The cinematic adaptation deemphasizes the piano by replacing it with images of African Americans capable of singing these melodies for themselves. As with opera, both recitative and aria provide narrative information, but the vocal parts of the film express more fully how the characters feel about an event, in the same way that Johnson's piano was able to elaborate the basic orchestral melodies. Jazz instrumentals mimic the movements of a train, identify the dangers of the city woman, and note a distinction between generations; the "arias" express the sorrows of the population in prayer and demonstrate the benefits of living in "Dixieland." With its dedication to unity, overt symbolism, and lack of narrative development, the structure of *Yamekraw* is perhaps more operatic than the literal "opera shorts" that Warner Bros. released.

Produced as Warners was revamping the image of the Vitaphone away from its association with the elite concert hall and toward the industrial and technological sources that inspired jazz, *Yamekraw* held a special place in the studio's catalogue. Even though the images themselves evoke a rural past, the speed at which they greet the eye demonstrates the fluidity of sound cinema. Johnson's rhapsody may have been written in response to Gershwin and performed for upper-class New Yorkers, but its music was intended to resonate with American listeners of differing economic backgrounds. With this piece as its foundation, *Yamekraw* sends a message about the potential combination of opera and jazz on screen and the Vitaphone as the voice of America. *Yamekraw* expresses the importance of great music, entertainment, and preservation, values that Warners had professed from the time of the Vitaphone's premiere. As such, the film mimics the discourse about the making of American music that called for a jazz-opera in the first place: rather than establish a national school of music or abandon the sonic history of its ancestors, American composers should exploit their limitations and embrace pastiche.[102] *Yamekraw* used images and sounds that referenced recognizable genres and styles and combined them in ways that reflected white Americans' discomfort with opera, jazz, and African American culture. Nonetheless, for all its ambiguity, *Yamekraw* could be the jazz-opera's first real triumph.

On a mission to foster "a national appreciation of good music,"[103] Warner Bros. constructed a catalogue it hoped would comprise the best music the United States had to offer. In so doing, however, it necessarily defined what "good music" would be, and it did so while pretending to withhold judgment on the jazz-opera debate raging in the pages of American music journals. With the transformations it made to pieces such as *Pagliacci* and *Yamekraw*, however, the studio made a very clear statement about both national music and American film. *Pagliacci* started as a piece that built on the Pierrot character of Italian and French pantomime. As it worked its way through Warners' executive offices, the opera became a signifier of Italian immigration, the sound of Jewish American pathos, and finally a tune so American that it forgot its roots altogether. *Yamekraw* was subjected to a similar broadening, resulting in a film that speaks about national heritage by dressing up the past in modernist imagery. It may have been defined as a form that has yet to arrive, but the jazz-opera was nostalgic even before it existed. It makes sense, then, that jazz and opera would come together most prominently in a studio intent on defining the past and preserving the present for the citizens of the future.

CHAPTER 2
Opera Cut Short

From the Castrato to the Film Fragment

Critics frequently used the word *charming* to describe American soprano Anna Case.[1] The daughter of a New Jersey blacksmith, she was famous for her purported lack of training and known as a light singer of serious music, capable of careful enunciation, particularly when singing in English, but unlikely to stray into the emotional depth of the German aria.[2] Case's career may have begun at the opera, but it was Thomas Edison who cemented her popularity. As the preeminent voice of the Tone Tests, a popular series of concerts demonstrating the lifelike quality of Thomas Edison's Diamond Disc Phonograph, Case had an affinity with mechanical reproduction that made her an ideal candidate to appear on the premiere program of Vitaphone sound shorts. Because it featured Case singing along with the Met Opera Chorus, her first film appeared to affirm the Vitaphone's high cultural status. Yet Case's second film, *Swanee River*, reveals the identity crisis experienced by both American opera and Hollywood cinema in the latter half of the 1920s. Although composers and the press were concerned with finding American voices to perform American music, engineers and studio executives had to figure out a way to respond to the threat that the dominance of American English would pose to its export market, and at the same time learn how to make synchronous sound acceptable to the American public. Case's second performance, recorded with ukulele player Roy Smeck and the Dixie Jubilee Singers, alludes to film's vaudevillian sources, but it also says something much more significant about the importance of song in defining the value of both opera and film sound during the period of conversion.

Like many of Warners' other efforts, the Case, Smeck, and Dixie Jubilee collaboration was opera with an American accent. Written by Steven Foster in 1851, "Old Folks at Home," the official title of the song featured in *Swanee River*, expresses the nostalgic longing of an African American man for the land of his youth. Though it might seem strange to select a seventy-five-year-old song lamenting the past to establish the vitality of a new entertainment medium, its appeal for singers lay in its broad range, octave leap, and, of course, American roots.[3] Perhaps Warners supposed that the combined familiarity of Stephen Foster's music and Anna Case's voice would align the Vitaphone with existing practices for distributing quality music to American listeners. Although conversion-era technology would have been capable of producing feature-length operas on multiple reels, this would not necessarily have been universally appealing. Contemporary audiences were used to hearing recordings of individual arias and experiencing autonomous songs in musicals, vaudeville, and stage revues. Similarly, opera shorts filtered the narrative out of the performance, separating the figure of the singer from the role that would otherwise contextualize her character. With Foster's melody and the collection of musicians chosen to perform it, however, *Swanee River* constructs a new story about American music that requires the contributions of white and black singers from folk, opera, and gospel traditions without accounting for their presence in the film or addressing the social and political problems that led to or stemmed from its production. As such, it resembles the fraught representation of American life commonly found in the staged jazz-operas.

Suffering the same fate as many of its jazz-opera predecessors, *Swanee River* was purged from performance history. Case's second film is nowhere to be found in a late-1920s Vitaphone Release Index, suggesting that it was pulled from distribution along with shorts starring fellow sopranos Rosa Raisa, Marion Talley, and possibly Mary Lewis.[4] There are a number of plausible explanations for the omission, ranging from regional restrictions on mixed-race ensembles to notorious problems with recording female voices. The disappearance of this short *in particular*, however, alludes to greater cultural concerns about the continued segregation of opera and jazz. Opera may appear on the same program as other musical styles, but it must signify in particular ways. In its quest to make American opera films, Warner Bros. would eventually cast aside its sopranos in order to promote a single male singer. Giovanni Martinelli starred in fifteen opera shorts for the studio during the same period in which Al Jolson represented the American jazz singer in a string of popular feature films. In spite of their distinct appearances and performance styles, Jolson and Martinelli play surprisingly similar roles. The assimilation narrative so frequently attributed to Jolson's films can also be found in Martinelli's history on screen; his appearances condense opera's European grand pageantry into a series of clearly articulated songs made to appeal to Americans. The promotion of the Italian Giovanni Martinelli over the American Anna Case tells us that it wasn't enough to find American voices; the Vitaphone had to make them.

This chapter explains how early sound cinema negotiated the distinct uses of opera in American culture to arrive at a set of gendered representational practices that would eventually become part of Hollywood's standard vocabulary. Edison may once have dreamed of producing cinematic grand opera, but the Hollywood sound shorts took a more minimalist approach, paring down the stage and reducing the chorus. Rather than transmitting the work of the masters, the short film commodified the opera as a salable song that was reliant on the signifiers of the European stage for its legitimacy, but remained wholly independent of its narrative context. As the differences between Edison and Hollywood of the 1920s illustrate, neither "opera" nor "cinema" is a singular entity; therefore, I refrain from seeking an all-encompassing explanation for their coexistence. I address the medium as a series of people, places, and texts that came together to create a group of films in a particular period. I begin by contextualizing the significance of "opera" for middle-class Americans in the nineteenth and twentieth centuries, showing how the aria became an American operatic vernacular. I then consider the gendered and ethnic performance of the aria and its effect on the style of these films, comparing the representation and relative success of the tenors and sopranos that sang for early opera shorts. Finally, I account for the persistence of the Vitaphone opera films throughout the conversion era in the face of the abandonment of the genre by the other major studios.

OPERA BEFORE VITAPHONE

"Opera" means something different for the shorts of the conversion period than it does for early Edison films such as *Parsifal* (1904), European televised productions such as Ingmar Bergman's *The Magic Flute* (1975), blockbuster Hollywood fare such as *Moonstruck* (1987), and the simulcast Metropolitan Opera performances seen today in multiplexes across the United States and Europe. Because of the variance of its screen appearances in the last century, we find in the literature about the opera film a prevailing desire to justify its existence. Scholars have addressed some of the more perplexing intersections: the prevalence of opera narratives in silent films, the presence of opera hits in animation aimed at children, or the popularity of live opera performances on screens typically used for action films.[5] Others, however, tend to pool all such instances together, in explanations that seem rooted in a persistent fantasy about the universality of the musical sphere.[6] Yet the transmission of music by particular technologies necessarily alters its capabilities for expression: whatever representational qualities music has on paper or in performance shift, depending on its mediation. In one of his characteristic polemics, Adorno claimed that the alterations made to the symphony by its on-air format ensure its incommensurability with "real" art. The characteristics of the symphony—unity, intensity, the suspension of time—are eradicated by the ether, which sets up a mode of consumption by which audiences listen for quotations, thematic fragments flattened by the lack of dynamic interchange and incapable of engrossing the listener in the manner in which she would be treated by the concert hall.[7] One could make a similar accusation against the conversion-era opera film. The lack of stereo sound and the restrictions on range imposed by the limits of the technological reproduction would not likely have permitted the construction of an engrossing soundscape. Adorno contends that this missing intensity transforms the symphony into mere "episodes" around which are placed "ballyhoo" or "radio sales talk." We can certainly find evidence of this presentation style in the structure of both the individual conversion-era opera short and its evening program, which situated arias among filmed vaudeville acts, live stage shows, previews for coming features, and an array of other attractions. Understanding the opera aria as variety act, recorded by a relatively new system and reproduced in a space not constructed solely for its reception, would brand the opera short with the stigma of Adorno's analysis. Yet what if the meaning of "opera" and "symphony" had not been as rigid as Adorno imagined?

The history of middlebrow artistic consumption has some bearing on why Hollywood studios turned to shorts rather than features as a means of presenting opera on film. Opera shorts could be seen as illustrated extensions of the opera records circulating in middle-class American homes or as partners of the contemporaneous "radio symphonies" heard in their living rooms. Indeed, the status these shorts attained for Warner Bros. in particular reflects the practice of collecting that Adorno sees as symptomatic of twentieth-century capitalism, which transformed melodies and the voices that make them into fetish objects "possessed" by record collectors.[8] Warners marketed its opera shorts in line with this logic but on a grander scale, creating a library of discs produced and circulated for the benefit of all Americans. The studio provided exhibitors with a Vitaphone Release Index, a catalogue that would enable them to select the sound shorts that best serve their patrons. An evaluation of the songs and singers that Warners preserved can tell us a great deal about the values of both the studio system and American culture during the late 1920s.

Although much of the scholarship on the relationship between opera and cinema assumes an "opera" is a fully realized work and treats "cinema" as a category limited by the feature film, such definitions are not only short-sighted (as it were), they also cannot account for a mode of fragmentary listening that is the key to understanding the place of opera shorts in the conversion period. It is important to base any argument about the emergence and subsequent rapid disappearance of the opera short on an understanding of how spectators understood "opera" prior to the introduction of synchronous sound and how the specificities of "cinema" altered that comprehension. The length of the short film, the representation of opera through audiovisual technology, and the organization of arias within each work led the major Hollywood studios to define *opera* as a series of highlights whose value to the studio depended on their ability to be played again.

The knowledge that these opera highlights had been recorded in order to be replayed in theaters around the nation shifts the expectations of the operatic spectator because no two performances of any live opera are ever identical. By this, I mean more than simply the idea that one diva might be a better Carmen than another, or that a singer might emphasize certain notes on Friday night only to change her inflection on Saturday. The changes made to individual opera productions as they traveled across the United States in the nineteenth and early twentieth centuries could be major. Indeed, such alterations shifted the source of meaning from the composer's hand to the local producer. This practice was familiar to silent filmgoers; the variability in film exhibition prompted Rick Altman to come up with the idea of "cinema as event" as an analytical approach, by which he wants us to consider the experience of the spectator as a singular exchange between the mechanisms of production and those of reception.[9] The importance of reception is especially evident when talking about early cinema: distributors provided prints, but projectionists and censorship boards altered them, which in turn encouraged producers to change how they would construct future products. This practice also applied to film music. Films were initially released with no suggestions for musical accompaniment, but pianists, orchestras, and trade columnists began to publicly recommend pieces to perform alongside individual films, choices that sometimes ran contrary to the intended tone of the picture and that resulted in the perceived need for producers to reign in meaning by providing ideas of their own.[10]

Thus the idea of seeing recorded opera in a theater conflicted not only with how audiences had been experiencing the cinema but, for many, with their experiences with opera in the United States. Just as projectionists and censors became editors and interpreters, local opera producers made decisions about the appropriate staging of various works for American audiences. As a result, touring artists often felt no obligation to maintain the integrity of an opera as it had been composed. The numerous opera companies that visited the United States throughout the nineteenth century were not required to perform the entirety of any given work and regularly inserted popular contemporary tunes in the place of some of the lesser-known arias.[11] Lawrence Levine notes that during this period operas were often presented on the same program as popular entertainment, such as farces or even dog shows.[12] Yet "opera" still retained a distinctive status that prevented it from being entirely synonymous with popular song. According to Katherine Preston, the tension between the notion of "opera" as popular music and "opera" as an aristocratic medium persisted throughout the antebellum era.[13] We can see that tension in the late nineteenth century with John W. Isham's Oriental Opera Company, which featured an all-black cast performing opera selections, burlesques, and cakewalks.[14] The poster for Isham's 1896 Broadway production of *Oriental America* (Figure 2.1) alluded to an array of American musical styles and symbols,

Figure 2.1: John W. Isham's *Oriental America* (1896).
Library of Congress, Prints and Photographs Division [LC-USZ62-28630].

but most prominently featured was an opera diva, gazing confidently at the viewer while the scores for *Faust, Lucia*, and *Rigoletto* lay strewn about her. Isham's promise to deliver forty minutes of grand opera was firmly situated within discourses that would make opera more accessible and more American while acknowledging both the elegance and the exoticism of the music. Thanks to new sites of performance (such as the cinema, the phonograph parlor, or the living room), shortened and creative programs like Isham's would continue into the twentieth century and influence the production and reception of the synchronous sound shorts.

In the nineteenth and early twentieth centuries, opera arias were familiar to Americans from a variety of social classes, albeit sometimes in arrangement or translation, and often without context. For example, Jenny Lind's much-touted 1850 U.S. tour did not cast her in full operas, but instead comprised a series of concerts in which Lind blended operatic pieces with folk ballads. She may not have elevated the American taste for music as much as her promoter P. T. Barnum claimed, but Lind did throw a wrench into what Levine calls the "sacralization of culture" that would result in the institution of an elite class of operagoers.[15] As John Dizikes points out, Lind's performances were not only important musically; they were also monumental in the creation of a new kind of singing star. Barnum remade Lind as an innocent and genuine personality, a Swedish girl promoted to challenge Americans' preconceptions of the histrionic opera diva.[16] Lind's diverse collection of songs was selected to showcase her talent while appealing to everyone. Lind's tour legitimized the recontextualization of the medium, freeing the idea of "opera" from its entrenchment in an aristocratic scene and defining it instead on the basis of the voice. As critics proclaimed her unparalleled genius, listeners began to measure other singers against a star who, despite her foreignness, possessed old-fashioned American values: she was loyal to her nation, morally upright, and humble, forging a formula on which the later operatic icons of the sound shorts would be based.

Jenny Lind united "high" and "low" art into a single vocal technique, defying contemporary movements to segregate American culture along class lines. Yet her influence was not permanent. As Levine argues, the distinction between "high" and "low" culture shifts with ideological currents. The elitist connotations given opera today resulted from both a drive to preserve the original language of the libretto rather than translate it into easily comprehensible English and a crusade to discipline audience behavior.[17] So even though Lind's variety concert format may have been replicated in Victor's record catalogue or Warners' Vitaphone collection, it is important to acknowledge that her nineteenth-century performance style had gone out of fashion by the time Warners recorded its first operatic short in 1926.

What happened between 1850 and 1926 that led to the creation of a cultural elite determined either to train the lower and middle classes to enjoy the opera or to exclude them from the experience? In part, the foundation of permanent symphony orchestras in the United States helped to establish "concert repertoire" as a genre to be set apart from more popular fare. Such institutions, launched, for example, in Boston in 1881 and in Chicago ten years later, performed a full symphony on every program, thus dismissing the notion that it was preferable to hear individual movements without context. Financial backing by industrial luminaries followed the naissance of symphonies and opera companies in major American cities, and with it the need to distinguish the "quality" art supported by such cultural giants from the more popular, and therefore less deserving, American stage. Thus a rift grew between shorter musical performances presented in vaudeville theaters and European works imported to premiere at newly constructed symphony halls and opera houses.[18] In fact, the Metropolitan Opera drew an even more precise line, separating popular Italian opera from its more serious German variant. Between 1884 and 1891, the company performed works only in the German language, even translating those originally written in Italian.[19] One could easily connect the growing distaste for Italian opera to New Yorkers' resentment of the city's Italian immigrant explosion in the late nineteenth century. Yet John Dizikes attributes Italian opera's purported lack of "seriousness" to its pervasiveness in the United States in the middle-to-late nineteenth century and its emphasis on the virtuosic vocalist rather than the composition as a whole.[20] When Italian opera reemerged as the genre of choice in opera shorts of the 1920s, however, its connotations of lightness, associations with immigrant singers, and, most importantly, emphasis on the capabilities of the individual soloist would prove essential to the Vitaphone's success.

Another reason for the change in opera's cultural status was the decreasing production of music by amateurs. As the phonograph became more affordable and began to replace the piano as the middle-class instrument of choice in the 1910s, the distinction between public and private performance sharpened to favor the consumption of music over its reproduction. Jacques Attali saw this phenomenon as a sociocultural shift from an age of representation to an era of repetition. According to Attali, alterations in musical style prefigure larger economic swings; thus one can hear, in the music of the late nineteenth century, the delocalized means of control attributed to the twentieth.[21] Because the source of cultural authority had become obscured, musical taste seemed intrinsic, naturalizing the value of opera over the folk song, in terms of its cultural sophistication and its economic worth. It may be true that some cultural forces in the twentieth century encouraged a stratified public culture, but the technologies of recording and reproduction that it heralded cannot be universally dismissed as exclusive, for they fostered the creation of alternative publics. It is with these neglected groups in mind that we ought to understand the 1920s opera shorts. Hollywood certainly did not expect a wholesale elevation of popular culture upon the introduction of sound, or it would not have continued producing jazz and comedy shorts. Because sound technology made filmed arias accessible during a time when the debate over the future of opera was raging, these shorts allowed the public to participate in a discussion about the place of American music and play a role in determining the sound of the American voice.

Though there were many famous exceptions, the taming of the audience from the distracted, disrespectful, and occasionally riotous masses of the nineteenth century to the silent crowds of the twentieth owes its success to the training of attention and the establishment of the proper reason for the performance. Highbrow events were, in Levine's words, intended for "aesthetic and spiritual elevation,"[22] leaving mere entertainment to the lowbrow centers of the twentieth century. Obviously such a split was never entirely pervasive, as conversion-era cinema's experiments with opera demonstrate. Moreover, Levine and many film scholars have shown the extent to which immigrant populations posed a problem for this absolute differentiation between high and low culture: upper-class citizens attempted to convert these new Americans to their standards of behavior at the same time that such groups established alternative sites for cultural consumption, threatening the validity of such mores.[23] As Jonathan Crary points out, however, this disciplinary process was not limited to the point of performance; it also influenced how composers designed their productions. For example, Richard Wagner was appalled by the audience's distraction when confronted with "serious" opera. Unsurprisingly, he associated highly attentive listening with long German operas and a low level of concentration with their Italian counterparts, claiming that in such works a few recognizable moments were all that required notice—a sentiment not only consistent with Adorno's observation but also making Italian arias particularly appropriate for a genre of films with room enough only for fragments. The audience's lack of focus, however, cannot be accounted for by its preference for Italian composition alone.[24] Both Crary and Rick Altman comment on the typical design of opera houses, which had long been such that social elites were encouraged to examine and talk to one another more than they were to concentrate on the events onstage.[25] Wagner proposed the forward-facing design of the Bayreuth Theater to quiet chatty crowds, but Levine notes that in the United States conductors and managers of major orchestras and opera companies held themselves responsible for hushing the audience, waiting for silence or even reprimanding individuals for unruly behavior.[26]

This brief survey makes apparent the multiple efforts that were under way at the turn of the century to change the relationship between spectator and stage, endeavors that shaped the reception of opera films by requiring a certain level of attention even as they reduced the time audiences were encouraged to engage any particular operatic work. In spite of an assumed legacy of Wagnerian accompaniment practices in late silent cinema,[27] Hollywood seemingly ignored the rest of the German composer's advice. That is, despite the sophistication they seemed to demand from audiences, the opera shorts produced at the end of the 1920s gave in to a preference for highlights by filming popular arias originating primarily in the Italian canon. What counted as an "American" opera film, then, typically included a nineteenth-century aria sung in Italian by a star known both for his recording career and his participation in either the Metropolitan or the Chicago Civic Opera. The identification of the opera short with both "high" culture and popular entertainment is therefore understandable when discussed alongside the shifting artistic standards of the early twentieth century, calculated changes in audience behavior, increased sites of performance, and the diffusion of new technologies for the presentation of opera among middle-class Americans.

SETTING THE STAGE

How many opera shorts were there? This is a difficult question to answer, owing to the loss of many of the prints. My research shows that Warner Bros. released sixty-five opera shorts between 1926 and 1932, while most other major studios produced just one or a handful of similar films.[28] Taking my cue from the American reception of opera sparked by Lind's tour, I base my identification of an opera short primarily on the vocal quality of the singer and his or her professional activity outside of the cinema. For example, when Frances Alda sings "The Star Spangled Banner," I label the release an "opera short" because she is an opera star. However, I believe that more than just the voice was at stake in defining what was received as "opera" in the conversion period. William Shaman includes Cantor Josef Rosenblatt's films on his list of Vitaphone opera shorts, though the kind of music he recorded was of such a different origin and style that it doesn't make sense to lump them with those of Martinelli. Rosenblatt may have possessed an incredible voice and entertained offers to appear on the opera stage, but the fact that he neither made that move nor recorded any shorts with operatic origins for the Vitaphone indicates that audiences most probably understood his music in an ethnic or a religious context.[29] The distinction between opera and operetta, however, is a more slippery slope. I justify the inclusion of some shorts otherwise falling under the latter category on the basis of their having been received in much the same light as opera proper in early twentieth-century American culture. Thus I have chosen to consider among the ranks John Charles Thomas, credited as an "Outstanding American Baritone"; Reinald Werrenrath, who performed both at the Met and on Broadway; Mary Lewis, whose Vitaphone shorts feature American songs as well as operatic pieces; and of course Anna Case. In fact, the line between concrete operatic performance and popular revue was increasingly blurred within the single short as the period progressed.[30] In 1929, Eleanor Painter combined an aria from *Carmen*, a tune by Irving Berlin, and a song from the Victor Herbert operetta *The Princess Pat* onto one reel.[31] Martinelli was now singing more than just arias, even deigning to include full production numbers by dancers or instrumental musicians in his later shorts. The Metro Movietone Revues of 1929 and 1930 mixed solos by Joseph Regan and George Dewey Washington with performances by comedians, dancers, and instrumentalists.[32]

The largest portion of opera shorts, both in terms of what was produced and what is currently extant, were released by Warners' subsidiary the Vitaphone Corporation. In addition, Edwin Bradley claims there were five significant releases by MGM, two by Fox, two by Paramount, and one by De Forest.[33] Because none of these films are available, I will surmise a bit where possible about their production by discussing the choices made regarding singer and repertoire within the context of other available films by these respective studios. I have also been able to examine one extant short by Official Films, though we can be relatively certain that more such independent productions were made and subsequently lost. In explaining why opera shorts looked and sounded the way they did in the 1926–1932 period, I examine the texts symptomatically, attempting to draw out the larger motivations behind their style and the selection of their stars.

For the most part the Vitaphone opera shorts adhere to a fairly strict editing pattern, introduced in late 1926 when the style expanded beyond the single shot. The films normally open with an extreme long shot that continues during an orchestral introduction and through the entrance of the main character(s). This is true whether the performance takes place in a conservatory, on a stage, or in a more fictionalized space. In spite of the diegetic associations produced by these sets, we can usually see the conditions of recording in the final product: it is obvious that the Manhattan Opera House or Vitaphone's Brooklyn studio has been transformed for the production of screen opera. Of the sixty-five Vitaphone shorts, twenty-six were filmed out of context, that is, in a drawing room or on an undecorated stage that has not been given a frame story, and all but five of these are collections of unrelated arias. There are four shorts about which I have very little information, and the rest were given some sort of visual setting related to the music at hand. Regardless of the furnishings, rarely are the objects included in any of these films of real value to an interpretation of the piece. Instead, the décor of each room is used to lend authenticity to the performance or to verify the singer's status.

Vitaphone Release number 890, a film released in 1929 and featuring Chicago Civic Opera tenor Charles Hackett, is typical of the studio's style. The film begins with a shot of an elaborate drawing room housing a baby grand piano. Wearing a tuxedo to complement his serious expression, Hackett enters from a door in the rear, crosses to the front of the piano, and bows slightly to the camera. As he begins singing, we cut to a medium shot, as if to focus our attention on his voice. Whenever Hackett pauses at the end of a verse, we cut back to a long shot, acknowledging the work of the accompanist, though without worrying ourselves too much about actually seeing him, since a significant portion of his body has been cut off by the frame. Finally, after Hackett finishes singing, he is given a long shot in which to complete a brief bow (which he does alone, without recognizing his pianist), and we fade out. The number of shots included in the short may increase as technology advances, but variations on this pattern remain relatively rare.[34] Indeed, this editing strategy seems to have made its way into the current crop of Metropolitan Opera simulcasts, where cutting tends to follow vocal and instrumental "action."[35] Warners' basic strategy of showcasing the body at the moment of vocal production in order to highlight the capabilities of its synchronization and draw attention to the quality of its musical reproduction not only is maintained throughout the era but extends far beyond 1932.

The fact that Fox, MGM, and Paramount devoted so few resources to producing opera shorts might be most productively understood by examining the role of opera in longer variety films. Fox's two Movietone Numbers featuring Richard Bonelli were released in 1928 while the five Metro Movietone Acts starring either Maria Kurenko or Titta Ruffo were all released in 1929. Paramount produced two shorts with Tito Schipa, one in 1929 and the other in 1930. [36] None of these films survive.[37] Yet we do have similar performances by George Dewey Washington, an African

American vocalist, and Joseph Regan, an Irish American singer, as part of MGM's Movietone Revues, which give an impression of the place of opera in the output of these studios. The Movietone Revues were two-reel affairs, each including four or five numbers that were generally performed in front of a curtain by musicians featured in MGM's other shorts. Since they have been created to replicate the stage, with the master of ceremonies addressing the camera directly, there was no hint of narrative organization or even a unifying thread. Instead, the operatic voices of Washington and Regan were emphasized by how they were set apart from the other musicians. Washington remained in character as a forlorn hobo for the entirety of his presentation, while Regan performed in front of potted plants or in an improvised conservatory. The bodily or decorative excesses of their numbers attempt to make up for the lack of editing; each is presented in a single shot.[38]

The simple cinematography of Washington and Regan's presentations could be explained as an effort to verify the liveness of the acts: they look and sound like they are performing on a stage. Yet this visual style is not a particularly good way to call attention to vocal quality. As the conversion to sound progressed, Warner Bros. made its Vitaphone opera shorts look more and more like narratives organized around the activities of tenors who had become recognized cinematic presences. Fox, MGM, and Paramount were relative latecomers to the presentation of operatic sound and as such lacked the time to develop a star image that would overcome the strangeness of opera's excess. These studios, unlike Warners, were unable to unify the notion of film stardom with the signifiers of operatic quality, and so they promoted their singers' ethnicities instead of their operatic talent. Rather than Americanizing the aria, Fox, MGM, and Paramount seem to be differentiating between opera and popular song in a way that failed to account for the historical role of opera in America. Taking these factors into account, we should find it no surprise that their foray into opera shorts was itself rather short-lived.

There are two other extant MGM films that give insight into how little interest the studio had in producing opera shorts and how willing it was to rely on a derivative style. In 1928, Joseph Regan combined "Mary Ann" and "Beloved" onto a single reel. Neither really qualified as opera, but the studio suggested they might do so by subtitling the film with Regan's status, "Irish American Tenor" (a move also made by Warners) and providing nothing else by way of context. The stage was also minimal; a luxurious curtain provided the background and some modernist geometrical pieces were positioned to frame Regan in a long shot in center stage. The entire film consisted of a single take, with the exception of the ending, during which a "curtain" wiped the screen to black and then opened again to give Regan time to bow. This approach to editing and set design was purposively exaggerated in comedienne Frances White's 1928 short. Grossly overdressed in a ruffled gown and feathered hat, White sang while standing next to a grand piano that had been draped in a scarf and set atop an oriental rug. Behind the piano was an expensive lamp and an ornate wooden chair, and behind them hung not one but two curtains. Each of these alone is a prop one would expect to find in a typical Warner Bros. short, but together they reek of the excess White tried to achieve with (what one hopes was) her intentionally overwrought voice. Moreover, White's film reproduces the curtain-wipe effect, though here it appears even between scenes. In its reference to a mode of address that Warner Bros. had largely abandoned by 1928 and its flamboyant mise-en-scène, MGM's self-reflexivity made something of a mockery of Warners' serious treatment of the opera.

Over the years the Warner Bros. opera shorts became more and more visually resplendent until they seemingly dispensed with opera altogether. The opera shorts from the early 1930s were not organized around single arias or operatic scenes, but rather invented scenarios unified around a larger theme, such as troubadours or gypsy excursions. There are additional stylistic changes worth noting as the era progressed. Bowing and other forms of direct address by the singer were replaced by title cards: information provided by the cinematic narrator in the form of written synopses that established the relationships between characters. The music salon setting popular for soloists and available for quick sessions was by 1931 integrated into a larger narrative frame, constructing the stage as a mise-en-abyme.[39] Finally, the compositions selected for production changed as well. Of the most popular operas recorded for the Vitaphone, most had traditionally been of Italian or French origin (with Wagner appearing only as fodder for satire).[40] Though there was one prominent German representative, von Flotow was highly influenced by the French *opéra comique*. His *Martha* makes the list three times, yet on two of these occasions it was "The Last Rose of Summer," the Irish tune incorporated into the opera and a staple of film accompaniment that was featured. Verdi is by far the most popular Vitaphone composer, with nine shorts attributed to three of his operas: *Rigoletto, Aïda,* and *Il Trovatore*.[41] He is followed closely by Gounod, with six recordings of *Romeo and Juliet* and four of *Faust*. By 1931, however, Giovanni Martinelli's shorts displayed a complete disregard for these worthy operatic luminaries; his last five releases mainly comprised popular melodies. Wagner would probably call this the ultimate triumph of Italian opera and the end of the Vitaphone as a serious promoter of "high" culture.

The majority of the opera shorts were recorded at the Manhattan Opera House, which had been leased by Warner Bros. in 1926. The site posed problems, however, thanks to the excess sound produced by subway construction, and it needed to be shut down for some time in 1927. This practical impediment has led some scholars to believe that most of the opera shorts were completed by the end of that year and simply held for release through 1931.[42] On the basis of this information, some have concluded that aside from honoring its contract with Martinelli, Warners did not pursue new operatic material after that year. There is, however, evidence that some of both Martinelli's and Charles Hackett's later shorts were produced in fall 1929 and winter 1930, and not at the Manhattan site. Vitaphone production records recovered at the USC Warner Bros. Archive for the Hackett releases numbered 899–900 and 916 as well as those for Martinelli's shorts 932, 944, 953, and 974 cite the Brooklyn studio as the recording location.[43] This indicates that the Hackett and Martinelli shorts released in late 1930 and into 1931 with even higher serial numbers must have been filmed after 1927, an assertion backed up by the noticeable increase in the number of shots and their stylistic complexity.[44]

Yet the question of whether or not those shorts released in early and mid-1929, featuring Frances Alda, Jeanne Gordon, Hope Hampton, Josef Kallini, Eleanor Painter, and Marie Vero, were filmed years earlier remains open.[45] All of the shorts in question were set in a drawing room and contain direct presentations of a variety of arias, a fact that certainly draws attention to the end of recording at the Manhattan Opera House. There were a few shorts released before 1929 that had been made in such a space, but the general direction was toward more complex backdrops and editing patterns. In 1927, for example, Beniamino Gigli's production of *La Gioconda* included an elaborate mock-up of a Venetian dock, Martinelli's two *La Juive* numbers featured a set built to resemble the ornate interior of the Cardinal's home, and Charles Hackett's short containing "Call of the Nile" and "Song of India" included two separate stages, one a desert oasis and the other a large tent.[46] The transition to drawing-room-only settings could indicate a strategy on the part of Warner Bros. to inexpensively maintain audience interest in opera shorts in order to bide time before fulfilling its contracts with Hackett and Martinelli. A letter to Martinelli's agent dated February 10, 1928, indicates that Warners was aware of its obligations to the star but was waiting for its Brooklyn studio to be completed before arranging dates mutually agreeable for production.[47] So even though the operatic releases became more stylistically and technically interesting, they also changed in another significant way: Warners began constructing shorts around fewer and fewer stars, eventually whittling down its lineup to eliminate singers such as Alda, Painter, and Gordon in order to feature the tenor exclusively.

HOW TO RECORD THE "FEMALE" VOICE

With the assent of the tenor voice came choices about visualizing the performer's body. Charles Wolfe has noted that Warners' emphasis on musical performances poses a number of questions that we ought to ask of all opera films:

> In what ways does the address of a performer to a camera differ from his or her address to a live audience, and is this difference acknowledged or compensated for in some way? How is a vocal performance on film framed or bracketed, set up or cut off? At what point and in what ways does performance become subordinate to, or comment upon, a fictional character an actor portrays?[48]

As we will see, these questions have striking implications for the representation of gender during the conversion to sound. Though its marketing materials would insist that there was no difference between live and recorded performances of its stars, Warner Bros. betrayed its own rhetoric by framing and editing male and female singers distinctly. Rather than respecting the concrete attributes of the characters written for the stage, these concessions to cinematic tradition reflected cultural attitudes about gender in ways that the screen made vividly clear. The studio thus distinguished live from recorded performances by relying on the audience's familiarity with the limitations of both technological reproduction and continuity editing to "cut off" women from the production of opera.

The argument that classical Hollywood cinema is structured so as to visually and aurally contain women is well known. Laura Mulvey claims that this happens at the level of the image; as spectacle, women are denied the narrative authority that belongs to men.[49] Kaja Silverman applies Mulvey's thought to the soundtrack, showing how women's voices are typically bound to the interior of the text. She associates men's speech with the voice-over and authorship and shows how women's voices are limited to the diegesis, with an emphasis on synchronization that ultimately signifies castration. However, in an important intervention, Silverman demonstrates that the traditional emphasis on feminine "lack" in psychoanalytic film theory conceals a castration that has already taken place. This primary castration exists, for instance, in the formation of subjectivity, when the Mother's voice is transformed into a Lacanian *objet petit "a,"* an object taken from the child when he becomes distinct from the mother and that now forms the basis of his desires. By placing emphasis on the fear of a possible (and perhaps more literal) castration, psychoanalysis attempts to divorce the male subject from the preexistence of a traumatic separation. The fetish object, then, exists not to disavow women's lack but instead to deny what men have already experienced. According to Silverman, the male voice regains its virility by extracting any possibility of verbal authority from female screen characters.[50] If we consider the conversion-era opera shorts through the framing devices identified by Mulvey and Silverman, we discover that their style works to fragment and restrict the female body, thereby refusing the soprano an enunciative role.

There were many attempts to produce both silent and sound screen operas prior to the introduction of Lee de Forest's synchronous sound system in 1922, but the known catalogue of his own De Forest Phonofilm Corporation includes only one straight opera short: the Sextet and "Mad Scene" from Gaetano Donizetti's *Lucia di Lammermoor*.[51] Its selection is significant. Lucia, bloody after killing her husband and wielding a dagger in full view of her guests, imagines herself wedding her true love. The scene speaks to the perceived dangers of the female voice. Left to sing on her own, she offers through her music what Susan McClary calls "a manifestation of the sexual excess the nineteenth century ascribed to madwomen."[52] Removed from the context of the opera, the scene seems to celebrate madness, the high E-flat at the end not a wavering suggestion of death but an artistic triumph. Capable of cutting up the body of a man and cutting out the "body" of the opera, Lucia embodies the act of castration that similarly enables the production of the opera short. Though no longer extant, De Forest's early effort reveals the condition that plagued female representation thereafter. Not wanting to be reminded of its unpleasantness, perhaps, and certainly not wanting to build a genre on the backbone of a "crazy" woman in a work that alludes to European excess, it is not a surprise that Lucia was not a popular figure on film during the conversion to sound.

In the Vitaphone opera films, female singers are disproportionately denied solo numbers; and when they do appear alongside men, they are generally prevented from dominating the scene. Of the sixty-five opera shorts produced by the studio, thirty-one of them star men singing alone (or bolstered by a chorus), seventeen feature female soloists, ten are male-female duets, four present two men together, and three involve three or more major players. There are no films that star two women without also including a man. The preference for men increases as the years go by: with the exception of Alice Gentle's Technicolor spectacle,[53] all eight Vitaphone films released in 1930–31 star either Giovanni Martinelli or

Charles Hackett. A similar fondness for the male voice can be found in the output of the other studios: seven of the nine films produced by Fox, MGM, and Paramount feature men.

The reception of the female opera shorts was often negative, which helped justify Warners' growing reliance on the tenor. Marion Talley's premiere, "Caro Nome," was famously unacceptable and was eventually eliminated from the roster of shorts accompanying *Don Juan*. Many critics attributed the tone of the film to a defect in Talley's voice rather than inadequacies in the recording process. W. J. Henderson of the *New York Sun* called her singing "intolerably piercing,"[54] while the *New Yorker* said of another of her films, "[She] is caused to utter sounds that could only be duplicated by the twittering of tightly-locked subway brakes."[55] After hearing the recordings of another female soloist (Ernestine Schumann-Heink), George E. Quigley, vice president and general manager of the Vitaphone Corporation, made a suggestion to Jack Warner: "it would not be advisable for this artist to record any numbers in the German language because of her manner of rendering same, which is very guttural and, therefore, not best for recording purposes."[56] The studio clearly had specific ideas about what female operatic voices ought to sound like, and their assumptions did not correspond to the model of the German prima donna.

Quigley's directive could be attributed in part to the popular preference for Italian opera, but it also makes a revealing statement about the gendered application of language: after all, Martinelli was permitted to sing *Martha*, and Charles Hackett songs by Schubert. Yet Schumann-Heink was a German-speaking contralto, not a weak soprano like those usually paired with stars such as Hackett, Gigli, or Martinelli, and she charged a fee for her services that approached their own.[57] Moreover, the seriousness that had been attributed to German opera by agencies such as the Met certainly had some bearing on how Schumann-Heink came to be represented on screen. A star of her influence performing artistically significant works in her native language would give Schumann-Heink the kind of authority that the cinema typically granted only to men. I contend that it was not merely the "guttural" nature of the language that resulted in her alleged recording woes, but rather problems arising from how Schumann-Heink's pronunciation was perceived as a gender crossing; that is, her "manner of rendering same," though certainly more "authentic" than the iterations produced by the Italian or American male stars, was nevertheless not what Warner and Quigley imagined as an analogue to the female body. Indeed, Deanna Durbin, the whimsical adolescent soprano picked by MGM to play Schumann-Heink in an anticipated biopic a decade later, would have been more aligned with Warners' goals.[58] As a punishment for exceeding the cultural trappings established for female singers by the Vitaphone Corporation, Schumann-Heink's voice was ultimately silenced.

Cases like that of Ernestine Schumann-Heink lead me to suggest that the conditions for picturing opera on screen required that visual restrictions be imposed on women's bodies as a way to limit the perceived power of their voices. This situation stems from the composition of the operas themselves. Catherine Clément demonstrates that the most magnificent arias of the nineteenth century were often assigned to the narrative moment of a woman's demise.[59] Michal Grover-Friedlander, on the other hand, claims that opera is *always* on the verge of disintegration: at the peak of her expression, the singer is about to expire, to lose breath, and with her disappears the music.[60] The creation of opera, then, is dependent on the liminality of the female voice; the pleasure in watching opera lies in the quivering uncertainty over reaching the highest pitch. Grover-Friedlander suggests that every repetition of her aria is another attempt to bring the diva back from the dead, a restaging of *Orpheus* that believes in the resurrection of Eurydice. Yet, as she notes, Orpheus always looks back. Indeed, the temptation of vision drives the operatic spectator, particularly in the cinema. Opera glasses, like close-ups, give viewers access to the diva's body. As Catherine Clément says, "the prima donna is a prisoner of machinery, and booby-trapped by a machination"[61] ; the desire for verification is too strong. Like the cinematic pornographer trying to represent female ecstasy, the opera producer attempts the impossible: using technology to reveal the workings of the throat.[62] With synchronous sound, film is simultaneously able to examine women's bodies and confirm the physicality of their voices, stripping them of the heavenly authority once given the castrato and that would from now on be awarded only to men.

The earliest Vitaphone opera shorts reduced the threat of female authority through decisive framing of women's bodies. A brief glance at the Vitaphone opera shorts of 1926 reveals that those featuring female vocalists contain far more edits. Anna Case's "La Fiesta" consists of nine shots, while Talley's "Caro Nome" is made up of six. By contrast, Martinelli's two earliest shorts are both only one shot.[63] Even Charles Hackett's first release, with its two separate sets, is content with a mere three shots. Embedded in the early visual strategies used to represent its female singers, then, is Warners' assumption that these women had something to prove. Male stars like Martinelli were allowed to remain distant from the viewer and endowed with the authority of the opera hall. In Kaja Silverman's terms, the early female shorts are required to provide evidence of synchronization while their male counterparts are more closely associated with the point of the text's production, their bodies capable of putting over the show without the aid of cinematic emphasis.[64] As such, reviewers' problems with Talley may be due more to the availability of her body than the quality her voice.

Even though singers like Ernestine Schumann-Heink were paid generously for their time in front of the Vitaphone lens, it does not necessarily follow that they commanded the authority exercised by their equally high-earning male counterparts. This gender discrepancy extends back to eighteenth-century Italy, where fully 70 percent of male singers on the stage were castrati[65] and were paid far better than were tenors and basses.[66] Yet because of their "unnatural" creation, the agency that we might award castrati remains questionable. Contemporary opera critics regarded their condition as a weakness. One observer described their state: "The sixteen young *castrati*...live up stairs by themselves, in warmer apartments than the other boys."[67] The castrato thus occupies an impossible space, mythologized beyond recognition, so that the "evidence" of his condition could never be enough to justify the tales that circulate about him. The rhetoric produced by Warners executives similarly marks women's voices as "unnatural," either too frail to be recorded by the Vitaphone or too strong to be appreciated by the public. Like the castrati, these female singers may have ruled the opera house, but they were ruined by the image of the body projected on them by the cinema and carefully controlled by the studio.

The first accounts of castrati in the Church come from the late sixteenth century, and the last castrato in the pope's employ was Alessandro Moreschi, who lived long enough to have made recordings in 1902 and 1904. These samples are widely available but may critics contend that they are a rather poor representation of the castrato's skills, having been produced late in the singer's career and released more than a century past his prime. Instead, historians analyze testimony that "proves" the superiority of the castrato's voice over both the soprano and the tenor, an argument based largely on the ornamental conventions of the period, but undoubtedly highly romanticized.[68] Yet castrati had a great influence on both the development of tenor technique[69] and roles later played by the soprano. Indeed, Naomi André sees the soprano as a hybrid construction showing that "the *sound* of the castrato voice was desired" even though "the *sight* of the castrato on the opera stage had fallen out of vogue."[70] Of course, it is not enough to attribute the vanishing of the castrato to fashion alone. Jennifer Jones grounds her account of his elimination in the general project of Romanticism, which replaced the value of his voice with the more "natural" sound of the tenor.[71] Susan Leonardi and Rebecca Pope, on the other hand, provide a litany of causes, from improvements in the Italian economic condition to the rise of comic opera, a form less reliant on the castrato figure.[72] Despite this insistence on his demise, the castrato did not disappear entirely. As Leonardi and Pope point out, the negative connotations formerly associated with castrati, such as vanity, coquetry, or excess, persist in the figure of the diva.[73] Whether or not the legacy of the castrato frees the cinematic soprano from imminent death, however, is another question altogether. A corrective to the monstrosity of castration, the film diva's voice conjures a more youthful Moreschi, while the camera makes every effort to assure us that we are seeing a *real* woman. Like her predecessor, who was finally recognized as a violent violation of the natural order, she too was removed from circulation.

HAUNTING AND MIMICRY

That the castrato's legacy lingers in opera's construction of gender can be revealed through a detailed analysis of two films released in 1926: Giovanni Martinelli's immensely popular "Vesti la giubba," in which he performs the most memorable aria from Leoncavallo's *I Pagliacci*, and Marion Talley's much berated "Caro nome" from Verdi's *Rigoletto*. Reading about the production and reception of these shorts with the history of the castrati in mind can help us understand why one would have been so universally praised while the other, like the sopranos in the Vitaphone films more generally, disappeared quickly. Indeed, we might see Pagliaccio as a direct descendant of the castrato; haunted by his impotence, the image of the clown asserts an ideal of wholeness aided by both the style of the short itself and publicity for the Vitaphone. Following Pagliaccio's lead, cinematic tenors generate images of complete bodies persistently undermined by the traces of their vocal training. Condemned to imitate the castrato's former roles, on the other hand, conversion-era sopranos are constantly forced to recognize their second-class status through the films' exposure of their inadequacy. This division works to promote the value of opera through the authoritative voice of men, who "naturally" lend themselves to electrical recording.

As the castrato's mythology of excess obscures his lack, so the clown's accoutrements are necessary for audiences to accept the authenticity of Martinelli's filmed performance. The costume requirement stems from the opera's libretto. *I Pagliacci* openly questions the clown's virility as he sings: "Are you not a man? You're just Pagliaccio!" The character goes on to accept the truth: without his "costume and the greasepaint and powder" he is neither clown nor man. The disguise, however, transforms the figure of ridicule into a reputable character with a long history on the stage. The aria itself is an expression of bitter irony about this transformation: instructing the singer to make audiences laugh in spite of his pain, the passion of the music suggests that the discrepancy between the singer's true feelings and the genre of his performance make him a better artist. Although he has been mocked and betrayed by his wife and friends and forced to wear a degrading costume, on the opera stage Pagliaccio escapes the trappings of masculinity prescribed by popular culture and becomes capable of sincere and sublime expression.

Martinelli's version of "Vesti la giubba" replicates the castrato's purported vocal excess. Martinelli slides into the word "uom" ("man"), emphasizing, perhaps, the uncertainty of his manhood, for he lacks a stable hold on the note itself. Immediately after singing this, Martinelli laughs, cruelly, at his own fate. His gestures reiterate the absence of masculine traits. Holding his right arm in the air, palm extended (Figure 2.2), Martinelli points to the empty space next to him, calling on us to imagine a "real" man standing there, one who could fill the stage without recourse to extensive bodily movements. The tenor's voice breaks before the line indicating his betrayal, and he spreads his arms widely above his shoulders, elbows bent, as if to acknowledge the inevitability of his experiences (Figure 2.3). Another break occurs just prior to the suggestion of his dying love, paired with a gesture that brings his fist down toward his waist, an imitation, perhaps literally of death, but more suggestively of sexual weakness (Figure 2.4).

Figure 2.2: The space of "man."
Frame grab from *Vesti la giubba* (1926).

Figure 2.3: Betrayal is inevitable.
Frame grab from *Vesti la giubba* (1926).

Figure 2.4: A weak gesture.
Frame grab from *Vesti la giubba* (1926).

The aria's most emotional moment and most expressive notes are found with the word "ridi," or "laugh." Martinelli slides into this final phrase, connecting the "ah" that precedes it in a manifestation of pain to "ridi" with a grand crescendo, and placing the full array of emotional possibilities within the reach of his own vocal range. The emphatic interpretation Martinelli gives the aria and his use of vocal and corporeal gestures to illustrate the lyrics (his own voice falters and spasms through the final line "the love that is destroying your heart;" his hands clap as the audience's would on the word "applaudirà") suggest that Warner Bros. was as concerned with representing the sufficiency of the tenor's body as it was with capturing any supposedly inherent qualities of his voice.

The first two Martinelli shorts, unlike those featuring Marion Talley or Anna Case, are composed of a single shot. This difference is important, for even though Martinelli's film is clearly a staged number intended to imitate a renowned live performance, Talley's and Case's verge on becoming cinema and may thus have been seen as less trustworthy, owing to the poor success rate of prior operatic sound film experiments with which they would logically be associated. Furthermore, the contrast between Martinelli's earliest shorts and those featuring sopranos demonstrates that we cannot attribute differences in editing solely to the restrictions posed by the need to maintain the consistency of the soundtrack by shooting with multiple cameras. All three performances were shot in 1926. So, why the gendered distinction?

Showcasing his body, even making it the center that holds the spectator's interest, called attention to the "naturalness" of Martinelli's movements and the "authenticity" of his voice. Contemporary reviewers cited the success of this enterprise: "None of the famous tenor's personality and tone was lost by the Vitaphone interpretation."[74] To this reviewer, the Vitaphone was simultaneously transparent and an agent in its own right, delivering Martinelli to the crowd without seeming to intervene. Mordaunt Hall of the New York Times noted how audiences were drawn to the singer's body: "The singer's tones appeared to echo in the body of the theatre as they tore from a shadow on the screen—a shadow that appeared earnest and intense in the delivery of Leoncavallo's well-known composition."[75] Here, the Vitaphone transformed Martinelli's screen image into a living thing, although what made it appear "earnest and intense" had undoubtedly to do with both his voice and the presentation of his body. Yet it was not merely the unification of body and voice that brought Martinelli to life, but the fact that he performed in a space. Before his voice entered the auditorium, Martinelli remained a mere "shadow," a term that echoes Balzac's description of his infamous castrato, La Zambinella, as "phantasmagorical" or "a form without substance."[76] Yet after his voice was ripped from the image, it filled the hall, bringing those within it together as a single body. Martinelli may have emerged from a world-class operatic institution, but his screen performance was democratic, capable of unifying listeners to appreciate the technological product of American ingenuity: the Vitaphone, paradoxically perfect in its inaudibility.

Unlike the raves given to Giovanni Martinelli, reviewers snubbed Marion Talley's short film, blaming its inadequacies on her "inexperience."[77] In his brief analysis of Talley's initial flop, Donald Crafton notes that disparaging remarks were often made about her appearance and origins; critics pointed to her Kansas City upbringing as well as her youth—she was only nineteen at the time of her Vitaphone debut—as reasons for her failure. Crafton rightly suggests that these same reviews often cited synchronization problems and concludes that these technical difficulties may have been one cause, if not the primary, of the condemnation heaped on Talley. I believe that the critical reaction to this short was more complicated. Rather than channeling audience fascination with the castrato through a historical lineage, the soprano must remain content to imitate his pain. Her roles and her tones duplicate those he once performed; she mimics his style at the level of gesture and voice. Martinelli's *Pagliacci* dispels rumors about the castrato's potential for contamination in the twentieth century; the soprano returns what we imagine we have securely repressed.

"Caro nome," drawn from the first act of Verdi's opera, was an immensely popular aria during the early twentieth century. It is also an older work, premiering forty-one years before Leoncavallo's piece, written by a composer who would prove a favorite with Vitaphone viewers. At the point in the opera where Talley's aria occurs, her character, Gilda, daughter of the hunchbacked Rigoletto, has just met her lover, a duke disguised as a poor student. In a sense, this aria is the antithesis of that performed by Martinelli. Although his Pagliaccio mourns a love he now knows to have been impossible, Gilda expresses the attainability of the heterosexual love affair. Her aria, about her suitor's "beloved name," may be based on false information, but the name she breathes is concrete, not merely a character type like Pagliaccio's comrades.

These differences make *Rigoletto* an appropriate choice with which to illustrate the dangers of the soprano voice. Indeed, Gilda threatens to capture the sexuality of the promiscuous duke by trapping him in a relationship with a "commoner." She sacrifices herself for her lover, killed in his place to satisfy the demands of her father, who pays someone else to do the offing. This narrative is not unlike the historical position of the castrato; disfigured at the instruction of the Church, he too gives up sexuality for his art, for the wishes of his patron. Yet Gilda poses a problem for the easy denial of the castrato's physical condition: she dies for the sake of love, always reminding us of what might have been. Verdi's Gilda is a remnant not only of the roles once played by the castrato but also of his body. By mimicking the castrato and endangering the expression of masculine sexual power, Gilda's fate must lie in death. The attainability of "feminine" sexuality expressed by the "Caro nome" aria ultimately leads to the destruction of her body. Placed in a burlap sack and mistaken for the duke, Gilda is punished for playing a part: her risk to masculinity is mitigated by the literal erasure of her body from the scene. The Vitaphone version of the aria performs a similar operation. The camera alleviates the threat of the castrato's return by chopping up the female body into recognizable parts.

The editing of the Talley short film pieces together multiple shots that emphasize the singer's face, particularly during the moments when she sings the highest notes. The film begins in an American shot; we are already closer to Talley than we were to Martinelli. Unlike Martinelli's film, which kept its distance and let the star's movements attract the viewer on their own, Talley's camera is particularly cruel to the few gestures she is able to insert. For example, her ascendancy of the staircase is divided into four shots, clearly timed to correspond to her vocal entrances, and producing the impression of a highly calculated performance rather than a spontaneous outburst of genuine emotion. If the stage diva reminds us of the castrato, now given a body from which audiences would not dare to shrink, her cinematic representation shatters the fluidity of the aria. This impression begins even before the film does. The opening credits promote Marion Talley as a "youthful prima donna of the New York Metropolitan Opera" rather than "Gilda," an assertive, if somewhat misguided, woman. Warner Bros. may have signed Talley hoping to repeat Geraldine Farrar's seductive screen successes a decade earlier, but without a full-length narrative to convince audiences of her star potential or a long take to validate her stage presence, Talley is just a "youthful" singing woman. Martinelli becomes Pagliaccio in the eyes of the public; Talley remains distant from her character. However, her body, like Gilda's, is contained, not in a sack but by the cinema that renders it visible. The closer shots provided at the moment of her enunciation call our attention to the synchronicity of the mechanism, a pairing that becomes all the more problematic when the conditions for its production go awry.

Though they appear stiff on the screen, Talley's gestures (or lack thereof) are arguably more "operatic" in the context of the period of their production than is the overstatement that colors Martinelli's performance. According to Mary Ann Smart, the operatic trend that synchronized bodies to music began to disappear in the late nineteenth century. The body remained the visual focal point on the stage, but its eroticism was implied less through physical movement and more by the connotations of the music itself. Romantic composers provided what Smart calls "a sensuous haze of sound" transforming the body into "more idea or aura than physical sequence of gestures."[78] Yet Smart celebrates mimicry where it continues to exist, seeing in it the potential for the redemption of opera's ill-fated women. The excess of expression could produce an opening for resistant readers, in which a composer's authorial voice might for a moment be overturned. However, in the two examples under analysis here, Martinelli's calls attention to his body with its redundancy of gesture, while Talley's attempts to distract from it by focusing on the voice. Why, then, should the reception of these shorts have been skewed so strikingly to accept Martinelli as the more "authentic" of the two?

As Gilda, Talley makes few physical movements: she primarily stands with her hands clasped together (Figure 2.5), occasionally sitting on a stone bench or mounting a staircase (Figure 2.6), objects and gestures that have little to do with either the melody or the libretto. In spite of their suitability for a twentieth-century opera hall, when captured on celluloid Talley's choreography is subsumed under the film's visual enunciation. The editing pattern lets Talley "speak" only within a predetermined range; the

Figure 2.5: Marion Talley's "youthful" expression.
Frame grab from *Caro nome* (1926).

Figure 2.6: Marion Talley's stage presence.
Frame grab from *Caro nome* (1926).

camera's closeness begs us to notice her "youth." The authority of the cinema precludes the possibility of the diva's excess. Instead of letting her act, the camera mimics the phrasing of the music through framing and editing. Rather than being given an outlet for expression, Talley is resigned to imitate the role forged for her by the castrato and approved by the practices of classical Hollywood cinema. Martinelli, on the other hand, was accepted as genuine while remaining outside the typical constraints of operatic practice. His voice was deemed worthy of the instrument that produced it; Talley's was not. Though there is much to be said about the patriarchal discourse embedded in discussions of the Vitaphone's frequency range, more important for the reception of these particular shorts are fears about the representation of the gendered body, concerns that persist into the years beyond 1926.

THE TENOR TAKES THE LEAD

In 1927 Warner Bros. began to release shorts with two or three key singers in each, in most cases "starring" Giovanni Martinelli or Charles Hackett "with" or "assisted by" a soprano. Rather than restraining the female body by distributing pieces of her across the aria, the duets and trios instead restrict her access to the camera by limiting her presence to shots that also include men. A good example comes from the prison scene in Gounod's *Faust* (1930).[79] The film begins with a title card that provides a narrative frame: "Marguerite, abandoned and mad, is visited in prison by Faust who has sold his soul to the devil. Faust urges her to flee with him and the devil, but she is redeemed by prayer." Despite its use of the passive voice (which might be read as a literary translation of the studio's visual strategy—a textual denial of Marguerite's potential agency), this summary implies that Marguerite should be the center of the scene. Yet the film opens with her character, played by Yvonne Benson, as nothing more than a small heap in the corner while the real action focuses on screen right, where the devil (Louis D'Angelo) and Faust (Giovanni Martinelli) enter the cell. The film then cuts to a medium shot, not of Marguerite but of Faust looking in the girl's direction with the devil posed somewhat artistically behind him, and the two begin to sing. The devil departs, after which we are treated to an even closer image of Faust, now alone in the frame and fretting over what to do. When we return to Marguerite again, she's rising from the floor in a long shot shared with Faust. Finally, at the entrance of her vocal solo and just as it seems that she will be granted permission to appear on screen by herself, a medium shot of her is interrupted as Faust bursts into the frame to deliver his lines. The two remain in this position for a time, but their gestures make it clear that Martinelli holds the real power. He clutches Benson's body to him and strokes her hair, a position from which she struggles to perform her part clearly. At last, Martinelli exits, leaving Benson alone to continue the number, or so it seems. As if to remind us of his operatic authority, Martinelli's hand enters the frame, something one might at first chalk up to an editing error, but when he steps into view some moments later, we realize that he was always capable of stopping Benson's expression, choking her weak grasp on the camera's gaze. Strangely, as Benson takes up her part again, the camera chooses not to follow her but instead closes in on Martinelli, who stands idly by listening to her sing. His perpetual dominance of the frame shifts our focus from Marguerite's moral struggle to Martinelli's operatic prominence and causes us to interpret the scene through the gestures of the familiar star rather than following the intentions of Gounod's composition.

As the example from *Faust* makes clear, opera shorts limited the vocal and sexual authority of the soprano in order to insulate the tenor from her threatening range. This approach was taken by other studios as well. Despite noted differences in its cultural values and production style, the representation of the female opera voice in MGM's feature films followed the approach taken by Warners' Vitaphone shorts.[80] In her first MGM release, Grace Moore, the Tennessee Nightingale and Met opera star, played Jenny Lind, the Swedish Nightingale. *A Lady's Morals* (1930) is primarily a romance between the singer and fictional composer Paul Brandt. On meeting Lind, Brandt informs her that she is "the most conspicuously pure woman of our time," a paradoxical description on which the sopranos of the first sound films were seemingly modeled, and one that justifies their control by a more sophisticated male artist. Though a rising star in her own right (and of course a "real" opera phenomenon), Lind somehow finds herself being tutored by the invented Brandt character, singing his music while he corrects her phrasing. Moore is placed in this scenario again in *One Night of Love* (1934), where she portrays a singer gifted with a good voice that must nevertheless be trained (tamed) by a man, this time a vocal coach with a musically suggestive name, Giulio Monteverdi.

In spite of the repressive work of the films' narratives, Moore's performances could be easily extracted from the bodies of these musicals and asked to stand on their own as signs of the star's vocal prowess. Indeed, according to the American film musical formula suggested by Jane Feuer, "a closed story is transformed into direct address through the agency of the musical number itself."[81] Able to communicate in ways barred to spoken language, songs—Feuer argues—open up alternative spaces through which the characters might address the audience or each other. From this perspective it would be possible for Moore to shun her diegetic training and sing directly to the viewer, who would in turn recognize her talent for what it was. This would work particularly well if viewers were given access to Moore with as little interference as possible, producing an encounter with the singer without the self-awareness of Vivian Sobchack's "echo-focus."[82] Producing her numbers in a single shot would certainly fail, for by 1930 such scenes would have felt quite different from the rest of the films and the genre that contained them, and would therefore make the apparatus more visible rather than less. There were ways to employ continuity editing that could have enticed viewers to be closer to Moore. Rather than attempt this, however, MGM filters Moore's address to the audience through the gaze of either Brandt or Monteverdi by editing the numbers according to a shot/reverse shot pattern whereby the value of Moore as both a woman and a singer is critiqued or affirmed by her male tutor. In the same way Martinelli came to Benson's assistance in *Faust*, MGM requires men to appreciate the soprano visually in order for her to succeed aurally. MGM's opera shorts are no longer available, but we might imagine that its presentation of the Russian Nightingale, Maria Kurenko, followed a similar logic.

Other than Kurenko's lost performances, MGM's other three opera shorts all starred baritone Titta Ruffo. The studio may have been thinking of Giuseppe De Luca's well-received *Barber of Seville* Vitaphone short when it signed Ruffo to perform the same piece in 1929. However, reviews were mixed. *Variety* called it "very worthwhile," though *Film Daily* suggested that the "work will mostly go for naught."[83] Ruffo's final film took a different approach and could well have suggested an alternate place for the baritone in MGM's output. Ruffo played the role of Nelusko in Meyerbeer's opera *L'Africaine*, for which the singer was well known. Notes on the film's production do not list the aria he performed therein, but it was likely "All'erta, marinar," given Victor's sales of Ruffo's rendition and the likelihood of the film industry capitalizing on performers' prior successes. In spite of its popularity, *Variety* published the curious claim that the selection of this piece would derail the short's reception.[84] "All'erta marinar" comes from the third act of *L'Africaine*, in which Nelusko executes his plan to take over Don Pedro's ship and murder all on board. The image of the resistant slave is certainly well outside the cultural context of opera on film during this period, but the composition of the work is unique as well. An unaccompanied number, it steers clear of some of the instrumental regulations of European operatic composition, in essence "freeing" the slave from the requirements of this form of expression. Nelusko is punished at the end of the story by committing suicide alongside Selika, who is the other foreigner in the plot, but the consequences for his uprising have obviously been cut out of the short version. Less threatening on disc because the performance is relegated to auditory blackface, on screen Ruffo's singing challenges audiences' beliefs about how opera ought to look and sound.

Following its dalliance with Ruffo, MGM released four feature films starring Lawrence Tibbett, the first American-born male singer to achieve operatic fame. Given the number of his Metropolitan Opera colleagues who appeared on screen, Tibbett's Hollywood stint should come as no surprise. The kinds of films he made, however, were telling. Nostalgic tales of Russian princes and memories of antebellum plantations place Tibbett in roles that fit neatly into Catherine Clément's typology of the baritone. Clément claims that in contrast to the tenor who provokes a rebellion against the regulations of the old guard, the baritone is characterized by "organized opposition" to these inevitable changes, characteristics that associate him with the wisdom of the earlier times.[85] In *The Prodigal* (1931), Tibbett performs "Home, Sweet Home" and a piece reminiscent of a black spiritual (but almost certainly written by one of the film's five credited composers), songs that position black Americans in an eternally happy past, hardly capable of the revolt carried out by Ruffo's restless Nelusko. Certainly Tibbett's baritone characters would seem out of place in a medium that needed to assert its novelty. Indeed, Warner Bros. made very few films with solo baritones, and those who did appear were limited in scope: Richard Werrenrath's contract was not renewed and John Charles Thomas's physical awkwardness in the music salon would certainly have lessened his appeal. We might even blame the brevity of Fox's foray into opera on its selection of Richard Bonelli to sing the classic baritone arias "Largo al factotum" and the prologue to *Pagliacci*. By contrast, Tibbett suited the MGM brand. Although he sold American musical novelty reliably at the Met,[86] Tibbett's films stressed continuity over disjuncture. On screen, he peddled an image of bygone days in which American singers were always successful. By casting the baritone as the lead in its features, MGM commented on its own status as an established studio, a place that boasted "more stars than there are in the heavens," and thereby left behind the brash representation of sound's revolutionary potential it had formerly sought to cultivate with Ruffo.

Unlike MGM, by 1927 Warner Bros. discovered that it was not making "opera films" but "opera shorts," and that the content of these productions, like the material that made up much of the Vitaphone Varieties, was not the story but the number. One might argue that the structure and style of classical Hollywood cinema works to strengthen narrative coherence, but this is explicitly not the purpose of the Vitaphone opera short.[87] Martinelli and Hackett's numbers do not "interrupt" a narrative in progress, for the original operatic story has little relevance for how these films function. Instead, these singers help collect arias, operatic fragments to be preserved by the Vitaphone for American audiences. The tenor's voice becomes both the material of the text and the means of its production. Such a shift subverts the foreignness of opera by instituting a rift between the singer—reconceived as an American personality through his association with Hollywood sound and the importance of his image for American cultural institutions—and the composer, silent in his European grave. Through the reformulation of opera as a mishmash of arias and genres and the emphasis on the tenor as the voice that makes sense of the mix, the audience is prevented from seeing the composer as the author of the film. In Vitaphone's reconstruction of "opera," the spectator recognizes the tenor as the rightful producer of the short and the aria it incorporates.

THE NARRATIVE BODY

Whereas the Vitaphone shorts of 1926 showcased the tenor's whole body, the later shorts became more cinematic, decreasing their tendency to replicate the effects of the stage. Through their direct address, the earliest Vitaphone opera shorts openly acknowledged the theatrical audience.

Later films, however, constructed minimal narratives that included observers from the cultural elite clearly capable of interpreting what they see and hear. In many of them, beautiful female characters adopt the role of viewers gazing appreciatively at the tenor. The physical presence of women is made superfluous, however, as the films begin to rely on knowledge of the tenor's extratextual status. In these shorts, tenors avoid becoming spectacle in and of themselves by the way their films reconstitute a selection of songs as a narrative unit and the male voice as the force that gives it meaning.

Cases of women looking at the tenor in opera shorts can be productively compared to films in which an opera has been staged for the benefit of a diegetic audience of mixed gender. Contextualizing the visual style of these films demonstrates how the Vitaphone transforms female performers into spectators and shifts the focus of the short from the content of the opera to the body of the tenor. One obvious instance of the female look occurs in a Charles Hackett short that combines two completely unrelated numbers, both of which are set abroad.[88] Behind the credit sequence stands a silhouette of a city, clearly marked as non-European, but otherwise unidentifiable. Hackett emerges onto a very stagey beach and lounges somewhat seductively on a blanket before beginning to sing. Exhibiting rather uncharacteristic behavior, Hackett moves very little, keeping his arms and hands inside his tunic; when they do emerge for just a moment, his costume for the second act is briefly visible. Hackett's first song, "Call of the Nile," written by the renowned American film composer Charles Wakefield Cadman, expresses a sentiment similar to that of his second number, "Chanson Indoue," by the Russian composer Nikolai Rimsky-Korsakov. In both cases, Hackett takes over for the author as an enthralled visitor, presumably educating the viewer about the foreign, but with a physical stance that shows his comfort in and dominance of the exotic.

One might be tempted to justify Hackett's immobility in "Call" by the need to conceal his clothing for "Chanson," but this is clearly not enough to explain the strangeness of the short. Since Hackett had to switch sets entirely for the second number, surely he would have had time for a costume change. The importance of his initial excessive covering could be made clear, however, if we were to think about how the female look creates a relationship between the two songs. Although the first number provides no diegetic observers for the tenor's performance, in the second Hackett is placed in an ornamented tent where two young women (who, given the song's title, are presumed to be Indian) sit kneeling before a chaise longue. As Hackett enters, the women bow before him and permit him to take their place in the front of the frame while gazing at him admiringly. Rather than remain in the pedestrian tunic he wore for the first number, Hackett is now dressed in finery; a golden robe covers his shoulders and a jeweled belt is wrapped around his waist. Hackett falls back on the chaise at the end of the number, out of breath with heavy arms, in ecstasy and exhaustion. Stilled by the face of femininity, it seems Hackett is no longer able to move at all. Although the first number might conceivably trap the spectator in a feminine position, drawn to the appeal of Hackett's voice and perhaps wondering what lies underneath his tunic, such a danger is alleviated by the mise-en-scène of the second song. The literal presence of women in the frame removes the ban on disclosing Hackett's body. Furthermore, visual references to India placed within the scene ask spectators to identify with Hackett's engagement with the location and the women who inhabit it rather than desire the star himself.

Hackett's short combines two distinct spectatorial looks that work together to form a template for viewing American film opera. These looks—looking at virile masculinity and looking at opera as a feminized foreign spectacle—function in a kind of relay. As Richard Dyer notes, fans are often attracted to stars of the same sex. Though we like to discuss this attraction in terms of identification, it may instead be more about providing what Dyer calls "the vicarious and disguised experience of gay feeling for non-gay audiences."[89] Because of the intensity of the music, the threat of homosexual desire risks amplification by the genre of the opera film. Hence these films situate opera in a fantastic space capable of isolating such a dangerous representation. The second look, then, establishes the strangeness of the opera in contrast to the everyday. The women in Hackett's film thus serve a double purpose. They not only distract the viewer from the sexuality of the singer by situating his body in a rudimentary narrative but also displace the feminization of opera itself by embodying its exoticism. In the context of early sound cinema, where the possibility for a synchronization error is strong, Warner Bros. was painfully aware that at any moment the voice of the singer might become dislodged. The closed circuit of these two looks, then, prevents us from studying too closely the source of the voice.

Such a structure of looks is essential to the American system of simultaneous sound recording used for the opera shorts of the conversion era. Because its rhetoric stressed the liveness of the exhibition experience, it was particularly necessary for the Vitaphone to communicate the tenor's presence by focusing on both his physique and his centrality to the body of the film in order to ensure that no one notices the machine. To understand the importance of this practice in a particularly American context, we might compare Hackett's short with a film starring the Italian tenor Tito Schipa. Schipa appeared in three conversion-era shorts in 1929 and 1930 (two for Paramount and one for RKO) and nine Italian features between 1932 and 1951. The first of Schipa's features, *I Sing for You Alone*, is primarily concerned with the status of the voice as object. Like many of the Vitaphone shorts, the film begins by showing us some diegetic spectators, though here they are men who appear extremely displeased with the performance of Schipa's character. It seems the tenor was unable to hit one of his notes, causing the audience to riot. Now stricken with stage fright, Schipa refuses to return to the theater. Schipa's friend becomes his physical stand-in on stage, a part that gets him both women and fame, while Schipa himself hides in the wings, singing. The story may be a rather self-evident metaphor for Italian cinema's mode of production (which relied on post-synchronous sound), but it also demonstrates a fundamental problem with Schipa himself. These spectators are not admirers, like those we find in the Vitaphone shorts; they are critics. *I Sing for You Alone* opens with a close-up of an angry operagoer, ready to pounce the moment Schipa makes a mistake. Something about Schipa's appearance invites this sort of response; unlike Hackett, Schipa on film looks stodgy, short, and timid. Perhaps a broader uncertainty over whether Schipa really could reach the high register inspired the plot of this film. It is clear that Schipa could not sincerely evoke the sensual looks awarded to Hackett, and thus would be unable to provide a sufficient distraction from technological shortcomings in the manner of the Vitaphone films. In the same way Titta Ruffo was a problem for MGM, Schipa's incompatibility with both male virility and feminine exoticism may have been partially responsible for Paramount and RKO concluding their brief venture into opera short production.

Unlike the Schipa and Hackett films, in which the distance between performer and spectator is impenetrable, women in opera shorts are often asked to play both roles. "M'Appari" from von Flotow's *Martha* is included in a 1929 Vitaphone short that features Martinelli with Livia Marracci, a relatively unknown singer and former winner of the Galveston, Texas, Miss Italy pageant. The short opens with three separate shots of Marracci, who is found flitting about the garden set and hiding behind a tree when Martinelli finally enters the frame. Throughout the aria, the camera repeatedly cuts away from the tenor to detail Marracci's mute responses to his words. Despite the emphasis on such inserts, in none of them is Marracci allowed to sing until the end of the number, when she joins Martinelli in an American shot for a final duet. Though Marracci does not prevent the spectator from gazing at the male singer, as with the "Indian" women in Hackett's piece, she does provide a significant visual focal point as well as a lesson in musical appreciation.

Most of the surviving opera shorts that show a larger audience as part of the story follow the visual organization of "M'Appari." For example,

Official Films's *Faust* is ostensibly a presentation of a "real" Metropolitan Opera performance. The first shot establishes the show we are about to see: a woman's hands are presented in a close-up, and in them rests a program announcing the Met's "Grand Opera Season" of 1928–29. The next shot tracks well-dressed patrons in the boxes and eventually stops on a pair of empty seats, to which a distinguished-looking couple are slowly finding their way. Throughout the twelve-minute film, which presents an extraordinarily condensed version of the opera, we are given two kinds of inserts: long shots of the crowd, followed by closer views of the initial couple. Strangely, rather than depicting the spectators in rapt attention, many of these shots show the woman whispering to her partner. We might at first assume her interruptions would disturb his listening pleasure; in fact, her mode of engagement with the performance and with her neighbor tells us a great deal about the relationship in which the film asks us to take part. The woman seems to inform the man about aspects of the opera he might otherwise miss: after one of her comments, he takes up his opera glasses and looks through them quizzically. The appropriate response to her coaching seems to be to increase the input to his senses, a difficult effect to register visually. The opera glasses, providing a literal close-up of the singer, are the most obvious cue the film has at its disposal for instructing the spectator in how to watch opera properly. By alluding to the glasses, the film teaches the viewer how to find evidence of the singer's skill and use it to interpret the value of the work, while at the same time suggesting that the cinematic spectator is better off than these folks, who need special tools in order to see a live opera clearly.

A 1930 Martinelli Warner Bros. short situates its diegetic spectators similarly, but no longer attends to the realism expected of opera films set in performance spaces like this one. Martinelli and his pianist begin to play a set of light music for a benefit concert after having been introduced by an emcee as one of the "great stars answering this country's appeal," an overt reference to the Depression.[90] The songs are ostensibly being performed for an elite crowd, but the concert itself has been put on for the greater good of an American public, who can, in fact, really hear it thanks to the Vitaphone. Yet there is a break from tradition here. In the other Vitaphone films that feature a tenor with a single accompanist, the piano remains the only audible instrument. In this short, although a piano is the only object sharing the stage with Martinelli, we hear an entire orchestra. Why are we capable of listening to a symphony that doesn't exist? By the end of 1930, Hollywood had provided sufficient training in listening to the operatic voice such that audiences might be trusted to fashion a narrative about the arias they heard around the figure of the tenor himself. Indeed, they would have been required to do this if they were to believe that this music was "opera" at all. We hear an orchestra because Martinelli has become capable of breaking the rules of the stage in favor of what would soon become conventions of the Hollywood film musical. The lyrical content of the songs has lost nearly all importance; what matters now is that Martinelli is singing them. Because he is what makes this concert both meaningful and profitable, cutting to closer shots of Martinelli's face, as Warners once did with Marion Talley and Anna Case, no longer poses the threat of fetishization, for the tenor is not a mere spectacle, distracting us from the plot of the opera or the words of the aria. Instead, the desire to see the tenor sing has become the justification for furthering the creation of opera on film.

We can see this process at work in two of the final shorts Martinelli made for Warner Bros., both demonstrating a complete reversal of the strategies employed in "Vesti la giubba." The earliest Martinelli film preserved the aria as an operatic performance, while these releases from 1931 are mishmashes of popular classical melodies with no reference at all to an opera stage. In the first of these films, Martinelli is a gondolier serenading couples as he rows along a river on a set built to resemble Venice.[91] As usual, Martinelli appears fully comfortable on the set, even though the camera gets closer to his face than ever before. On high notes and other moments of dynamic stress or tempo change, Martinelli the gondolier stops rowing while the camera cuts to a medium close-up, providing us with the opportunity to examine the throat of Martinelli the singer. Shifting emphasis like this allows us to comprehend the two roles the star has been asked to play; the poor worker, blithely performing a tune in its proper environment, and the famous aesthete, demonstrating how any melody can be transformed into high art with the "right" voice. Martinelli's final film, "Gypsy Caravan," blends familiar eastern European melodies with the strains of Tchaikovsky's *Nutcracker*. The gondola short reminded us of the singer's Italian background; "Gypsy Caravan" represents the ideal position of the generic immigrant in the audience. As narratives were being constructed around him, the meaning and place of "opera" changed to support what Martinelli could offer. These films integrated the Italian tenor into the melting pot of American popular culture and opera into the variety act.

By the time his contract with Warner Bros. came to an end, Martinelli had succeeded in making women unnecessary for the production of opera on film. Completing a transformation that began with the erasure of Marion Talley from the shorts' output, the women in both "Sorrento" and "Gypsy Caravan" are finally able to say nothing at all. These women continue to gaze at the tenor, swoon at his voice, dance to impress him, and acknowledge his talent, but they no longer have any reason to sing. As the castrato helped to silence the soprano centuries before him, the tenor aided in her cinematic banishment by naturalizing the place of opera in sound film production.

Despite critics' adoration of Martinelli and Warners' promise to collect important voices for future generations, the melodies he performed were far from timeless. The predominantly Italian origin of the arias recorded during the conversion era indicates that regardless of efforts to discipline the viewer and "sacralize" opera as a medium, the film industry held particular assumptions about the attention span and social status of its audience. As the stylistic procedures of sound film solidified, the function of the opera short as an educational tool shifted as well. Opera shorts stopped including descriptive title cards or relying on the strong hand of a cinematic narrator and instead made stories centered on the tenor's voice. The conversion era's attempts at opera were thus distinct from those typically produced before the availability of synchronous sound, for these were no longer adaptations of single works. These shorts neither foretell the grand merger of opera and cinema in the European "opera film" nor presage the class-based signification associated with opera in the Hollywood blockbuster. By elevating the tenor's body to the level of textual production, the conversion-era opera short essentially accomplishes a *de*sacralization of opera, eventually enabling the medium to speak the same language as jazz.

CHAPTER 3

Selling Jazz Short

Hollywood and the Fantasy of Musical Agency

In 1931 Warner Bros. released a short film with the misleadingly euphemistic title *Sax Appeal*.[1] The story concerns a miserable saxophonist named Joe Penner, whose repeated attempts to improve his musical skill are thwarted by his father, a junk collector, who insists that Joe accompany him on his route. Joe boards his father's wagon, saxophone in tow, only to discover that being an inadequate musician makes him a superior junkman. As Joe and his father drive through town, they are bombarded by rubbish thrown at them by characters hoping to be speedily rid of Joe's noise pollution. Having amassed more clutter than they would by relying solely on the salesmanship of the father, the men leave the residents in peaceful silence. The "appeal" of the saxophone here has little to do with its sound, nothing to do with the sexual connotations of jazz music, and everything to do with its ability to generate a profit. Joe's lack of musical aptitude nevertheless channels the flow of capital in the right direction. In addition, by transforming the saxophone into a punch line the short erases many of the negative stereotypes that were often associated with the instrument and its manifestation in jazz. Jazz's urban menace is voided by the backwardness of the film's rural setting, the music's infectiousness is negated by the townspeople's desire to eliminate the means of its transmission, and its sensuality is denied by the domestic focus of the story. Although Hollywood is rather like Joe's father in its exploitation of jazz for economic gain, *Sax Appeal* belies any reading of jazz as a simple signifier of race and sexuality.

Sax Appeal may have neutralized the sexual and racial connotations of the saxophone, but jazz in conversion-era films was typically assumed to be far more threatening. Theodor Adorno, for example, reads the open piano lids in Hollywood jazz films as signs of castration's lurking menace,[2] to which we might oppose the closed (clothed) lids of the opera shorts, whose pianos are more tastefully dressed. For Adorno, spectators are subject to castration by listening to all sorts of records, since such activity replaces active musical production with passive distracted consumption. Jazz records, however, are especially dangerous. This is because, according to Adorno's functional definition, jazz is made for dancing. Whether live or recorded, then, jazz provokes a physical response. Motivated by the impulse to "tear into rags,"[3] the listener instinctually celebrates his weakness. Despite Adorno's assertion that jazz is more the product of capitalism than of African American culture, underlying his premise is the assumption that in a musical context, blackness is a signifier for castration. [4]

Whatever the racial and musical problems with this argument (and there are many), Adorno is not the only theorist to have connected black music and castration. In his study of blackface, Eric Lott claims that nineteenth-century blackface minstrelsy articulated both the threat of black sexuality and its defeat by the white body.[5] The music and its attendant stories may have institutionalized distinct African American stereotypes, but in the end it was harmless white men acting out these roles. Such an arrangement returned with the foundation of sound cinema, particularly with regard to Al Jolson, whose resurrection of blackface helped displace African American authority at the very moment when black jazz musicians were able to sing for themselves on film. Yet as Alice Maurice has shown, accompanying Jolson's rise to fame was a movement to employ sound technology in the service of African Americans, drawing attention to the spectacle of the black voice in order to conceal the shortcomings of the machine.[6] In Adorno's theory of aesthetics, the castrating force of capital eliminates the distance between the serious and the popular by replacing them both with mere melodies. In other words, it didn't matter what these voices sang; what was important to Hollywood was that they sounded black.

Rather than endorsing the view that jazz is a byproduct of capitalism or advocating an essentialist position that sees African Americans as the only group capable of authoring and performing jazz, I want to suggest that the jazz *voice* might be used to undermine the commercial conditions under which the music was produced, thus revealing the historical circumstances in which it arose and the current climate in which it continues to speak. This view is in line with what Paul Gilroy calls "anti-anti-essentialism," or, a perspective that "striv[es] to comprehend the reproduction of cultural traditions not in the unproblematic transmission of a fixed essence through time but in the breaks and interruptions which suggest that the invocation of tradition may itself be a distinct, though covert, response to the destabilizing flux of the post-contemporary world."[7] The jazz voice articulates the continued relevance of race to the production and dissemination of music even in cases where the style would seem to have to progressed beyond its origins in a particular community. Of course, the idea that we could hear the voice this way challenges Adorno's low expectations of the jazz audience: so all-consuming is the dominance of melody and rhythm in Adorno's conception of modern musical listening that he does not permit internal critique. Like many accounts of jazz history, Adorno's work pays scant attention to the multiple ways the voice can be used, instead relegating it to the status of a fetish object. The vocal fetish he decries is always associated with a proper name: Louis Armstrong's voice or the "voice" of the Stradivarius are for him "holy properties like a national trademark,"[8] which listeners can own on records that they accept as a substitute for an experience and an age. Iconic voices like these condense the time and place of production into a familiar sound, which becomes the very "fixed essence" of Gilroy's formulation, producing a version of history that ignores the evolving sound of music and its changing importance for American culture. The jazz voice is capable of much more variance than Adorno acknowledges. What do we do, for example, with voices that fail to assimilate?

When we sing without words, it becomes much more difficult to label the voice. Like opera, jazz is particularly prone to moments where the voice moves beyond signification; scatting and humming, jazz vocalists play not just with rhythm and melody, but also with language and identity. In such moments, the jazz voice is both separate from and wedded to the music, forcing a radical rethinking of the nature of song. Because they are "meaningless," these noises are unavailable for fetishization: instead of substituting for the whole, they question the stability of the piece. Nathanial Mackey calls scat the "apparent mangling of speech" that communicates the horrors of lynching.[9] Indeed, Mackey explains, the sounds of a voice without content can be more meaningful than one with lyrics. An "inarticulate vocal line," for example, can become a "willful dismantling," a "loud critique of available options" for expressing what otherwise might be left unsaid.[10] In Gilroy's terms, then, the jazz voice is not an outright refusal of language; nor is it a commercial experiment in vocal performance. Instead, it both refers to a history of real oppression and reflects modern musical conventions that are also made available to the recording industry.

If Adorno is right that popular jazz has already been culturally coded as a castrated form, then nonsense syllables work as critique precisely because they cannot be appropriated. Thus these sounds reveal the violence done to African Americans only because commercial recordings have trained us to read black voices as we do castrati, created by a force that marked them as strange, secretive, and available solely for pleasure. Like their operatic counterparts, jazz voices speak truth when they say "nothing." As the film industry struggled with how it should sound, Hollywood commodified jazz, selling it in shorts that advertised the potential of the conversion. Yet slipping through the cracks of these films are not only fragments of bare jazz voices, but equally nonsensical jazz images. There are severed shots, self-contained stories, or ambiguous "symbols" for which we would struggle to find meaning. How each studio presented these pictures and voices, moreover, says a great deal about what each thought jazz ought to mean, and how the music's citation of history was to be safely contained by the technology of the individual studio.

Jazz images, like jazz voices, are not accidental. They are akin to what Mackey describes in the incoherent voice as "a mix of exposé and refusal" in that they reveal a truth about the cinema's relationship to jazz and reject the unproblematic absorption of the music by the rest of the film.[11] The incoherence of jazz images lies in their inability to be integrated into the diegesis. Although the makers of these films produced and edited these shots, it would be disingenuous to attribute their multiple occurrences and variations to a single authorial hand. The images seem almost to spring from the music itself, or perhaps from the mind of the spectator, who may have been hearing it apart from the image and generated a visual source. Yet they do not arise apart from the technologies that make them visible. As Mackey describes the quality of Louis Armstrong records: "The sense I have is that we're being addressed by a barely audible witness, some receding medium so heart-rendingly remote as to redefine hearing."[12] The scratches on the record combine with the scratchiness of Armstrong's voice to make this sound a testament to music history. Similarly, the cinema is a witness to jazz origins and uncomfortable about what it sees. Its expression of discomfort is the jazz image, allowing us to understand the body of the film as Vivian Sobchack does: "as the film's means of perceptually engaging and expressing a world not only for us but also for itself."[13] Inserted into an otherwise complete narrative or musical setting, jazz images have the power to tear apart not only the film's fiction but also the fiction that the viewing experience is all-consuming.[14] This produces a profoundly unsettling effect in which spectators are forced to confront the fragmentary nature of the film text; unable to find an explanation for the image within the context of the story, they must search outside of it, for historical information that may call the entirety of the representation into question.

The history of "jazz" as a musical description is fraught with tension. The negative connotations of the term in the early twentieth century caused some musicians to avoid its use, while its present associations with artistry tinge the word with elitism. This fluctuation in the meaning of "jazz" permits jazz and film scholar Krin Gabbard to be extremely inclusive in his definition. For example, in spite of the fact that *The Jazz Singer* (1927) contains little in the way of "real" jazz,[15] Gabbard insists that because of how the music signified at the time of its initial release, Jolson's feature film debut is indeed a "jazz film." I share Gabbard's view that it would not be useful to impose present-day connotations of musical terminology onto the past. Thus as I did with the opera shorts, I label a "jazz film" one that would have been recognized as such by Hollywood and its audiences during the period of conversion, regardless of whether the soundtrack meets the more recently defined musical prerequisites. Despite the connection between jazz music and American identity that has been acknowledged by many scholars,[16] conversion-era jazz films waver in their efforts to locate jazz in opposition to the "good" cultural object and to write the music into a narrative of progress by showing how jazz produces cultural synthesis.

This chapter examines the appropriation of jazz music by three major studios during the conversion era. I argue that Warner Bros., Paramount, and MGM all constructed definitions of jazz to reflect the ideals represented in their promotion of sound technology. The differences reveal that the conversion era was rife with confusion over the significance of jazz and the cultural role of film sound. Furthermore, how each studio asserted its own technology as a means of grafting American values onto a potentially dangerous musical style demonstrates that concerns about the place of jazz and the value of sound cinema were fundamentally linked. Whereas the dialogue and lyrics typically found in the Warner Bros. shorts attribute the creation of jazz to rural, Southern, African American amateur musicians, the films themselves include primarily seasoned and mostly white professionals. As such, Al Jolson provides the perfect image of nostalgia; his baritone naturalizes the Vitaphone and helps offset the impression of cultural elitism suggested by the promotion of Giovanni Martinelli's operatic tenor. For Paramount, jazz is a problem best solved by the cinema. The Paramount films center on a jazz fan who misrecognizes the function of the radio and phonograph and attempts to join performances in progress by Louis Armstrong and other popular stars. By building a narrative around such a hapless and enthusiastic figure, Paramount exposes the dangers lurking within the technologies of sonic reproduction and proposes the supervised space of its own sound stage as a solution to jazz's potential for corruption. MGM jazz shorts tend to put the white female body on display, identifying jazz as a visual spectacle rather than associating it with actual musical sounds. The "M-G-M Dancing Girls" often credited with this work transform perilous places into sites for the exploitation of unsuspecting men, yet they do so at the expense of their own musical agency. Reflecting the conflicting perspectives exchanged in the jazz-opera debate with which this book began, jazz shorts upset the desire to simply celebrate jazz as the musical articulation of American experience. Instead, they show how each studio told its own story about where jazz came from, a tale that corresponded to the specificity of the sound technology on which it was reproduced.

WORKING ON THE RAILROAD, PLAYING IN THE BAND: AL JOLSON AND JAZZ AT WARNER BROS.

Warners' initial image of "jazz" was not a glamorous cityscape but a shanty cabin occupied by an established performer invested in nostalgia. Al Jolson's *A Plantation Act* (1926) was part of the second program of Vitaphone shorts, a lineup that also included Willie and Eugene Howard's *Between the Acts at the Opera* and a solo by Metropolitan Opera singer Reinald Werrenrath. Yet in spite of its continued presence, the new program upstaged opera with a different kind of voice: the Howards' skit lampooned the opera and Werrenrath's recital was not given any special recognition. Jolson's number, however, went on to serve as the prototype for Warners' representation of jazz. Later shorts starring white performers followed Jolson's lead, developing their narratives around traditional American songs reconfigured as "jazz," a practice that lent itself to ridicule by the African American musicians featured in the studio's black-cast shorts. Moreover, Warners' reliance on phonographic discourse situated Jolson within larger concerns over which bodies should be allowed to produce jazz music. By associating jazz with a distinctly American past, Warner Bros. not only anchored the music in a particular historical trajectory; it also stabilized the reception of the studio's sound technology.

Al Jolson was perceived as a natural entertainer. For renowned stage critic Gilbert Seldes, Jolson was possessed by a kind of dæmonic spirit that made his performances "the easiest seeming, the most effortless in the world."[17] Jolson had been incredibly popular in one-man stage shows before appearing on film; he was famous for his characters, singing, and sentimentality, but his primary appeal was his exuberant energy. He started in minstrelsy but developed this reputation in his vaudeville days, when he would walk the aisles and sit on the edge of the stage talking directly to his audience until all hours of the night.[18] This intimacy extended to his earliest film roles, where his direct address to the camera made sense in light of his well-established star persona. For some critics, it was shocking that such a maneuver should translate to the screen. One *Billboard* columnist predicted Jolson's demise the day he encountered a crowd unwilling (or unable) to serve as fodder for his patter.[19] Perhaps we can credit the Vitaphone's rhetoric of liveness for Jolson's initially easy passage to cinematic fame. Although, as Krin Gabbard notes, Jolson was constantly creating and then abandoning identities for himself and his characters,[20] his distinctive sob was accepted as a real expression of his sentiment. Seldes calls each of these personae an "image of longing" that would seem to reflect on his own life story, transcending as it does the caricature of blackface.[21] His biography was well known, and the "inspiration" he received from watching African American jazz musicians was reiterated by Warners' press materials and used to justify the singer's affinity with blackface. In many of these stories, it was his African American valet who advised Jolson to put on the burnt cork for the first time.[22] Even if such tales were largely fabricated, it is impossible to understand Jolson without acknowledging the influence of black performance styles on his own. As Henry Pleasants remarks, the whistling and other embellishments on which Jolson's act relied were improvisatory moves that mimicked the style of "true" jazz.[23] Jolson had been making recordings for some time before he appeared on film, thus it should come as no surprise that Warners' publicity highlighted his easy adjustment to film sound technology. As the pressbook for *Say It with Songs* announced: "His voice records perfectly. The same resonant quality that causes the nerves of an audience to tingle at a Jolson personal appearance, registers."[24] Jolson's natural vocal ability was repeatedly pinned to his black muses; the origins of his "jazz" made his cinematic performances seem as effortless as those he had been giving on stage for years.

Every movement Jolson made on stage or screen was calculated, yet because his numbers reminisced about an ideal American past, these gestures were quickly associated with an older performance style. For example, Jolson's blackface *Plantation Act* includes three songs: "The Red, Red Robin," "April Showers," and "Rock-a-Bye Your Baby (with a Dixie Melody)." The last of these is the most significant, both for how Jolson characteristically addresses the camera as "Mammy" and for the introduction he gives to the number. In what is presumably a justification for selecting songs with such sentiment, Jolson claims that his "little Mammy songs" are "the fundamental songs of our country" and compares them to "Mother McCree," as made famous by Irish tenor John McCormack. By putting "Mammy songs" in a comparative national context, Jolson attempts to neutralize their racial significance. At the same time, Jolson's performance posits an alternative "Mammy song" as an ideal the Vitaphone can never reach. His promise that "a million baby kisses I'll deliver, if only you will sing the Swanee River," must, of course, go unanswered, for the Mammy he serenades no longer exists. There was, of course, a significant gap between the period Jolson recalled and the time of the recording of *Plantation Act*. In the same way the Vitaphone opera shorts preserved the popular music of the previous century rather than modern works, so Jolson's short brought back an earlier music reclassified as "jazz."

It is important to note that not all the songs featured in *Plantation Act* have the markers of jazz sound.[25] Yet the way Warner Bros. amplified Jolson's image and gestures and the manner in which it contrasted his short to the operatic numbers produced simultaneously suggests that the studio associated jazz with a rosy picture of plantation life. Wanting to mark jazz clearly as such, Warner Bros. selected a few key visual elements to rearticulate across its body of films and used music of a particular period and style, even if on the basis of sound alone that music would not be strictly identified as jazz. By bringing Jolson to prominence, Warners ensured that jazz retained its historical significance and posed little threat to the technology that promised to preserve America's past.

Following the model of *Plantation Act*, the Warner Bros. jazz films are typically heavily laden with nostalgia. Like its opera productions, most of the studio's shorts released near the end of the conversion era and into the 1930s enclose a series of musical numbers within a minimal narrative in order to logically account for their presence. Yet the earlier films rarely take great efforts to narrativize their selections or provide a setting for their presentation. A 1928 short featuring Blossom Seeley and Bennie Fields is typical: it begins with a shot of a curtain that opens to reveal a stage with two grand pianos, which are draped with expensive curtains and surrounded by an excess of potted plants.[26] The presence of draperies and foliage elaborately arranged in a grand ballroom provides jazz with the cultural capital to make it worthy of the viewer's attention. Indeed, the musicians (who are usually all white and male) are almost always dressed in tuxedos, face the camera rather than one another, and often perform beneath an enormous crystal chandelier.[27] If the names of the orchestras are not recognizable on their own, these elements, like a Beethoven bust prominently placed in an opera short featuring the American baritone John Charles Thomas, inform the viewer that these performers are reputable musicians who belong in such a setting.

As if to reinforce the image of jazz as an established musical genre, the shorts are edited without accounting for the improvisational techniques of the jazz performance; instead, the cutting of these films bears a strong resemblance to the Vitaphone's 1926 recording of *Tannhäuser* by the New York Philharmonic. The jazz short habitually opens with an extreme long shot that introduces the entirety of the orchestra, cuts to closer shots that reveal smaller groups when their instruments are heard, and then goes back to the opening shots for the *tutti* sections. Warners did occasionally alter its style. For example, *Paul Tremaine and His Aristocrats* (1929; Figure 3.1) provides an exception to this formula that ultimately produces an even more conservative reading of "jazz." Rather than a stage, the short begins with silent stock footage of a train leaving a station, accompanied by musical imitations of a locomotive. Unsurprisingly, the band's first number is a jazzy version of an American standard: "I've Been Working on the Railroad." Thus, even the urban or technological connotations of jazz music emphasized by the instruments' ability to mimic the machine are transformed into mere symbols of folk history.

Figure 3.1: Warners' refinement of jazz.
Frame grab from Paul Tremaine and His Aristocrats (1929).

Of course, the selection of the train was no accident. According to Lynne Kirby, the silent cinema had at its beginnings succumbed to the allure of the railroad, an attraction built on technological kinship, economic incentives, and the aesthetic potential of the moving camera, among other things.[28] Kirby notes that concurrently with the recognition of various national cinemas in the 1920s, trains on film began to take on national characteristics, standing in for the values held by particular cultures.[29] The presence of the train footage in Tremaine's short, or later in *Yamekraw* and other Warner Bros. films, suggests a continuation of the trend identified by Kirby, but with specifically musical overtones. As early film distributors often did, Warners had already made extensive use of trains and other moving vehicles in its advertisements in order to illustrate the modernity and miraculous capabilities of the Vitaphone. Like early train narratives (and the trains themselves), which brought the social classes together in the same space, the Vitaphone's appropriation of the train suggested its capacity for unity in its ability to assemble Americans in the name of good music. Associating the train with jazz, as these films implicitly do, prompted a different interpretation. The trains at the beginning of the jazz shorts are seen only from the outside. They approach or whiz by the camera, both referencing the astonishment such images aroused in early film audiences and reproducing the point of view held by those not lucky enough to afford a ticket. In the context of "I've Been Working on the Railroad," then, these are trains as seen by the workers themselves, in stark contrast to the well-dressed white musicians now singing their music. Jazzing the folk song on a stage in a ballroom thus saves it from its less prosperous roots; Paul Tremaine takes a song describing the excruciating working conditions of African Americans and immigrants and turns it into a dance tune. The Warner Bros. shorts typically continue this tradition by positioning folk symbols in a narrative that folds jazz into a tidy story about the past, even when the music they feature cannot all be easily certified as jazz and even when the films can boast no narratives themselves. For example, Paul Tremaine and his Aristocrats end their performance with a medley that, the bandleader notes, "might have been seen and heard on one of the old Mississippi River showboats." By situating "In the Evening by the Moonlight," "Oh Susanna," "Swanee River," and "Mississippi Mud" on such a journey, Tremaine constructs a nominal story through which the viewer is intended to interpret these tunes. Indeed, this medley and the musical styles through which it sequences operate more like a montage, providing glimpses into the lives of African American Southerners that have clearly been exaggerated for white audiences. The offensive lyrics of "In the Evening" not only set the tone for what is to follow but reveal who it is that Warners credits as the authors of jazz:

> In the evening by the moonlight,
> you can hear those darkies singing.
> In the evening by the moonlight,
> you can hear their banjos ringing.

Although a third party clearly produces the music we hear, the description of its muses and the style through which they are evoked cause us to understand the white performers as failed conduits for an experience we can no longer access, one that perhaps only the oldest members of the audience can fully appreciate.

The loudness and placement of the banjo in the short film combined with the instrument's prominance in the song's lyrics give "In the Evening" a particular nostalgic sensibility. Initially an instrument fashioned by slaves from northwest Africa, it was popularized in the 1840s and 1850s by the minstrel act. After becoming an integral part of ragtime, by the mid-1920s the banjo was central to Dixieland jazz, and its distinctive sound became identified with a recognizable New Orleans style.[30] In Tremaine's film, after the introduction of the medley we cut to a shot of the banjoist, situated at the front of the stage, awarded an atypical close-up for a brief solo moments later when his instrument is acknowledged by the lyrics. Of course, the following number, "Oh Susanna," is a song about a wayward banjoist from Alabama, a reference not lost on Tremaine's group. The banjoist finally becomes one of three singers of "Mississippi Mud," a song popularized by the Rhythm Boys three years before its appearance in the Vitaphone short. Like "In the Evening," "Mississippi Mud" envisions a carefree African American band dancing in perfect rhythm with only their bodies to guide them. By relying so heavily on an instrument that would likely be heard in the fantasy "original" performances on which these tunes were based, Tremaine invokes the banjo as a signifier of African American musical identity while absorbing it into a sanitized spectacle that informs us about black culture from a distance.[31] Dressed to the nines and visibly accomplished on their instruments, the "Aristocrats," "Ambassadors," or even the "Five Pennies" seem about as far as one can get from "beating their feet on the Mississippi mud."

Warner Bros. often seemed conflicted about its own interpretation of these American songs, a state it revealed in what I have labeled "jazz images," visions of an alternate history that slip their way into the dominant narrative created by the studio. The jazz image can emerge through lyrical suggestion, alterations made to the lighting or mise-en-scène, or most strikingly, through the use of stock footage and superimposition. An example of the first case has already been mentioned in the words to "In the Evening" performed by Paul Tremaine's band. As Tremaine and the other white men stand facing the implied audience, singing the song matter-of-factly into the camera, we cannot but be reminded of a much livelier group of singers who would play their banjos for the "old folks" of yesteryear. Visualizing this performance while hearing Tremaine's straightforward style, we recognize the rift between the voices cited by the text and the ones we can actually hear. The film proposes that Tremaine's Aristocrats have refined these early sounds, turning them into music appropriate for American audiences. And yet, Warners' constant mining of the past for jazzy material is not unlike its obsession with nineteenth-century Italian opera. In both cases, the film uses the lost voice for inspiration without fully accounting for its absence. Thus the style of both the opera and jazz shorts produced by the studio attempt to compensate for the sound that alludes representation; the soundtrack replaces the castrato or the oppressed black American with something more "modern," while the image divulges Warners' discomfort with this solution.

Jazz images crop up in attempts to disguise the origins of the performers or increase the artistry of the short. An example of the first of these circumstances is *Rhythms* (1929), which opens with an extreme long shot of Leo Reisman and the nine members of his Hotel Brunswick Orchestra in silhouette. Even though the name of the band implies that the kind of setting given Tremaine's orchestra will soon emerge as the reality behind the strangely lit space,[32] the silhouette leaves us uncertain about the racial makeup of the group. Certainly Warner Bros. produced some films staring African American musicians, and shadows and silhouettes were often employed in black-cast shorts or used to signify blackness on film (indeed, Jolson's blackface character in *The Jazz Singer* is referred to as his shadow).[33] Although the opening shot soon makes way for Warners' typical luminous ballroom, the editing teases us by periodically returning to the silhouette, as if to dislodge the meaning of the cinematic shadow. In addition, some of the shots include hanging plants, while the first number played by Reisman's band, "The Water of Perkiomen," is accompanied by stock footage of rivers and streams. Unlike the old Southern scene conjured up by Tremaine's song, these peaceful images of nature reinforce the associations Warner Bros. tries to give this music by placing its musicians in "safe" spaces. The silhouettes, however, prevent this operation from succeeding fully. As it had with the selection and recombination of operatic arias, Warners decontextualizes the song in an attempt to recontextualize it within the signifiers of the short. By turning to the silhouette, the director attempts to both authenticate the jazziness of the music and confirm the cultural merit of the musical film.

The jazz image in *The Audition* (1932; Figure 3.2) speaks even more resolutely than Tremaine's lyrics or Reisman's silhouettes, refusing to conform to Warners' recontextualization of jazz as a series of songs with a black American past that can be easily appropriated by white musicians. The short starts predictably: a band appears in a studio performing for a film producer. Just as he tells the manager that the group cannot expect to be seen on screen without a singer, the film seems to conjure up Hannah Williams, an energetic white woman, to perform a version of "Get Happy" infused with the religious articulations typical of an African American female vocalist. Thus it is no surprise when, immediately following her act, she tells the producer that she'd like to see the band perform on a Southern set. Thrilled by the idea, he suggests that they put the men on a levee and blacken them up. Then something strange happens. Just as the producer utters this last suggestion, we clumsily cut to a shot of the band on the levee, but without the burnt cork. *The Audition* then proceeds to visualize

Figure 3.2: Historical superimposition.
Frame grab from *The Audition* (1932).

the scenes described by the typical Warner Bros. jazz short through a series of superimpositions that function as multiple frame narratives while the band plays "Here Comes the Showboat." As we move back in time, getting progressively closer to those watching the showboat "chug, chug chugging along," we leave the band behind and are instead presented with images of the "real" African Americans depicted by the lyrics. Instead of adding to the narrative, however, the black characters seem to interrupt the tune, reminding us about the uncomfortable historical circumstances under which this great mobile entertainment center of the past had been constructed, a version of events eschewed by the upbeat performance style of the music.

Clearly created at some point after the producers had abandoned their plans for a blackface scene, this particular jazz image is available only to the cinema. In fact, the superimposed sequence is constructed as a collage of the exhibition experience in the classical Hollywood period. With what presumes to be documentary footage, shots from more theatrical productions, and the cartoonish appearance of the Three X Sisters in polka dotted dresses, we have an image that puts the brief history of the cinema's representation of jazz on display while at the same time announcing itself *as* representation through the foregrounding of the water, as if to say that this mere *reflection* of jazz is the closest the studio will come to presenting the "truth" of its production. Indeed, superimposed historical images recurred in Warner Bros. films throughout the 1930s. Shorts like *Isham Jones and His Orchestra* (1933) combines shots of military drills, trains, towers, and Russian buildings over our view of the band playing a jazzy version of a Rachmaninoff prelude; *Ben Pollack and His Orchestra* (1934) similarly splits the screen to arrange the "tramping feet," "birds that sing," and "bells that ring" contained within the song "Beat of My Heart" next to a heart that frames the singer's face; and *Red Nichols and His World Famous Pennies* (1935) dissolves a shot of the band performing "When It's Sleepy Time Down South" into a series of plantation images seemingly ripped straight from the lyrics. By the middle of the decade, Warner Bros. had found a way to reappropriate this particular jazz image as a standard visual shorthand so that it no longer threatened to escape the diegetic dictates of the song.

There were shorts that featured black performers and visualized the jazz image through the actions of a particular musician. For example, *Harlem Mania* (1929) with the Norman Thomas Quintette constantly threatens to come apart at the seams. The short opens with an African American baritone singing "Sleep Baby Sleep" in a voice full of vibrato. An unseen pianist plays chords that sound at odds with the singer's more traditional performance style, while a drummer provides fills that seem just as disconnected.

Indeed, the group cannot sustain this presentation style for long; the act slowly moves from a musical number to something of a spoof in which the drummer, unable to stay in his seat, spins about on the floor and dances on his chair, managing to keep time, but clearly putting his body above the importance of the music. One could easily read this scene as racist buffoonery; smiling for the camera and clowning around, the drummer cannot keep his act together. Yet I prefer to see this routine as another kind of jazz image. Because the tunes they play are known, having been appropriated by white performers for decades and included in several other Vitaphone shorts, these musicians are using their bodies to make a pronouncement about the absurdity of Warners' standard interpretation of jazz. A similar moment comes in *Pie Pie Blackbird* (1932), when Eubie Blake, his band, and the Nicholas Brothers are baked in a pie, yet keep on dancing after being burned to a skeletal crisp. It is a ludicrous image, but one that defies the offensive stereotype of the black crow. Associating themselves with the nursery rhyme after which the short is named, the musicians sing on after the pie is opened and refuse to be devoured by the king.

Black performers were not the only ones to use their bodies in excess. Like *Harlem Mania*'s drummer, the white violinist in *Jazzmania Quintette* (1928) is undoubtedly the most energetic figure in the short. He blithely hops atop the piano, does a duet with a female singer, and detaches his bow so that it fits around his instrument, forcing him to play the melody in nothing but double-stops (which he does admirably). The most notable part of his performance, however, is the rendition of "I Ain't Got Nobody" on a Stroh-Violin, an instrument invented for pre-electrical recording in which the violin's wooden body was replaced with a horn in order to make amplification possible. Rather than providing an opportunity for a showpiece, however, the musician actually seems restricted by the instrument. His playing becomes more subdued and follows the melodic line much more closely than it had previously. Yet as soon as he switches back to the regular violin, his improvisational vision returns, leaving the viewer to wonder what the purpose of the brief chorus had been. The image of the Stroh-Violin is not without novelty appeal; presumably most viewers who had never set foot in a recording studio did not have the opportunity to see and hear the instrument in action. But as a reminder of the process of recording, the Stroh holds a strange place in this film. Its failure to project might paradoxically be understood as a demonstration of the Vitaphone's potential. An electrical recording process with its own method of amplification, the Vitaphone could exceed the limitations that led to the creation of the Stroh. The contrast between the violinist's "naturalness" with the traditional violin and his awkwardness with the Stroh illustrates how the

Vitaphone is capable of presenting "real" music by improving on the technology of the phonograph.

The awkwardness of the Stroh-Violin demonstrates how important it was that Warners sell the Vitaphone as an appropriate producer of jazz. It wasn't only its reappropriation of African American musical tradition that made jazz "safe" for consumption: the studio needed to remind the public that its technology enhanced the capabilities of the phonograph, particularly with regard to the invisibility of the jazz performer. As Paul Young points out, "Phonograph recordings of 'coon' songs had raised the alarming question: 'What happens to the "love & theft" of blackface when there is no face?' "[34] The ability to amplify the sounds coming from the disc allowed the phonograph to be heard *en masse*, providing a defense against the "contamination" of those most vulnerable to manipulation. As Pamela Robertson Wojcik shows, women were perceived to be particularly susceptible to the emotional power of music and were often punished for challenging the masculine control of technology.[35] By placing decisions over music making squarely in the hands of the studio and (generally male) projectionists and theater managers, the Vitaphone avoids the potential for feminine indiscretion. Moreover, the standardization of the exhibition experience encouraged by recorded sound lessens the likelihood of dancing and other "infectious" behavior, in spite of the exaggerated exceptions to this rule that appear on screen in African American figures such as the Nicholas Brothers or white singers who attempt to evoke blackness, such as Hannah Williams. Finally, synchronization ensures that the voices we hear belong to the bodies we see. This is especially important for jazz, a musical style in which the ratio of black performers to white is higher than in other genres.

Guarding the cultural project of the Vitaphone, Warner Bros. produced jazz shorts that rejoined the signifiers of music created for African American audiences and the style that was sold to white Southerners and redirected the combination toward the middle class. The conversion to sound may have given Hollywood an opportunity to return to minstrelsy,[36] particularly with the stardom of Al Jolson, but the use of blackface in the Vitaphone jazz films appears awkward with respect to the African Americans now fully visible and audible—and sometimes appearing on the very same program as a blackface short. As such, blackface may well be a citation of the sorts of traditions defined by Gilroy's discussion of anti-anti-essentialism: a harkening back that exposes anxieties over the technological upheaval of contemporary entertainment, but whose own significance has shifted to reflect those very cultural changes. As Corin Willis has shown, the real difference between the presentation of live blackface minstrelsy and blackface on screen was Hollywood's encouragement of co-presence, which placed actors in blackface alongside African American performers.[37] Willis argues that co-presence leaves a trace of minstrelsy's violence on the film itself. The conversion-era Warner Bros. jazz shorts may not contain many co-present acts, but they produce a version of historical co-presence that gives the white singer even greater legitimacy. By having Jolson ventriloquize the Mammy, Warners simultaneously maintained its status as an authority on jazz and concealed the relationship between the studios and the black actors they employed.

THE JAZZ "FETCHITIST" AT PARAMOUNT PICTURES

Anything you can express to the public is jazz.
                    Louis Armstrong[38]

Although Paramount did not employ many African American performers until near the end of the conversion era,[39] those black-cast jazz shorts that featured black musicians stressed the authenticity of the music by refusing to fictionalize the names of its performers. Attaching a narrative to a preexisting song, the studio paradoxically gained the freedom to be more creative with the representation of its stars. The culpability of the performers in the disreputable schemes that are often the basis of the plots of these films is displaced onto the technologies of jazz reproduction, suggesting that despite the innovation of its films Paramount was skeptical about the place of jazz in American society. As I illustrate through an analysis of two of the studio's shorts, *Rhapsody in Black and Blue* (1932) and *Musical Doctor* (1932), jazz for Paramount was the ubiquitous sound of a popular culture simultaneously hidden from view, a music heralded boldly over the airwaves from a corner of Harlem impossible to navigate, or a harmless brand of home entertainment subsequently banished from domestic space. The status of jazz in the Paramount films remained conflicted because, unlike Louis Armstrong, the studio was uncertain what exactly it could "express to the public."

The construction of fantasy in *Rhapsody in Black and Blue* is emblematic of Paramount's efforts to erect a division between the public and private consumption of jazz. The film opens with a sequence that acknowledges the source of the music: spinning discs come into view to announce the credits and are followed by a shot of a phonograph playing a record clearly attributable to Louis Armstrong. After we are given ample time to make the connection between Armstrong and the music, a longer shot reveals that the trumpeter has acquired a rather untalented accompanist. An uncoordinated but exuberant man sits next to the machine, drumming on pots and pans, much to the chagrin of his wife, who would rather he finish mopping the floor (Figure 3.3). The character is modeled after Stepin Fetchit, Hollywood's most popular African American actor, whose antics classify him with Donald Bogle's category of the "coon," a buffoonish black comedian.[40] As was often the case with Fetchit, whose laziness was the basis of both humor and mayhem, our character foolishly fails to remedy his household neglect, which results in a shattered vase. As a consequence, he is accosted by his wife, who sends the man off dreaming to Jazzmania, where he is made king of a soapy wonderland inhabited by Armstrong's band playing the title song.

Arriving in the mythical land of Jazzmania, our character finds Louis Armstrong dressed in a tattered leopard skin that exposes his bare chest. There has been extensive backlash against Armstrong for agreeing to be featured in a way that aligned him with a stereotypical "coon" persona. Yet applying Henry Louis Gates, Jr.'s notion of "Signifyin(g)" to this film, Krin Gabbard has shown how Armstrong turns a costume meant to demean the

Figure 3.3: Paramount's "Fetchitist" plays with the phonograph.
Frame grab from *Rhapsody in Black and Blue* (1932).

African American actor into a symbol that speaks to his own sexual prowess.[41] For Gates, Signifyin(g) is an African American trope in which the sign of the oppressor is doubled, turned on its head to critique the limitations of white language.[42] Used for more than playful insults, Signifyin(g) "constitutes all of the language games, the figurative substitutions, the free associations...wherein the materiality of the signifier...not only ceases to be disguised but comes to bear prominently as the dominant mode of discourse."[43] In Gabbard's reading, Armstrong's singing and hamming for the camera are completely distinct from his trumpet playing. When he picks up his instrument, Armstrong's clowning is instantly transformed into authority, his haphazard lyrical recitation into an intricate and virtuosic solo. Gabbard convincingly argues that Armstrong's hypermasculine trumpet performance, which is characterized by his posture and the achievement of high pitches facilitated by the star's endurance and physical reach, Signify on the limited roles allotted him by Hollywood typecasting.[44] It is important to note here that were Armstrong to sing in the range that he achieves with his trumpet, the meaning of the performance would be significantly altered. Singing is culturally coded as an expression of an interior state; its association with femininity further increases the higher one goes up the musical scale. Louis Armstrong's voice is famously low and scratchy, which proves advantageous in *Rhapsody*, for it allows him to blend in all sorts of sounds that become indistinguishable from words. Such meaningless moments make it difficult to wholly attribute the intention and function of the song to either Signifyin(g) or buffoonery.

These meaningless sounds proliferate during the film's featured song, "I'll Be Glad When You're Dead (You Rascal You)." Armstrong utters slurred and incomprehensible syllables, makes guttural noises, does spontaneous lyrical changes, and punctuates his performance with comments like "yeah" or "look out there" which he directs at the band. All of this is, of course, a kind of improvisation, but more importantly, it demonstrates the instability of the jazz voice. These vocal shifts instruct us not to take this performance as the final word on anything; Armstrong might be joking around, he might be intoxicated, or he might be demonstrating the absurdity of the scene. Whatever the intention, he seems to find the song hysterically funny, a strange sentiment to have when the lyrics tell the story of a cheating wife and a husband dreaming of the day when her lover dies. The origins of this irreverent vocal play might be found in scat singing. Brent Hayes Edwards reads a familiar legend about Armstrong's accidental invention of scat: while recording "Heebie Jeebies" in 1926, Armstrong supposedly dropped his lyric sheet, making up the forgotten words with other syllables.[45] According to Edwards, scatting replies to melody; interpreting a phrase, adding emotional emphasis, or quoting other canonical works, scat usually functions as commentary. In this film, however, Armstrong doesn't respond by scatting. His performance is more an excess of mumbling, which seems to carry an uncertainty about his place in this recording. Rather than overruling the confusion, his assertiveness heightens the film's ambiguity. Indeed, the only shot that might be attributed to our hero's point of view is taken of Armstrong's back, in what is essentially an image of obfuscation. By the time of the film's release, Movietone had become the industry standard. Yet the ability of sound-on-film to capture reality, as its advertising so often claimed, is called into question by the contrast the film makes between the realism of the record and the fantasy of the story. Though one gets the impression that this record exists outside the space of the text, the superimposed transitions between dream sequence and reality clearly bracket the tale of Jazzmania as the property of the cinema. The suggestions of Armstrong's commodification made by the opening image and sound of the record are denied by the troubling dream sequence. Questions about what Armstrong is doing here and how much he is in on the joke would appear to have confused Paramount as much as they did later jazz critics.

It seems that Armstrong's behavior may be both dangerous and contagious. Unable to appropriate the star's musicianship, the enthusiasm of the Fetchit imitator spills over into the home—to ruinous results. In Jazzmania, however, the lead character's appreciation of Armstrong's music is appropriately channeled. As king of the imaginary world, he is able to make requests of the band and have his wishes fulfilled. Jazz is thus coded as a musical style best heard publicly, lest one tread down the dangerous road of the amateur. As a former vaudeville performer and producer, Jesse Lasky, one of Paramount's main founders, would have had a different relationship to jazz than that of the Warners, who had been hesitant about the music's artistic merit.[46] Unsurprisingly then, this model of public consumption corresponds to Paramount's promotion of famous jazz figures who, unlike Warners' performers, need no additional symbols to be recognized. The democratic potential of the phonograph so praised by the Vitaphone is chastised by Paramount as a danger to the productivity of both jazz performer and nameless citizen.

Rhapsody in Black and Blue essentially tells the story of how sound-on-film helped jazz escape the hazards of phonography. Indeed, the film has the best of both worlds: the diegetic phonograph authenticates the performance, marking Armstrong as commercially and artistically viable at the same time that it serves as a launching pad for a narrative that undermines the superiority of the machine. *Rhapsody* suggests that the phonograph is

the basis for a realistic encounter with live jazz musicians that is fully realized only as a dream, and only within Paramount's own recording facilities.
The distinction between the couple's drab home and the bright Jazzmania
is emphasized by the construction of a sound space that supports the contrast between reality and fantasy. *Rhapsody* begins and ends with the sound
of the record; the volume of its pops and scratches in the home compete
for attention against a stilted conversation written to elaborate a fully fictionalized scene. Jazzmania, however, has its sonic priorities in order: in
Armstrong's world, music is much more important than dialogue, which
is suitably inserted between numbers rather than shouted over the top.
Moreover, the structural position of Jazzmania mirrors the Signifyin(g)
that Gabbard attributes to Armstrong. Even as scholars have read Stepin
Fetchit as a figure that complicates the very stereotype he worked to
cement in American cultural memory, so his representative here can be
credited with more than mishap.[47] After all, it is from his imagination that
Jazzmania springs, and through his dream that Armstrong's virility comes
to fruition. The laziness of the Fetchit-like character results in a fantastic
space in which the elements of his labor became props to aid the image of
Armstrong as a powerful African American performer. The agency Gabbard
attributes to Armstrong is thus possible only because of the Fetchit stereotype. By using the phonograph to lend jazz an air of authenticity and then
constructing a narrative to justify the number, *Rhapsody* distinguishes
between jazz as a destructive force of distraction and jazz as a productive
ingredient in the creation of cinema.

As a counternarrative to *Rhapsody in Black and Blue*, *The Musical Doctor*
(1932) presents a very different kind of "jazz" but inserts the "Fetchitist"
as a figure who functions like a jazz image, literally interrupting the logical
flow of the narrative and the rules of musical production within it. Rudy
Vallee is the head of a musical hospital where he oversees a class of spe-
cialists, teaching them diagnostic methods, remedies, and operating procedures. Most of these, of course, consist of Vallee singing something, usually
"Keep a Little Song Handy," a cure-all that ensures "nothing can ever go
wrong." In all of these practices he is assisted by Mae Questel, the voice of
Betty Boop and a jazz icon in her own right. Together, Vallee and Questel
transform jazz from a signifier of vitality to a soothing agent. In one notable
scene, Questel comes across an anxious patient seemingly suffering from
"Pagliacci," a word he exclaims excitedly while jumping repeatedly from his
bed. Questel quiets the man by singing her characteristic "boop-boop-be-
doop" in his ear. Another patient stricken with "musical starvation" is put
on a diet of musical styles, the menu for which is communicated through
Vallee's version of jazz. As the short draws to a close, Vallee croons to his

patients over the Televisor, an imagined television that broadcasts his voice into each room, calming their nerves and putting them to sleep.

Though the hospital's patients and doctors are almost all white, there is one exception. An emergency call brings Vallee into the operating room, where he meets an African American man with a self-proclaimed case of "black fever." The man describes his symptoms lyrically: "I've been missin' all the kissin' from my Alabammy Mammy pains." Vallee nods sympathetically, responding in song that this is just what he expected, and that he'll need to operate. Acquiescing, the man expounds: "I got those yearning to returning to my Alabammy mammy pains." Vallee then administers an anesthetic, which turns out to be a phonograph recording of Brahms's lullaby, and "operates" by singing the first few bars of the "Mammy" ballad through a bullhorn. The "operation" a success, the doctor returns to his rounds and leaves the man to recover.

Seemingly referencing Al Jolson, Vallee offers sentimentality as an appropriate treatment for the ailments of modernity. In so doing, he performs something of an operation, for Vallee's amplified song invades the ear, interrupting the man's dreams and shaping his imaginary, just as Hollywood jazz as a whole helped mold public opinion about what jazz music ought to be. As such, the allusion to Jolson and cinema implies a larger institutional operation that "lifts" jazz from its traditions to be used for other ends. Here jazz is a cure for, rather than reflection of, technological and social shifts in the first decades of the twentieth century. The acting style of many of the hospital's patients implies that they have had some sort of nervous breakdown, while the film itself proposes that too little music results in physical and mental anguish. Jazz, then, gives Vallee the ability to heal the sick, worn down by the stress of modern life. Yet the emergency case seems different from the others; the image of the "Fetchitist" reminds us of a history of real pain inflicted on real bodies, which becomes particularly palpable when compared to the ridiculous ailments of his fellow patients.

Like the Fetchit character in the Armstrong short, this similarly nameless man misunderstands his place in jazz production, calling on Rudy Vallee to invade his body rather than tucking the singer away in a record on the shelf. Indeed, the character embodies the danger of crooning that Allison McCracken observed in contemporary reactions to Vallee's radio performances. Thanks to advances in microphone technology, the intimate sound of Vallee's radio voice was intensified, causing women to swoon and men to shy away from this perceived threat to masculinity.[48] Since he is unable to separate himself from Vallee, the man in Musical Doctor is addressed as an abnormality, one who cannot be treated solely with a dose of the Televisor.

As was true of the husband in *Rhapsody*, this character cannot seem to control his body; thrown on the gurney, he writhes in pain and begs for help from the star. Seemingly rewarded for his actions, he's the only patient in the film permitted to sing along. Yet like Armstrong's "Fetchitist," this man is also rebuked: silenced and "cut open," he's never heard from again. In fact, the film concludes by erecting a technological apparatus to ensure that none of the other patients repeat the African American's mistake, mediating Vallee's voice with a televisual device that replicates the relationship Paramount seeks with its audience. The film's technological invention mitigates against the recurrence of the jazz image.

Paul Young points out that films of the 1930s often pictured television as a public medium that nonetheless maintained an intimate relationship with the viewer.[49] Here, the Televisor simultaneously broadcasts Vallee's performance while dispensing it as "medicine" to individual patients who appear on the screen as Vallee turns the dial. The Televisor answers the predicament of the "Fetchitist" by confirming the cinema's ability to frame and deliver stars without the dangers of the personal encounter. As Young claims, rather than present instantaneous transmission as a problem for film in general, *The Musical Doctor* offers Vallee as the ideal cinematic spectator, capable of controlling the image even as he "knows very well" how it works.[50] However, the Televisor also responds to another important imaginary device featured in *The Musical Doctor*. The film opens with Questel seated at a musical organ that doubles as a telephone switchboard. As she answers calls, impatient voices are represented visually with a close-up of a pulsating light mounted on top of the instrument. Questel's distinctively nasal tone, an odd representation of professionalism, serves to heighten the distortion produced by typical pairings of technology and the human voice already implied by the irate image of light. Although these initial shots suggest that jazz and machinery have no business being together other than for comedic effect, the inventive medical treatment made possible by the Televisor offers a nearly miraculous union of Vallee's soothing jazz voice and film sound technology. Thus it is not just any medium that can represent jazz; Paramount offers the public/private space of the cinema as therapy for the chaos of modernity.

Paramount's jazz films contradict Adorno's notion that the radio produces listeners who see themselves as temporary owners of the snippets they hear and are incapable of being absorbed by the music.[51] Vallee's patient and Armstrong's fan run into trouble because they *fail* to treat the song and its singer as commodities. Signifyin(g) on the restrictions on African American representation enforced by the entertainment industry, these unnamed stereotypes surpass the limitations on musical appreciation purportedly imposed by sound technologies. Like Stepin Fetchit, the black jazz aficionado refuses to follow the rules and ends up contributing to the production of jazz music in ways barred to the white viewers for whom these films are largely intended. Similarly, the man ill with "black fever" has failed to recognize the implied racial restrictions of the hospital and demands to be seen by Vallee in person, even as the rest of the patients receive mediated treatment. Indeed, it is the fans' misunderstanding of the regulations for "proper" jazz consumption that produced these encounters. Making "noise," howling, banging, and calling out, the "Fetchitist" indicates that the spirit of this music is his, even if he receives no profit from its sale.

Far from promoting a deviant reception of jazz, however, Paramount positioned itself as the answer to the problems created by its crafty characters. Both *Rhapsody in Black and Blue* and *The Musical Doctor* conclude by punishing their unbilled musicians: the jazz-loving husband wakes up to a silently revolving record accompanied by the recriminations of his wife, while the "black fever" victim is put to sleep and silenced. By creating narratives that fail to resolve in favor of the live appreciation of music, Paramount suggests that jazz might be more appropriately consumed in another way. The danger of listening to jazz at home is not that existing technologies are too poor to accurately represent the music, but instead that they might be too successful and inadvertently reproduce the bodies of the jazz singers themselves. Thus these films demonstrate the necessity of supervision when sound technologies are used to promote jazz. The studio's own eminent recording facilities, which it proudly displays at the beginning of many of its musical shorts, provides the proper context for jazz appreciation. The "Fetchitist" of the film text is a warning to the fetishist viewer, who would be better off leaving the production of jazz to Paramount.

MGM, JAZZ, AND THE DANCING GIRL

In advertisements produced throughout the conversion era, MGM equated the quality of its sound system with its stars. One 1929 *Photoplay* ad was typical: "Living, breathing, laughing, loving, dancing, singing—M-G-M stars appear before you in all their brilliance, in stories that are masterpieces, directed by masters."[52] The films referenced in *Photoplay* may be the studio's high-end features, yet it was clear that MGM saw stars as the key to its success in both feature-length and short films. Announcing its acquisition of thirty famous Broadway musicians and comedians in a promotional campaign for its new lineup of one-reel sound films in 1928,[53]

MGM characterized its Movietone shorts as star vehicles, a definition that extended to its presentation of jazz. By 1932, however, MGM's representation of jazz had changed a great deal. Instead of highly paid professionals performing without much in the way of cinematic emphasis, the studio employed a series of lesser-known comedians in shorts that stressed their extraordinary use of Technicolor over their talent. Jazz in these films was similarly transformed into an anonymous spectacle: performed by a scantily clad troupe of dancing girls, jazz had become both an attraction and a source of anxiety for the characters in the stories, who tended to tie its production to the dangers of female sexuality. The association of jazz with women nevertheless proved advantageous for the narratives of the short films and for MGM itself. In both cases, jazz naturalized capitalist production while purporting to lift the morale of the American public in a time of economic hardship.

MGM's editing style in 1928 resembled the approach found in Warners' earliest musical shorts. Performing numbers pieced together with few-to-no edits, singers who could nominally qualify as jazz artists took to stages decorated with very little in the way of props. The studio's release schedule in the latter half of that year demonstrated its commitment to this jazz ideal. Hardly a week went by when at least one of its Metro Movietone shorts was not devoted to "jazz" singing by Marion Harris, the Ponce Sisters, George Dewey Washington, or Walt Rosener.[54] These shorts were among the first batch of twenty-six one-reel films MGM decided to produce, and the studio imagined that the set would be shown for years as theaters staggered their conversion to sound: "We will accumulate a library of this class of product. As it has no age factors, the first releases will usually be as desirable as later releases for houses just installing sound equipment."[55] In spite of MGM's rhetoric of durability, the shorts bear the markers of early synchronous sound production. The first Ponce Sisters short is a single take, while Marion Harris performs her numbers in three. Walt Rosener and his Capitolians have been given twenty-three shots, but the editing style is very straightforward, reflecting the manner usually used for bands by Warner Bros. two years earlier. Moreover, the Ponce Sisters, Harris, and Rosener all acknowledge the audience by bowing at the end of their acts, a practice that faded fairly quickly at all the major studios. Thus, even though MGM may have thought its shorts would never grow old, their style made such a presumption impossible.

Although they looked very different from the colorful comedic jazz shorts that followed a few years later, the Ponce Sisters and Marion Harris films (of which there were two and four respectively)[56] nonetheless prefigured the representation of female sexuality that would become the trademark of MGM's version of jazz during the waning years of the conversion. The Ponce Sisters' first song in their first production, "Too Busy," laments the inattention of a lover but provides a plan for female revenge: "Wait 'til you want me honey, then it won't be so funny, when I say that I'm too busy for you." In spite of their chaste tennis costumes and tasteful hairstyles, the sisters propose using their bodies as weapons in a war of attraction. However, the lyrics of their second number, "I'd Rather Cry over You," suggest that their vengeance strategy had not been as successful as they'd hoped. In both songs, the sisters use identical "jazz hands" and other gestures that suggest a minimalist depiction of the synchronized motions that the M-G-M Dancers would perform in later pictures.

Billed as "The Song Bird of Jazz" in her first film, Marion Harris is dressed in a sleeveless imitation crinoline gown replete with two corsages, her bobbed hair being the primary symbol of her residence in the Jazz Age. At first, Harris cannot think of a song to perform, but thankfully, Irving Berlin supposedly calls her on the telephone and proposes "Afraid of You." Her jazz credentials thus established, we cut to a medium shot, in which Harris sings Berlin's recommendation directly into the camera, stretching out her bare arms to fill up the entire frame. This move not only calls attention to Harris's body, it also announces her authority over both jazz music and the presumably male addressee of this particular number, an attitude that directly contradicts the lyrics of the song: "Assure me, and cure me baby, 'cause I'm afraid of you." Her performance style thus turns a number about an insecure young woman into an ode to female sexuality. Harris's second song returns to the long shot with which we began, though she now extends herself into much of the newfound space. Her lanky body moves in an even more striking fashion, causing us to interpret the lyrics of the song in a suggestive fashion. "We Love It" describes the bliss of newlyweds in spite of their impoverishment, leaving it up to the viewer to imagine what it is they do after 9:00 p.m. when they lock the door. Both Marion Harris and the Ponce Sisters are incredibly tame in comparison to the M-G-M Dancing Girls, but they nonetheless suggest that jazz might be a musical style particularly suited to assertive women, a dangerous proposition for some, but for a studio whose films often rely on strong female personalities, one that might be logically explained.

The M-G-M Dancing Girls are no shrinking violets, yet their anonymity gives them much less authority than Marion Harris or the Ponce Sisters were able to exercise. The dance troupe is a key feature of both *The Devil's Cabaret* (1930) and *Over the Counter* (1932), two-reel musical comedies each with a story concerning a corporation's troubled revenue. In each case the Dancing Girls use jazz to rescue a floundering business. *The Devil's Cabaret* opens in hell, where we see Satan (who bears a striking resemblance to Vincent Price) gleefully filling in a large ledger. We soon come to realize, however, that his affairs are not as rosy as they appear. Satan and his assistant reveal that far too many people are finding their way to heaven, forcing them to come up with a new plan for luring clients to the underworld. The assistant begins handing out guns, cards, and other signifiers of vice, which proves to be a moderately effective strategy. However, his campaign really kicks off when he sings a stagy jazz tune: "Come Hot It Up with Me." He immediately attracts a troupe of backup dancers, the M-G-M Dancing Girls, dressed in traditional (but turquoise) waitress uniforms. As the song progresses, the women prove that the key to a successful business strategy lies not in the product but in how it is sold. The assistant recedes into the background and the tempo slows, its melody taken over by a seductive muted trumpet, to which the women sway while taking off their clothes in unison (Figure 3.4). Wearing nothing but lacy undergarments and tap shoes, the women swoon into the camera as it provides a tracking shot of each face—a technique that would become characteristic of Busby Berkeley's style a few years later. Having successfully passed into hell with the diegetic spectators in tow, the dancing girls perform a leggy and synchronized tap ballet. The

Figure 3.4: Conversion-era striptease.
Enlargement from frame grab of *The Devil's Cabaret* (1930).

suggestiveness of the ballet becomes too much even for hell's proprietors, who announce on its completion that men and women must retire to their separate dormitories. Hell's new citizens respond with a resounding "no," preferring to continue "hotting it up," not with these corporate stooges but with women who obviously know what to do with jazz.

The story of *Over the Counter* is similar. The opening shots are of a department store chairman dictating a letter to his liberal-minded son that strongly disagrees with the latter's efforts to modernize the business. It seems that the son's innovative plans have scandalized the stuffy managerial staff. All of his improvements to the store include the M-G-M Dancing Girls performing some kind of service for male patrons, each of which proves a big hit with customers. The most popular of these services is "check your husbands," which "liberates" women from their tiresome men so they might be free to "spend their hard earned dough," while the men not only watch a dancing spectacle but also get intimate with the performers. Each of the son's proposals is more successful than the last, until the father finally accepts his successor's rightful place in the institution and embraces his own misogyny; clutching two women to him, he proclaims, "That boy has some great ideas." Most of these ideas have been put to song, much of which would be considered low-quality Tin Pan Alley jazz. The music and its rhyming lyrics smooth over the appalling story, for the point of these shorts is not the comedic exchanges between men but the presentation of the female dancing bodies. The revisions to department store policy conceal the labor of production and consumption by drawing attention to these women, who are, of course, the commodity that the film itself has been created to sell.

In all their pre-code glory, the M-G-M Dancing Girls evoke images of burlesque, disturbing the studio's prior efforts to present jazz as a musical style perfected by professionals that could be easily incorporated into its expensive feature productions. While Marion Harris may have projected a strong female sexuality that was unique to her own jazz style, the Dancing Girls are more than ready to strip off their clothing in order to make a profit for their proprietor. This was not a unique situation. Peter Stanfield points to the importance of the striptease in the history of jazz on film, noting that although it was often linked to exotic names and places, the strip act was distinctly American. Stanfield identifies blackface and burlesque as the two ends of Hollywood's representation of jazz; one marked the beginnings of Hollywood's interest in the music and the other encompassed the female sexuality and dying urban culture that characterized postwar cinema.[57] That we find evidence of these extremes in the same period but belonging to separate studios should not be surprising. In the same way blackface justified Jolson's nostalgia and rooted the Vitaphone's reception as descendant of the phonograph, the invocation of burlesque gave MGM a glittery image of easily earned capital in an era that yearned for prosperity. MGM paired its relatively late investment in sound with an equal dedication to novelty: the two-strip Technicolor that would have been an attraction in its own right could also be used to highlight what these women were (or weren't) wearing.

As Robert Allen wrote with regard to nineteenth-century American theater: "All that had been repressed in the righteous, moral, conservative middle class's conquest of the theater returned in burlesque."[58] The exposure of the M-G-M Dancing Girls reveals the crass commercial strain of jazz that had been elided in both the Warner Bros. performance shorts and the narrative exploits of the Paramount "Fetchitist." First popularized in the United States in the 1840s, burlesque was primarily a working-class entertainment that celebrated the transgressions of social values largely through its exhibition of women's bodies.[59] Allen points to the historical association of burlesque women with black minstrelsy, citing one particularly vocal critic who claimed that because of their popularity among minstrels, certain musical instruments ought not to be used by women on stage.[60] Since we rarely see a band performing within them, the MGM shorts ask us to infer the relationship between the M-G-M Dancing Girls and the music we hear. In the 1920s, efforts to refine and define jazz led to presumptions about the ease with which the term may be applied. Certainly the films rest on a very loose definition of what jazz ought to be. Yet just as these women have been created to serve capital, so the jazz we hear is decidedly commercial. Its nonspecificity is not unlike the anonymity of the women themselves, but its interpretation rests on the correlation between loose women and black music that troubled burlesque theater from the outset.

Siegfried Kracauer's image of the mass ornament provides a useful framework though which to understand the role of the M-G-M Dancing Girls and the studio's construction of jazz. The mass ornament is an inorganic "girl cluster" that has been created for no purpose other than self-presentation. In spite of their revealing clothing and the close framing of their more intimate parts, Kracauer claims that combining women in this way produces a distinct lack of eroticism. Instead, the mass ornament mirrors the conditions of contemporary capitalism, which effaces the totality by requiring laborers to focus solely on the tasks they perform.[61] Certainly this describes the functional purpose of the Dancing Girls in these two MGM films. Yet it also identifies the position of the Dancing Girls at the studio itself. The studio's tag line, "More stars than there are in heaven," did not, of course, apply to the Dancing Girls, who were branded as studio property.

Similarly, the jazz in these films is not identifiable by song, composer, or style. Instead, the commercial jazz reflects MGM's attitude toward music and the Fordist environment in which its composers operated. Wherever one attributes its origins, jazz is a musical style characterized by its ability to mix and evolve, traits that would seem to contradict the requirements of the studio era's mode of production. The Dancing Girls, then, are a visual manifestation of the conditions of musical labor that make the star image possible.

The initial skepticism about the market value of the female body expressed by the proprietors in the MGM shorts is simultaneously an anxiety about the place of jazz music in American society. Equating jazz and sex, MGM's productions seem concerned that shifting musical tastes would result in the inevitable alteration of social mores. Men abandon their wives for the rhythmic gyrations of scantily clad chorus girls in *Over the Counter* or gleefully choose a hell with cohabitation rights over a heaven without them in *The Devil's Cabaret*. In *The Wild People*, another 1932 MGM short, women have taken over responsibility for courtship entirely, even proposing marriage to men. In all these cases, jazz is the catalyst for such "indecent" behavior, provoking physical movements that men find impossible to resist and that would seem to empower the women that exert them. Of course, these women are unnamed employees working for these same men. Having helped produce efficient businesses then, the M-G-M Dancing Girls gladly abdicate responsibility for their jazz incursions. In the 1930s MGM shorts, jazz is identifiable by the presence of the Dancing Girls rather than the sonic attributes debated by composers and critics. As anonymous visual pageantry, jazz served MGM's spectacular brand image while at the same time undermining its concentration on quality star productions. The result was a conflicted appropriation of popular song that conveyed visually the potential for disturbances in the flow of capitalist production purportedly alleviated by the films' narrative conclusions. The M-G-M Dancing Girls produced jazz images that provoked spectators to reconsider their relationship to individual films, women's bodies, and the commercialization of jazz.

After the end of the conversion era, Warner Bros. produced a two-reel short that could easily be *Sax Appeal*'s opposite. *Operator's Opera* (1933) proposes a remedy for the telephone company's inefficiency that begins by exploiting the sexuality of its female workers. The manager proposes changing the "girls" into "hot numbers" by having them sing the news of crossed wires or bad connections to appease disappointed customers. The infectious practice spreads throughout the city, where the long distance enactment of musical entertainment becomes the norm. Applying a "voice with a smile," the operators use the malfunctioning technology to transform the home into a performance space where dancing is preferable to completing a business transaction. As the manager exclaims, "You see, what you're really doing is humanizing the telephone."[62] The anthropomorphosis that began with the infusion of sex alters the meaning of communication. The "Operator's Opera" is technological *jouissance*; no longer defined by its function, the telephone becomes a conduit for physical expression itself unbound by genre. By the end of the period, then, Warner Bros. had revised its educational mission to account for the necessity of pleasure. Thus the meaning of the "opera" performed by the operators is evacuated even as the specificity of the telephone turns out to be nothing but a pretext for word play. Like the jazz in *Sax Appeal*, the opera of the later short is employed in the interest of capital. Yet in both cases, music does not so much fix technology's defects as render them inconsequential. Jazz and opera are no longer needed to draw out the defining characteristics of film sound technologies, for by 1933 the Vitaphone existed only as a corporate arm of Warner Bros., its disc campaign abandoned in the face of practical and economic obstacles. As sound-on-film became the industry standard, jazz on film receded to the background; but with opera, it remained integral to the texture of the classical Hollywood film score.

CHAPTER 4

Opera and Jazz in the Score

Toward a New Spectatorship

The medium of the classical Hollywood film score was largely symphonic; its idiom romantic; and its formal unity typically derived from the principle of the leitmotif.
Kathryn Kalinak, *Settling the Score: Music and the Classical Hollywood Film*

The film-music scholar needs to be vigilant against inherent biases in analytical tools that were developed to study absolute (instrumental music)...indeed, nearly every kind of music written or performed in the twentieth century has appeared in the movies.
David Neumeyer and James Buhler, "Analytical and Interpretive Approaches to Film Music (1): Analysing the Music"

As with music for the theatre and programme music, film music exemplifies for better or worse, as it were, the marriage of the world of music with the visual world of images. Thus the so-called "extra-musical associations" which plague historical musicology are in many instances more-or-less actually embodied in the work *per se*, a priori exegesis or hermeneutic interpretation.
William H. Rosar, "The *Dies Irae* in *Citizen Kane*: Musical Hermeneutics Applied to Film Music"

Thanks to a wealth of publication in the last three decades, it is no longer possible to claim with any sincerity that film music is a neglected component of cinematic scholarship. From the 1980 issue of *Yale French Studies* edited by Rick Altman to the influential critical work done by Claudia Gorbman and Michel Chion in the mid-to-late 1980s (and continuing today) to the historical surveys and composer interviews of the 1990s, and finally, to the detailed analyses of popular music produced in the 2000s, film music is anything but invisible and unheard.[1] The canonization of some of this writing, moreover, has made "film musicologist" a meaningful label, carving a place for an academic concentration that benefits from the knowledge of two discrete disciplines. Yet cinema scholars and musicologists continue to be trained very differently, and as a result many of us remain uncritical of the origins and influences of our object. Rather than assuming that film music has been modeled on the unifying practices of Wagner and treating instances of non-"classical" music in classical Hollywood cinema as anomalies that protrude from an otherwise Romantic score, we ought to listen to the organization of musical sounds in 1930s cinema, many of which had their roots in conversion-era opera and jazz shorts. In fact, I propose that opera and jazz are not exceptions to Hollywood's Romanticism but instead constitute the foundations of classical Hollywood film music.

When we recognize the existence of opera and jazz as the essential components of the classical Hollywood film score, we are doing more than merely glimpsing cultural codes; we are changing how we conceive of spectatorship. It would be a worthy (if incredibly time-consuming) task to draw up a list of all the opera and jazz quotations in classical Hollywood films. Even if we accomplished this feat, we would have proven only that opera and jazz are two among the many genres that influenced composers and arrangers in the years following the conversion to sound. Though we might sway an analysis of an individual film by identifying such citations, our imaginary list would change little about the predominant understanding that the film score is essentially diluted classical music. Instead of embarking on this long and fruitless excursion into history, I take film musicology as my starting point, moving outward to reexamine the primary texts that have enabled its conception of Hollywood's Romanticism. I return to the idea of the jazz-opera as a genre, picking up the conversation nearly a decade after it first began and locating it in the context of American film sound.

The ideal of the American jazz-opera, a form that would join aesthetics and accessibility, represent a nation of immigrants, and foster a new generation of creators, composers, and listeners, became a possibility once again as Hollywood standardized its approach to voices and found a place for the nondiegetic score. That this happened in ways not imagined by Otto Kahn and his cultural contemporaries should come as no surprise. The foregrounding of sound technologies in the promotion and production of music during the conversion era contributed to an increased awareness of the acoustical properties of exhibition spaces, which could have proved a hindrance to musical appreciation. Yet the regular comparative reporting on sound systems' musical capabilities in newsletters and trade journals suggests that listeners were also tuned in to the quality of the music they heard.[2] Robert Spadoni's characterization of the conversion-era audience as "medium-sensitive viewers" could be productively extended to account for musical listening outside of the theater, which, with the growth of radio and the introduction of records targeted at specialized markets throughout the 1920s, had more opportunities than ever to prosper.[3] If people were listening to recorded or transmitted music more frequently, they were also sharing their knowledge of the technologies that allowed them to do so in magazines and clubs devoted to radio and phonography.[4] American music was being innovated by and for the technological advances of the period, and leaving behind the segregated spaces of the opera hall and jazz club. It was also leaving behind the differences created by the variations in sound-on-disc and sound-on-film technologies in favor of standardized sound recording and reproducing practices agreed to by the Hollywood majors.[5] Although distinctly national approaches to constructing sound-scapes remained throughout the 1930s,[6] in the United States, with the help of technology, integration certainly sounded possible.

Integration was happening on a corporate level as well. As the major studios sought to exploit the musical sensitivity of their listeners and maintain the continuity of the soundtrack from live accompaniment to the recorded score, they were faced with prohibitive copyright fees. As Katherine Spring notes, movie theaters in the 1920s had public performance licenses with ASCAP, allowing them to use compositions by its members.[7] Yet these rights did not apply to recorded soundtracks. To compensate, studios began buying stock in individual music publishers or purchasing publishing houses outright. Warner Bros. made such a move by procuring Witmark & Sons, a decision that was more than partially responsible for the sound of its cartoons and feature length scores.[8] The publishing houses that interested Hollywood usually originated in Tin Pan Alley, a street in New York famous for turning out commercial melodies written in the thirty-two-bar, AABA form often identified interchangeably with popular jazz. According to Ulf Lindberg, there were three main sources for Tin Pan Alley's conversion-era sound: "sentimental ballads" dating from before the turn of the century; African American influences, such as ragtime, blues, and jazz; and inspiration drawn from white middlebrow poetry and European songs.[9] The musical combination of these forces was recognizably American. Notably, Tin Pan Alley's most esteemed representative, Irving Berlin, whose "Alexander's Ragtime Band" was a bestselling song in the 1910s and the foremost representative of ragtime in popular culture thereafter, was among those solicited by Otto Kahn to compose the jazz-opera. Certainly the studios' promotion of jazzy tunes would have been connected to their newfound ownership of pieces like these. Of course, Tin Pan Alley was no stranger to operatic quotation.[10] Yet much of the Italian opera the Hollywood studios continued to reference belonged to the public domain, and thus posed no threat to their bottom line.

Tin Pan Alley's mode of production was unsurprisingly similar to that of the Hollywood studios. Describing the publishing houses as "song factories," Reebee Garofalo notes the homogeneity of their output, which was reinforced by a publicity machine that fended off outside influence.[11] The mechanical nature of the system is detailed in *How to Crash Tin-Pan Alley,* a 1930s songwriting guide that outlines an extensive list of steps for the aspiring tunesmith, most of which involve outsourcing everything but the melody to "professional" lyricists, arrangers, and manuscript transcribers. The manual also provides a list of acceptable subjects, which includes "love songs, songs of joy," and "the moon over any place songs," but excludes "slang expressions," "comedy gags," or "organization songs."[12] Indeed, between 1920 and 1940, 85 percent of American popular songs were based on the theme of love.[13] This statistic demonstrates the suitability of Tin Pan Alley music for Hollywood during a period in which, according to Mark Garrett Cooper, studio films were organizing their narration around the requirements of the love story.[14] In spite of the fact that Tin Pan Alley is an American phenomenon, Garofalo points out that copyright for its songs was still granted on the basis of European conventions regarding single authorship, melody, and lyrics.[15] Clearly this system cannot adequately describe the *use* of the music in classical Hollywood cinema, which requires that viewers draw a relationship between melody and image. The songwriter is rarely considered the author of a film, and indeed, the rhetoric of film music composition tends to subordinate the message of the music to the meaning of the picture. The extent to which this approach produces an adequate analysis of film music's function, of course, is more than questionable. Although Spring points out that Hollywood's publishing takeover was largely abandoned by 1931 owing to the financial hardships of the studios and the unpopularity of their musical films, she claims that its business dealings had set standards for composition that continued in the classical Hollywood era.[16]

In spite of the movement toward musical and corporate integration, we must not pretend that racial segregation during the conversion era was limited to live performance. The practical application of technologies cannot exist apart from the ideologies of the culture that invents them. The promotion of sound films stressed technological innovation and made viewers more sensitive to the apparatus, but they also privileged certain voices, naturalizing some sounds while expunging others. Sound technologies, both inside and outside of the theater, asserted that only certain types of music were worthy of preservation and likely to adapt to the market. After short films had established a practice of experimenting with opera and jazz as spectacular attractions, Hollywood composers got down to the business of writing music not intended to draw attention to itself. Yet the forces that asserted the compatibility of opera, jazz, and the apparatus did not just go away. Having helped to form the practices that became the standard Hollywood mode of address and the identity of the individual studios, opera and jazz remained just as present in the Hollywood score as they did in American public life. Moreover, the incorporation of European music into American cultural products was just as prominent in film as it had been in orchestral and operatic productions, as many of the composers who contributed to the sound of the typical American soundtrack were recent immigrants (Erich Wolfgang Korngold, Miklós Rózsa, Max Steiner, and Dimitri Tiomkin to name a few). Thus, even if it appeared that studios like Warner Bros. had abandoned their educational mission, they were still bringing culture to the masses by way of talented composers trained at European institutions. The democratizing potential of jazz so noted by those who sought to "jazz the classics" during the 1920s continued to exist after the conversion, as film music was infused with American values. The jazz images and sounds that persist into the 1930s challenge any reading of the score as a coherent whole and open up the experience of music to associations created by spectators in their encounter with the film.

Essentially, I am arguing that the classical Hollywood film score operates like a jazz-opera, which is to say, as an impossible entity, always unbound and incomplete. I have claimed throughout this book that opera and jazz can be productively analyzed through their relationship to the human voice, which can excise a sound from its context, a move that mirrors the position of the song or the aria, itself capable of splitting off from the larger work that only seems to contain it. This chapter continues this practice by reading the leitmotif as the operatic articulation of a theme, which, like the song, always carries the possibility of vocality. I base this theoretical interpretation on two of the film score's historical antecedents: Tin Pan Alley jazz and Italian opera. This works because, contrary to popular and critical opinion, the classical Hollywood film score bears very little resemblance to the Wagnerian *Gesamtkunstwerk*. Indeed, Scott D. Paulin has shown that the constant invocation of Wagner in historical discussions of the score has been used to "repress knowledge of the constitutional lack of unity in film."[17] Paulin credits the common misreading of the film score as Wagnerian to both a desire for film to appear a more unified art and an economic imperative on the part of the producers and exhibitors to appeal to the middle and upper classes. Yet these same goals were pursued by the industry's adoption of Italian opera as a model of vocal performance and a source for instrumental citations. Hollywood's embrace of Tin Pan Alley similarly served both aesthetic and economic ends: it presented short melodic segments that could be easily implemented without the need for musical development and that contained lyrical suggestions that could be cross-promoted with sheet music and record sales. Whereas the Wagnerian leitmotif was a dramatic tool that the composer originally identified with the orchestra rather than the voice,[18] the cinematic leitmotif is a particularly singable melody more liable to break away from the film than it is to draw it together. As Paulin points out, contrary to Wagnerian compositional practice, suggestions for musical accompaniment (such as those compiled by Erno Rapée in his famous anthologies for silent-era pianists) based their justification for the match between melody and film on the concept of "appropriateness" rather than any inherent similitude between image and sound.[19] Thus the same melody could be used to designate a wedding, a chase, or a nation in film after film. This practice continued into the sound era. Far from unifying the individual text, the cinematic leitmotif promises to return both within and outside of the cinema.

Reviving the hope that the jazz-opera would translate the American spirit into a work accessible to the nation's inhabitants but expressing itself aesthetically to the world, Hollywood cinema in the 1930s seemed uniquely capable of convincing the musical elite to create popular art on a wide scale. Though there were certainly other attempts at blending "high" and "low" culture during the decade as a result of the New Deal public arts grants, such a confluence became normative (and less controversial) in the cinema in a way that it did not on the stage.[20] This difference can be attributed to the financing available to composers working within a relatively stable field, Hollywood's reliance on the recording technologies used by the music industry, the studios' acquisition of publishing houses, and the standardization of film exhibition. Despite this consistency, the classical Hollywood film score encouraged a spectator who was not a submissive recipient of meaning, but an active listener capable of drawing connections both inside and outside of the text. To explore this claim, this chapter concentrates on the music of feature films from the conversion era and into the 1930s, showing how the practices for representing opera and jazz in the more experimental Hollywood musical shorts wove their way into the ordinary sensibilities of American film sound.

Film musicologists have relied on the term "classical" Hollywood cinema to mean what it says. For Bordwell, Thompson, and Staiger, the Classicism of Hollywood cinema enables a critique of its products as the result of a group style similar to that of other artistic movements: "the principles which Hollywood constitutes as its own rely on notions of decorum, proportion, formal harmony, respect for tradition, mimesis, self-effacing craftsmanship, and cool control of the perceiver's response—canons which critics in any medium usually call 'classical'."[21] In her pioneering analysis of the classical Hollywood film score, Claudia Gorbman concurs with a definition of *classical* based on the material and aesthetic constitution of a film: "To use the term 'classical cinema' means understanding this cinema as an institution, and a class of texts which this institution produces."[22] Caryl Flinn claims that "classical" is appropriately applied to music for two reasons: it refers to the set of principles already in place to regulate the studio system and it calls up the compositional procedures of the eighteenth and nineteenth centuries. Yet she is careful to distinguish the Classical period from the Romantic era, where she locates film music's historical lineage. Like Bordwell et al., Flinn identifies the studios' organization of labor as key to the development of classical Hollywood sound. The arrangement of creative personnel paired with the ideological goals of Romantic composition ostensibly instituted by Wagner resulted in what Flinn labels a "classical conception" of the Hollywood score: "But what does this classical conception of film music entail? Simply put, it maintains that the score supports the narrational information already provided by the image."[23] In other words, "classical" Hollywood film music has been envisioned as a cog in the machine designed to churn out the Hollywood story.

From the perspective of production, this model makes good sense. The studio music departments operated much like its other creative parts: systematic and efficient, the individual units had little sway over the outcome of their labor. Working under strict time constraints and after the final visual product was complete, the composer gave his sketches to an arranger, who passed along his notes to a copyist, who transcribed the music for the orchestra, which was usually conducted by someone else altogether. It is easy to see how this procedure replicates the general practices described by Bordwell, Thompson, and Staiger with regard to the typical Hollywood mode of production. In opposition to *auteurism*, they analyze the requisite functions that led to the creation of a typical Hollywood film. Yet the application of this paradigm to music making has been called into question. Flinn notes that unlike the rest of the music department personnel, the composers themselves were not unionized. According to her, this led to an inflated understanding of their creative input, a false sense of authorship that remained at odds with their meager salaries and loss of copyright.[24] Of course, composers were not just arrangers, and since they did write their own material, it would be misleading to deprive them of the prestige that comes with their title. Nevertheless, classical Hollywood is rife with sonic fragmentation and musical recycling despite any desire on the part of composers to read their output as continuous or directives from the studios that scores be individualized for every story. The devotion of each soundtrack to many musicless minutes and the proliferation of a particular melody across multiple texts exposes the Taylorized construction of what is supposedly a singular creation. By regularly breaking the regulations of "Classicism," Hollywood film music reveals the gaps in the system.

From the analyst's point of view, the idea that music exists to serve the narrative is seductive in its simplicity. In general, the stories that Hollywood composers tell about their own work emphasize how they reinforce the story, trying to make what they do "match" what already takes place in the image. Flinn describes how composers developed techniques to underscore dialogue, allowing the story material to come to the fore. This led to an impression of integration that Flinn critiques as an illusion of perfection.[25] Gorbman suggests that sound and image work in "mutual implication," noting that any combination of music and image creates an effect different from that produced by either sound or picture alone.[26] Kalinak adopts Gorbman's process, taking pains to point out that both sound and image contribute to the progression of the narrative. In spite of these valiant attempts to correct the myth of music's inferiority, many viewers continue to assign it a supportive role.

Efforts like these to hear film music as something other than a reinforcement of the image have been available for some time. Theodor Adorno and Hanns Eisler's now "classic" *Composing for the Films* approaches the possibility from the perspective of the practitioner. For them, typical Hollywood film sound makes the image more commercial: "It converts a kiss into a magazine cover, an outburst of unmitigated pain into a melodrama, a scene from nature into an oleograph."[27] Rather than engage the "bad habits" that encourage such a process, Adorno and Eisler suggest that Hollywood composers avoid the "classical" music that lends itself to cliché. However, they are quick to point out that even modern music, once placed in the context of Hollywood, can be all too easily emptied of its revolutionary value. Although their critiques of Hollywood film music have been well noted,[28] less often discussed are their own musical experiments on which they base their book's findings. Working without the ideal partnership they desire for composers and directors, Adorno and Eisler could pair nonclassical music only with donated footage. The results, they claim, were unable to definitively break music from its secondary status: "the new musical material was helpful. But it, too, was subordinated to the primacy of the dramaturgic and was not used indiscriminately in the manner of a composer writing autonomous music, but viewed in accordance with functional requirements."[29] They conclude that the Hollywood mode of production makes it impossible to understand music apart from the image, however "modern" it may aim to be.

Thus, to reiterate what is by now a fairly obvious point, system matters. Hollywood's mode of production prevented Adorno and Eisler's experiments from having any real impact. Completed before the music began, the image always asserted itself too strongly. As Adorno and Eisler attempted to sonically shift their footage away from "saccharine" interpretations, the institution of the classical Hollywood assembly line precluded even these participants from connecting too deeply with the meaning of the final product. Despite their ire over the tendency of composers to justify their music in the image, Adorno and Eisler's conception of picture and sound as separate input streams can lead to no other outcome. This may explain why, in trying to get away from notions of parallelism and counterpoint, film musicologists sometimes find themselves right back where they started. Perhaps the source of this issue is in critics' faith in "Classicism." The coherence attributed to "classical" Hollywood film music and that stems from Bordwell, Thompson, and Staiger's use of terms like "harmony" and "tradition" to define it can lead to assumptions about the effects of scoring. Maybe Adorno and Eisler's problem was not with the mediocrity of the visual texts they received, but with their own efforts to disrupt the harmony so expected by the viewer, to throw a wrench into the compositional tradition. In describing the outcome of their work, the authors lamented, "the musical results achieved are due as much to this conception of the film as a unity composed of heterogeneous elements, as to the composer's interest in the tendencies of modern music."[30] Adorno and Eisler's approach to the culture industry may prompt them to attempt a more radical critique of Hollywood's products, but their experiment tended to affirm the potential of classical unity rather than call attention to the disparate parts that make up a film.[31]

Rather than grasp the classical Hollywood film as either a fully unified work or a text that can be divided into individual tracks of meaning that are cohesive unto themselves, I propose that we accept the essential fragmentation of the score as a basic interpretative tool, that is, that we search American film sound for remnants of the song. I suggest that we resist dating the commencement of classical Hollywood scoring with Max Steiner's *King Kong* (1933) and instead reexamine musical composition during the conversion era to demonstrate how the "harmony" we think we hear may not be at all representative. The "classical" template has led film musicologists to credit Romanticism with the responsibility of forming the essential Hollywood soundtrack, resulting in an analytical mode that all but ignored the contributions of opera and jazz. By reading opera and jazz as structuring components that diffused the content of the narrative fiction film, we can reformulate classical Hollywood cinema as a technological interpretation of the jazz-opera.

THE ROMANTIC LEAP

In her analysis of Hollywood's compositional mode, Caryl Flinn reveals an ideological conflict between the rhetorical position of American film music and the Romantic sounds it seems to incorporate: "whereas Hollywood classicism downplays the role of music, late nineteenth-century Romanticism openly celebrates it."[32] Despite this difference, scholars before and after Flinn are apt to analyze film scores as if they were listening to sparsely orchestrated Romantic symphonies. As Adorno and Eisler noted, it makes little sense to talk about leitmotifs in the traditional sense with regard to a form that denies ample time for harmonic or emotional development.[33] Why, then, do we continue to deride the meagerness of film's musical ideas while treating them as equivalents to Wagnerian themes? Flinn answers this question by claiming that Hollywood cinema relegates music to the backdrop of the spectator's consciousness, thus implying the fullness of the Romantic idiom without exposing its own lack of resources. Although she provides historical and aesthetic reasons for its appropriation, it is Romanticism's "utopian promise" that she claims ultimately drew the form to the attention of Hollywood composers. But what about Hollywood's listeners? What if, as spectators familiar with the multiple and disconnected performances proliferating in musical shorts, we refuse to read Hollywood through this illusion of wholeness? What happens then to its alleged Romantic score?

Like most film musicologists, Flinn is careful to distinguish between Classicism as an ideal pursued by the cinema and the "classical era" of musical production defined after the fact. Yet in their search for Classicism, scholars could just as easily have been more literal, arguing that the film score functions more like Mozart than Wagner, more like a sonata than a nineteenth-century German opera. In some ways, this claim could be convincing: the finale "recapitulates" a theme often introduced in the film's "exposition" during the opening credit sequence and "developed" throughout the film in a variety of emotionally charged situations that could otherwise be labeled "keys." That this could be read as the form of a single movement in a otherwise larger "score" should be evident when we imagine all the parts of any film that do not correspond easily to the articulations of the musical theme. Yet like Romanticism, Classicism, whether in the form of the sonata or otherwise, would do little to explain film music's abrupt entrances and exits, its peculiar combinations of instruments, its repetitive tendencies, or its willingness to recede from audibility. Flinn claims that the individuating characteristics of Romanticism maintained an illusion of authorship for composers grappling with an unfair system of labor.[34] Perhaps the appeal of Romanticism for scholars is similar: the illusion of wholeness allows us to subsist in a familiar form of analysis without challenging the fundamental differences between Richard Wagner and Max Steiner.

Although the desire to find an anchor for the institution of classical Hollywood cinema is compelling, this privileging of the composer could easily result in an understanding of the score as a unified document that can be distilled to a single meaning.[35] Such a move is typical of what I am calling the "Romantic leap": the presumption of coherence based on a set of principles imposed externally and shared by the texts in a given group. This kind of reading has become essential to the conversation on Hollywood film music. For instance, Claudia Gorbman's foundational book on the subject outlines seven compositional tenets of the classical Hollywood film score:

1. "Invisibility"—The source of the music should not be present in the image.
2. "Inaudibility"—Spectators should not be acutely aware of the score's performance or effects.
3. "Signifier of emotion"—Music both creates a mood and refers to the feelings of the characters.
4. "Narrative cuing"—The score aids the film in telling the story, either by representing a particular viewpoint or by explaining the meaning of the action.
5. "Continuity"—Music lends the image track a sense of coherency by making the editing less noticeable.
6. "Unity"—The score is structured around repeated elements, the effects of which bleed into spectators' perception of the narrative.
7. Any of the above rules may be broken as long as it is to honor another of the tenets.[36]

Since these principles appear in a chapter devoted to the work of Max Steiner as the paradigmatic Hollywood composer, it is unsurprising that they take for granted a conception of the score as a continuous and complete work of art. Gorbman's first two principles, invisibility and inaudibility, identify the score as nondiegetic musical material that takes a back seat to the audience's perception of the image. By leaving out diegetic cues, Gorbman characterizes the score in a way that may not be entirely representative of how a listener hears a film. Her third and fourth rules describe how the score relates to narrative material. As an emotional prompt, the familiarity of distinct musical devices may trigger preordained feelings in the spectator. The score can also refer to events in the story by establishing leitmotifs for particular characters or emphasizing the meaning of certain actions. These traits imagine the score working to flesh out the image track, creating an even more tightly woven text. The fifth and sixth principles emphasize this point further. Gorbman's continuity rule claims that music stitches together pieces of film that might otherwise have appeared disconnected, while her imperative of unity directly asserts that the score must be formally conceived as a totality. The final tenet states that a composer may disregard any one rule to serve another, preserving the apparent harmony of music and image.

Cementing Gorbman's principles, film musicology's Romantic leap makes it difficult to talk about opera and jazz except as metaphors, which is perhaps why critics are notorious for suggesting that a particular film is "like an opera" or "feels improvisatory like jazz" without saying exactly why.[37] It is easy to see how, within a Romantic framework, both opera and jazz would violate almost all of Gorbman's rules. The scholarship on jazz and film usually deals with moments where the music is readily "visible," either because it is diegetic (Louis Armstrong's appearances are pronounced cases) or because it has been composed by an important figure unseen within the film itself (Miles Davis's score for *Elevator to the Gallows* [*Ascenseur pour l'échafaud*, 1958, is perhaps the best known example). A similar problem arises for opera: films containing a diegetic appearance of the opera (*Night at the Opera*, 1935) or adaptations of an opera (*Carmen*, 1915) supply much of the literature. Because they are presumed to be atypical, opera and jazz are assumed to be fully "audible." As a result, we seem to believe that opera and jazz are unable to subtly activate emotional responses or point to understated narrative events. Moreover, since they are often examined as isolated incidents in an otherwise Romantic score, it is difficult to imagine either opera or jazz making a major contribution to cinematic construction. Could it be that in our desire to justify the value of film music, we've classified the score with an ear deaf not just to the persistence of opera and jazz but also to the essential discontinuities of the Hollywood film score?

There are three main reasons the idea of a continuous and cohesive classical Hollywood film score modeled after a Romantic compositional or discursive framework is fundamentally unsound:

1. It is not historically accurate.
2. It misrepresents the relationship between the mode of production and the final product.
3. It tends to reference a psychoanalytic mode of spectatorship constituted with little regard for the soundtrack.

I will address each of these concerns in turn. First, film musicologists often justify their unifying readings of the score by linking classical Hollywood to the silent era. Pointing out that silent films were typically accompanied by continuous music, scholars tend to assume that after a period of indecision, in the 1930s Hollywood reached a period of stabilization during which the score reverted to a less intrusive version of its early 1920s iterations.[38] Claudia Gorbman goes back even further, rooting Hollywood's love of music in the literal meaning of melodrama, reaching from ancient Greece, through the nineteenth-century French stage, and into the American vaudeville theater.[39]

It is important that in trying to explain the persistence of music we not neglect the disparity of its functions. To illustrate this claim, Rick Altman shows how difficult it is to identify a normative practice for more than thirty years of musical accompaniment by exploring the history of film music as a conflict between exhibitors' agency and producers' control.[40] The fact that such a tension persisted during the silent period forces us to rethink the notion that the soundtrack of the 1910s and 1920s could serve as the basis for a cohesive classical Hollywood model. I am not referring here only to Altman's assertion that some early films were indeed silent. Instead, I want to point to his conclusions to note that even if music was usually present, it was not necessarily comprehended "continuously." That is, though studios or prominent pianists and conductors suggested themes for particular films, and even on occasion provided scores, what audiences usually heard was a collection of melodies, some of which they recognized and others they did not. If we are going to argue for a consistency in musical styles from the silent to sound eras, we have to account for the variety of music that made up the silent film "score" and acknowledge that a recorded extension of this model would likely feel just as disjointed.

Second, it is illogical to acknowledge the constraints faced by composers under the studio system but ignore the inevitable results of their servitude. Because he usually created the score after the rough cut was complete, a film composer's music always signifies in relation to the image. Any analysis of a score's unity would be nonsensical without continuous reference to the picture. This is not to say that film music cannot be interesting or valuable in itself, but it does mean that it is not absolute and should not be treated as such. This assertion returns us to the middle epigraph that opened this chapter, which suggests that the methods created to analyze instrumental music are inadequate for the study of film music. To take Neumeyer and Buhler's remarks further: it is not only the variety of musical styles that makes it difficult to construct a standard musicological analysis of these texts, but Hollywood's mode of production also contradicts the possibility of treating the score as a unique object. Of course, there were exceptions to this compositional rule. Max Steiner's score for John Ford's *The Informer* (1935) has been critically hailed for both its sound and its process: Steiner's admirable effort is the result of having worked closely with Ford during the script and shooting stages, an unusual practice for even the most established Hollywood composer.[41] Although it is precisely this fact that should *prevent* this score from becoming an archetype, it has nevertheless been given special prominence in more than one critical discussion of the standard Hollywood film.[42]

From the perspective of the studios, moreover, scores were little more than lists of musical selections requiring rights clearance. Many of the pieces that made up the silent film score, of course, originated in operatic and jazz contexts, and these citations continued into the conversion era. Thus the newly organized music departments compiled cue sheets of the melodies included in each film, being careful to note the number of measures used of every piece so that accurate fees might be paid to the music's publisher. For example, the list for *Love and the Devil* (1929) includes four separate selections from Bizet's *Carmen* and one twenty-three-bar quote from Verdi's *Aïda*, in addition to many functionally titled "classical" pieces ("Agitato Pathétique," "Mysterioso Dramatique") and tunes that nodded to jazz and the popular ("Suite from the South," "Through the Ages").[43] Any hint of unity in these lists can be found only in relation to the theme or setting, and it would not depend on the musical properties of the works themselves. *Adoration* (1928) tells the story of a Russian princess, so its musical cues range from Tchaikovsky's *Nutcracker Suite* and Rachmaninoff's "Prelude in G Minor" to the "Volga Boat Song" and several other Russian folk melodies.[44] Similarly, the score for *The Terror* (1928) included cues with titles such as "Weird Night" and "Gruesome Tales" that allude to the film's status as a ghost story.[45] Because it was disparate and referential rather than unified and absolute, the conversion-era score bore a striking resemblance to its silent predecessor, a similarity that continued into the classical Hollywood era and made the establishment of music publishing deals all the more pressing.

Third, we ought to be cautious about applying image-based models of spectatorship to the soundtrack. Indeed, the conception of the score as an amalgamation of melodic fragments complicates how music can be addressed by film theory. For example, Michel Chion claims that listeners isolate the voice from other sounds: "A film's aural elements are not received as an autonomous unit...other aural elements, notably background music and offscreen commentary, are triaged to another place, an imaginary one, comparable to a proscenium."[46] By allocating it to a secondary space, Chion conceives of music as an audible rubber cement: because it is "offscreen" the score can patch together pieces of film that might otherwise be recognized for their difference. However, the voice does not work the same way. Voices lure spectators into an invisible scene, a space off limits to the diegetic realm. In Chion's vision, these voices can then become the unifying principle of a film: for example, the female "screaming point" in films such as King Kong (1933) and Psycho (1960) produces a vortex into which the rest of the narrative descends, while the disembodied voice in The Testament of Dr. Mabuse (1932) provokes a quest for the source that drives the plot.[47] In the model of film music I will propose, however, music is always potentially vocal, so it would make little sense to separate the operations of film music from those of the voice more generally.

Though his critique is not reliant on the place of the voice, Ben Winters shares a similar conception of the fundamental nature of film music. Unlike Chion, Winters claims that reading film music as an aspect of the narration and assigning it nondiegetic status may often prove reductive. Instead, he challenges film's basic realism to assert that not only could we perceive film music as available to the characters onscreen, we could also imagine its capacity to manipulate those characters, whether they acknowledge its presence or not.[48] There are some obvious examples one could come up with to demonstrate this claim (to Winters's suggestion of the zither in The Third Man, 1949, we could add a film such as Dario Argento's Suspiria, 1977, where the obtrusive and seemingly nondiegetic music by the prog-rock band Goblin starts and stops with visual effects and appears to rouse the main character's concerns), but the basic premise that such an active role could be played by film music is an important one. When paired with the latent power of voice, film music not only has the ability to act on the text, it has the potential to break it apart.

The notion that music contributes to the envelopment of the spectator relies on the possibility for cinematic suture, a term typically defined along visual lines. Daniel Dayan has famously condensed discussions of this practice in his definition of Hollywood's "tutor-code," that is, the means by which "the presence of the subject must be signified but empty, defined but left free."[49] This process is enabled through shooting and editing techniques such as the shot/reverse shot, whereby the spectator's identification with the film is interrupted by a momentary awareness of the frame that evaporates when another character appears to close the gap. This has been imagined musically as well: Claudia Gorbman notes that scholars like Adorno and Eisler had earlier acknowledged the concept of suture as a function of film music, albeit under another name.[50] Certainly it is easy to see that if we classify the score as a binding mechanism, we can show how it contributes to the spectator identifying himself as the film's uncritical recipient. Yet the incorporation of this model into musical analysis leads us a priori to identify sound as a continuous support for the unique subject, who is built on visual relationships. What is banished here is not only the subject's awareness of herself, foundational to theory of the cinematic experience developed by scholars like Vivian Sobchack and touched on throughout this book, but also the difference inherent in the sounds of the score.[51] If we had begun with the materiality of the film score rather than imported concepts appropriate to the Romantic symphony or developed for the image track, we might identify a different production of subjectivity altogether.

THE FAILURE OF THE SYSTEM: SCORING AND SUBJECTIVITY

By addressing the score as the fragmented construct that it is rather than the Romantic unity it pretends to be, we can see how classical Hollywood cinema can, and regularly does, suggest imaginary spaces apart from the diegesis but bearing little resemblance to the proscenium or the womb. These spaces are created through the fleeting relations the soundtrack takes up with the image, moments generated by the spectator and opening onto patterns that refuse to be absorbed by the narrative. This works because the spectator is never as fully intertwined with the machine and its projection as apparatus theory would have us believe. As Sobchack puts it, "The human body never entirely incorporates the technology that enables its perception and expression."[52] The subject compelled by the musings of the cinema is not a mindless placeholder entangled in an ideological snare. It becomes even more difficult to make the case for absolute absorption when we try to imagine a model for suture that would take into account listening as a perceptual act. Dayan described suture as a two-shot process: "The reverse shot has 'sutured' the hole opened in the spectator's imaginary relationship with the filmic field by his perception of the absent-one. This effect and the system which produces it liberates the imaginary of the spectator, in order to manipulate it for its own ends."[53] Although William Rothman shows how the suture mechanism would not necessarily have to conform to the bourgeois ideological position Dayan assumes it to take, he nonetheless retains the privileging of sight as the means by which spectators are led to position themselves in relation to the film.[54] Yet even Dayan's own definition of suture inadvertently invites us to notice sound: "Classical cinema establishes itself as the ventriloquist of ideology."[55] In other words, the cinema *speaks*. Yet it does not have an identical conversation with every listener.

To understand the possibility for such a multifaceted cinematic exchange, we might turn to Francesco Casetti's application of enunciation theory, which complicates a visually based conception of cinematic suture. Casetti claims that a series of subjective shots makes a statement: "I make you gaze, you equally as her," with regard to the character from whose eyes we now see.[56] Here too, Casetti presents the organization of images as a basis for unity, yet each in his typology of four gazes becomes a linchpin not just for images but also for sounds. Moreover, in "hearing" this statement, the spectator becomes aware of himself as its intended recipient and of the sensual experience in which he is now engaged. In Sobchack's terms, this constructs a double perception; I am newly attuned not only to the filmmaker's use of the camera to construct the character's point of view but also to how the projector asks me to gaze similarly.[57] Along those lines, I want to suggest that concentrating on the spectator as a listening subject allows us to make considerable alterations to the formulation of absence typically associated with the concept of suture. In order to describe the operations of classical Hollywood film music and the function of opera and jazz as constitutive elements therein, I define the score as an image-sound relation that splinters into alternate meanings capable of being more or less directed by the ideology of the film. Thus opera and jazz are not mere kernels of recognition but tantamount to the large and small forms that shape the score and can derail the authority of the gaze.

How is this conception of the classical Hollywood film score different from that outlined by this review? Although I do think it misguided to assess the score as a unit, I do not believe that film musicologists have led us astray in identifying its primary element. To be clear, I am not arguing that the score is free of leitmotifs, but I am saying that the leitmotif functions in ways that we have been hesitant to recognize. That is, the leit-motif is not just Romantic; it is operatic, and this very origin shatters what might otherwise be read as a self-contained score. Performed by both the orchestra and the singers, the operatic leitmotif is capable of moving from denotative to connotative value and back again. I do not want to suggest that a Wagnerian definition of the leitmotif necessarily would have oper-ated this way, or even to invoke the structure of opera in general. Instead, I call on the centrality of lyrical content to Hollywood film music from the time of the sing-alongs in early nickelodeons, through the musical puns of the 1910s, to the theme songs of silent films in the 1920s, and to the Italian opera and Tin Pan Alley jazz on which many of the conversion-era shorts relied.[58] My conception of the operatic Hollywood leitmotif acknowledges these multiple spheres of influence by noting the kinds of melodies that become thematic material while at the same time recognizing the history of the studios' reliance on the ideal of the opera to establish a template for listening to synchronous sound.

As is appropriate in observing the leitmotif's cinematic ontology, what I call the "score" includes music that has traditionally been termed both diegetic and nondiegetic. I have constructed this inclusive definition for a number of reasons. First, in the conversion era in particular, it was likely that what initially seemed a nondiegetic cue would eventually be incor-porated into the narrative. For example, even though most of *The Public Enemy* (1931) is free of accompaniment, the tavern scenes contain music by a pianist who is usually produced to justify its existence. *Svengali* (1931) works much the same way in its employment of sound bridges. The non-diegetic cue that initially appears to be accompaniment easily becomes diegetic background music in the following scene. This potential for diegetic grounding continues even when nondiegetic music becomes the classical Hollywood norm. It is always possible for the music we hear to be explained by the presence of a dance band, wandering musician, radio, or some other more outlandish device.[59] This is not to say that music works the same way whether or not it is visualized. It does mean, however, that film music is always capable of being snatched up by the image, forced to signify, or, in Ben Winters's terms, capable of being heard by the film's char-acters. Second, diegetic music, such as that described in the scenes from *The Public Enemy*, is often just as "unheard" as music that remains in the wings. From the spectator's perspective, then, it would be meaningless to say that *The Public Enemy* has no score while *King Kong* (1933) does. Third, diegetic cues recorded after the conversion may read as if they had been produced on the set, but they are usually no more "live" than the music we typically call accompaniment. The convention of playback in the Hollywood musical attests to this fact. Finally, the fundamental character of the leit-motif ensures that it remains free to form new constellations of meaning, regardless of whether it originated over the airwaves, on a jukebox, or with a hundred-piece orchestra.

Sergei Eisenstein famously envisioned a relationship between image and sound that mirrors the one I've been describing:

> Music demands to be set free from the purely routine and to transpose the theme onto a somewhat different plane, a somewhat different dimension....Because music in sound film begins at the point where the usual pairing of sound and image gives way to an arbitrary unity of sound and depiction; that is, when actual synchronization ceases to exist. As long as the depiction of a boot is linked to the sound of a violin, then it can have no relationship to the creative process but, when the violin is separated from the boot, and rests on the face of the person speaking, that is when your action starts.[60]

Although he was writing against the ideological effects supposedly produced by the unified Hollywood score, Eisenstein's remarks in fact accurately describe the unwitting position of music in the classical Hollywood film. Any attempt to securely attach a theme to a character or object is almost certainly thwarted by the meandering visual field. For example, though David Raksin might intend his memorable melody to call up an image of the character Laura in the 1944 film that bears her name, we might instead, seeing Waldo as it plays, attribute the song to him and queer our reading of both film and song. Moreover, Raksin composed his score after the film had been shot and under a strict deadline, meaning that like most Hollywood composers he had little say over where and how his music would ultimately be used. [61] The film always returns to Laura—the search for Laura, the friends of Laura, obsession with Laura, love for Laura. Contained in a melodic strain, Laura is a question posed by the text. But *Laura* can only ask; the wandering elaboration of the melody and its extension into the space of the spectator provide an undetermined answer. Thus even in a theme score as tightly organized as *Laura's*, there is significant room, as it were, for Raksin's boot to become separated from his violin.

Taking my cue from Eisenstein, I will explicate the difference between my operatic revision of the leitmotif and its traditional interpretation by giving two readings of *Don Juan* (1926), Warners' first feature with a Vitaphone score. It is readily apparent on an initial hearing that the continuous score accompanying the film is intended to replace the theatrical live orchestra. As such, the music maintains the traditional attributes of the 1920s silent film score: "invisible" players, wall-to-wall music, multiple melodic themes, excessive repetition, emotional referencing, and sound effects (the sounds of bells and clanging swords are particularly apparent).[62] A dominant reading would make connections between the themes and the film's characters, showing how the repetition of musical ideas both drives and echoes the narrative, unifying the text, while an oppositional analysis would restore the leitmotif to its operatic origins and by analyzing its role in fragmenting the narrative and revealing its potential for vocalization. I will begin with the former.

Don Juan opens with a prologue that justifies the title character's Romantic exploits. We are introduced to what appears to be a loving family: Don José, Donna Isobel, and little Don Juan. Accompanying the father is a melody played by the French horns, a bold theme that is later reorchestrated to include the entire string section. When we see the child, we hear a lighter melody performed by flute and pizzicato strings. A dwarf enters the scene, unsurprisingly escorted by a clarinet quotation from *Till Eulenspiegel's Merry Pranks*, Richard Strauss's symphonic tale of the mischief-making German folk hero. It seems, then, that the film closely adheres to Kathryn Kalinak's explanation of classical Hollywood's imperative: "every character should have his own theme."[63] But wait, what about Donna Isobel? Not only does *Don Juan* fail to award little Juan's mother a leitmotif of her own, it also keeps most of the other women in the film from acquiring a distinct musical identity. Thus the score is neatly able to reflect the legendary character's opinion of the fairer sex, an impression he gained by watching his parents. When Juan's father is called away from the family home at the beginning of the film, Isobel engages in a Romantic tryst, which is, unfortunately for her, observed by the trickster dwarf. The music illustrates the scene: as each character appears (lover, son, and dwarf), his melody emerges, often mingling with the others in a sonic translation of the central conflict. When Don José returns at the bidding of the dwarf to banish his unfaithful wife, his theme silences the others. What had once sounded Romantic during an embrace between José and Isobel has become angrily accented, and finally, mournfully sparse as it marks Juan's sadness over the departure of his mother and the conclusion of the scene.

A traditional leitmotivic analysis of the prologue to *Don Juan* would argue that the cuckolding of the father determines the direction of Juan's future. As the winner of this thematic dual, Don José's leitmotif has proven itself capable of communicating both valor and sorrow. Although it is entirely directed by the narrative, this reading is not uninteresting, for it provides a glimpse into the gender politics of the classical Hollywood score. The male lineage is awarded the entire range of expressive power while the female characters are restricted to stereotype. There is, expectedly, one exception.

Adriana, the virginal daughter of an unwelcome Duke and Juan's resistant love interest, has her own theme. Typically, then, other than the figure whose purity restores the mother to audibility and converts the son to monogamy, women in *Don Juan* are visual and musical surrogates for one another.

Revising this reading would require revisiting the notion of the leitmotif as a resource for operatic expression. Ideally, the leitmotif would so tightly wind the listener's emotions with a character or idea that even when the visual referent disappeared, the audible suggestion of the music would bring back the sensations associated with it. The interpretation of the leitmotif's unifying function arises not only from its integral place in the action but also from its mutability; a theme may return in a melodically, harmonically, or instrumentally altered form to develop the opera's ideas and integrate its themes. The cinematic leitmotif is historically less impulsive. For example, Rick Altman explains how orchestras in the 1920s would often adapt a theme from a preexisting work rather than compose a special one for a given film.[64] Both because of its need for recognition and its hasty application, this practice necessarily lessened the available variations on the theme. Yet what seems to be a restriction might also trigger a renewed understanding of the leitmotif. It is precisely the repetitive nature of the classical Hollywood film score and its apparent *lack* of musical development that leads me to classify its leitmotifs along the lines of Eisenstein's boot. The Hollywood leitmotif must be thought of in relation to the image, not as a purely musical device. In the same way that the operatic leitmotif alters its idea with every iteration, so the classical Hollywood theme carries with it the possibility of combining with new images to create situations that fail to correspond to their original intentions. This is, of course, very different from a symphonic conception of thematic material, which not only depends on musical development but also provides no opportunity for the sudden visualization or vocalization of the melody. Let us see how a potentially visual and vocal leitmotif would alter the above impression of the prologue to *Don Juan*.

An operatic reading of *Don Juan* recognizes the leitmotif for its repetition rather than its variation. Indeed, it is difficult to ignore the repetition of the prologue's four central themes, interpreted above as musical analogues for the film's main characters. The melodies themselves vary only slightly (instrumentally and dynamically), and they are stylistically independent enough that one has no trouble distinguishing the entrance of one from the departure of another. The analysis given here pinned these melodies directly to the narrative, reading their interaction as a musical illustration of the plot. Viewed silently, however, this prologue gives the impression not of a sympathetic man scorned by women but of a very cruel husband and father: Don José leaves a dwarf to spy on his neglected wife, deprives his son of a mother, and kills her lover by entombing him in the wall of the castle.[65] Heard as an expression of Romanticism, the leitmotifs cause us to attribute José's actions to righteous anger. However, I do not believe that the spectator is so easily duped.

What would happen to this interpretation if we recognized the role of the spectator engaged by the music's enunciation? To do so, let us briefly consider how Francesco Casetti's four gazes construct the viewer as the receiver of the discourse generated by the text.[66] Extending our understanding of the gaze beyond the visual field and using Casetti's categories, we would say that his first gaze, the objective shot, in which no character in the film is made obviously responsible for the image, is most like the nondiegetic score, unattributable to any single cinematic agent.[67] Because we assume that its characters cannot hear the music we do, it would appear that *Don Juan* occupies this position most of the time. Casetti's second gaze, the impossible objective shot, is one in which film exceeds its capacity for realistic production, causing us to identify with the apparatus. Casetti gives the intense redness of the sky when Atlanta burns in *Gone with the Wind* as an example. A sonic analogue would be a case in which film music asserts itself as a product of technology. *Don Juan* would likely have fit this category thanks to the uniqueness of hearing a fully recorded score in 1926.[68]

Interpellation, the third gaze, takes place when a character within the film looks into the camera. This would be mirrored by diegetic music, in which the musicians bare themselves to the audience. The title card telling us that the soundtrack to *Don Juan* has been "played on the Vitaphone by the New York Philharmonic Orchestra" manifests interpellation at its most basic level, as a literal address to the audience from the makers of the music. Finally, the subjective shot, Casetti's fourth gaze, is more commonly referred to as the point-of-view (POV) shot. This would be most easily paired with point-of-audition (POA) sound, an effect where we hear like a character in the fiction.[69] Examples in *Don Juan* would be the sounds made by the swords or bells that become audible when in close-up, suggesting our psychological affinity with the film's characters.

Casetti notes that it is impossible for the viewing subject to notice all of these gazes all of the time. Instead, "The subject of the enunciation ... is recognizable only through fragments, a series of indices internal to the film."[70] Although the fiction cannot function if the viewer continually detects his own role in constructing the film text, these fragments nevertheless continue to assert themselves both visually and aurally. In the case of *Don Juan*, all four gazes are audible in the soundtrack we hear at the opening of the film and in the leitmotifs contained therein. What first seems to be an objective soundtrack might in fact be mostly attributable to the emotional POA of Don José. On both occasions when José enters the room, he looks directly into the camera, an interpellation. Both the visual and the aural aspects of the scene then follow José's pattern of looking: the shot structure and the leitmotifs that accompany the images are centered on José and the objects and people he sees. Thus the leitmotivic articulations are not the property of an invisible narrator; they belong to Don José. With the exception of the love theme played while he is away, the variations on the leitmotifs could be attributed to José's attitude during varying points in the opening sequence. Yet there are problems with attempting to unify the score around a single figure in this way. Don José is not present for part of the prologue's action; he disappears from the film entirely soon after the sequence draws to a close, while some of the themes we have heard thus far return in the body of the film. Moreover, an impossible objective sound arises to counter the dominance of Don José. The reference to *Till Eulenspiegel*, by the notoriously complex Richard Strauss, draws attention to the orchestra's technical skill, reminding us that what we're hearing is no small-town band. By breaking up the authority of the implied narrator, as well as his substitute in Don José, this application of Casetti's gazes to soundtrack reveals the fragmentary traces of enunciation that exist in the Hollywood film score.

Thus the four gazes reflect the spatial orientation of the spectator, but they cannot entirely determine his relationship to the film. For example, because the repetitive music in *Don Juan* calls attention to itself (both because of the audibility of sound technology and because many of the melodies are familiar), it prevents diegetic absorption and frees the viewer's eye to wander.[71] What we notice immediately is that Don José, like the adult Juan, is played by John Barrymore. Rather than accept his behavior as either cruel or justified, we might instead connect the melody to a particular gesture we recognize as distinctly the actor's own. The extratextual association releases us from having to embrace the character as defined by the narrative. We can then see how the leitmotif reveals that the status of women in *Don Juan* is a problem. Reading the film's music through a Romantic lens absorbs us into the diegesis, creating a world in which Don Juan's misogyny fails to trouble the women around him. An operatic interpretation, however, might recognize a tension between the narrative construction of Don José and the star text of Barrymore. Impossibly associating the music with both at the same time, we can no longer use the melody to justify José's treatment of his wife; nor can we accept that an idol like Barrymore would engage in such cruelty. Women, who are no more sonically represented in this reading than they were in the last one, are suddenly positioned as a roadblock to ideology.

Rather than enforcing passive spectatorship, the operatic leitmotif encourages a state of expectation. In part, this is because music and image require different conceptions of space. In Dayan's model, the shot/reverse shot structure opens a gap in which I am momentarily the recipient of the look in shot one, only to close off this potential with the looking back of shot two. The rerouting of identification causes the space I had just occupied to be absorbed by the space of the film.[72] As we have seen with the application of Casetti's alternative, an exchange of musical themes rather than shots produces a number of possible results. Like shot one, theme one communicates to me, but unlike shot two, theme two is nothing like an answer. Instead, the space produced by theme one (the space where I receive the music) can be identical to the space referenced by theme two, or it can be a space shared by my ears and those of a character, the apparatus, or potentially heard differently by all of us. The music accompanying images of Don José and the dwarf are not telling each other anything (presumably José is already aware of the dwarf's sneakiness or he would not have entrusted him with the responsibility of trapping his wife); instead, they cause me to draw together relations within and outside of the text. Rather than encouraging me to accept the unity of the diegesis and the meanings presented therein, the multiplication and variation of what are often preexisting leitmotifs ensure that I am always reminded of the space where I continue to exist. Far from an audible adhesive gluing the pieces of film together into a coherent narrative space, the film score is instead a producer of Sobchack's "echo focus," announcing the means by which we are perceiving the world of Don Juan.[73] Rethinking the operatic leitmotif as the basis of the score imagines classical Hollywood as a cinema dependent on my active participation; if a film coheres at all, it is because I am present outside the text, forming clusters of meaning not explicitly directed by the narrative.

The potential vocality of the leitmotif is, of course, most audible in films that thematize opera overtly. For example, *One Night of Love* (1934) contains a nearly continuous musical score that integrates original film music with well-known operatic arias. The film tells the story of Mary Barrett, aspiring American opera singer (played by an actual American singer, Grace Moore), who arrives in Italy to study with the tyrannical Giulio Monteverdi, with whom she, of course, falls in love. Opera in the film musical is often structured in opposition to jazz or other popular music,[74] but here the division between the two is nonexistent. Part of the reason for this may be the music's origins. Victor Schertzinger, the composer of the newer melodies, is also the film's director. Schertzinger's song "One Night of Love" is played by an orchestra during the credit sequence and then heard again in the opening of the film, when Grace Moore sings it in a radio audition. Immediately, then, we are alerted to the value of the number as a structuring device; wrapped into the title of the film, its presence on the air makes it capable of traversing spaces. The song returns a number of times throughout the film and in a variety of ways that culminate in a bizarre conclusion, which finds Mary in her Metropolitan Opera debut. Paralyzed with fear, Mary mounts the stage and sees Monteverdi, hidden from the audience. Instead of presenting the authentic *Madame Butterfly*, however, the music at this moment offers a blend of Schertzinger's tune and Puccini's score. Mary makes her entrance and "One Night of Love" fades into the opera; if we hadn't heard either piece before, we would be unable to separate the two. The film score has woven its way into the opera score, and the popular song into the aria, where it seems to have belonged all along.

The operatic context of *One Night of Love* makes explicit the general condition of the leitmotif in American cinema. It clearly serves as a thematic thread and organizes the film's musical material, but the leitmotif also exposes a key assumption of film scoring that usually goes unrecognized by the text: these melodies are made to be heard. Musicals acknowledge this fact by presenting the score in the manner of Casetti's impossible objective shot: placing the audience in awe of the medium's capabilities, musicals complicate the diegetic-nondiegetic boundary, make realism irrelevant, and revel in excess. *One Night of Love* is typical of how Hollywood film scores transform moments of interpellation, which might generate discomfort, into moments of subjective sound, situating the audience with a listener in the diegesis. This is a movement from what Michel Chion calls a "zone of audition," in which what we hear reflects the spatial geographies of the film, to a "point of audition," in which we hear through the ears of a character.[75] When Moore begins to sing, interpellating us into the film, we are abruptly made aware that we have been eavesdropping, that the melody we've been hearing belongs to this space and not our own. Like the glimmer of the sardine can floating on the waves in Jacques Lacan's memory, Moore's entrance marks the abrupt appearance of the pervasive gaze.[76] We suddenly realize that the musical wash of sounds that pretends to fill in the diegetic fissures of *One Night of Love* has actually known all along that we have been listening.

Ostensibly working to close this gap, the production of Moore's voice is aligned with the story of her romance. The film sanctions our listening by asking us to identify with Monteverdi, who overhears everything from the radio audition to the exotic Met debut. Our listening *in* becomes a listening *through* Monteverdi's ears, and works with him to approve of Moore as a love interest. Yet this is a cover that ultimately fails. As the large form of the score, the leitmotif attempts to assure us that all is well, that any infractions on hearing can be rerouted to events within the diegesis. But its vocal origins, the fact that it could at any time be sung, and the connection it has to sound technology (that is, the operatic foundation on which sound films were introduced to the American public) make such a closed text impossible.

Although I am identifying the operatic leitmotif as the basis of the standard Hollywood film score, there are, of course, alternatives to how film music functions. Moreover, such deviations in Hollywood practice can occur more frequently in music than in dialogue or the image, for not only were Hollywood executives capable of ignoring the score's representational possibilities, the compositional process was not a focus of the Production Code Administration; nor was it carefully regulated outside of those boundaries. Therefore, there are many films from the 1930s and onward that have very little musical material or that use more original approaches to the incorporation of music. In light of these exceptions, the classical Hollywood film score continued to represent the values through which Americans understood opera and jazz during the conversion to sound. The preconceived notion that film music disappeared for several years while Hollywood worked out the kinks in its sound systems and then returned to mimic the accompaniment style of the 1920s silent film is false; music was there all along, not just in the short films discussed in this book but circulating throughout American culture, where composers—often the same composers who later worked in the film industry—were manipulating operatic and jazz material. Film music was not composed in a vacuum: the waning of European opera's influence, the circulation of race records, the increase in the airplay of jazz, and attempts to create a jazz-opera on stage all influenced the sound we eventually attributed to Hollywood cinema. The voice that connects opera and jazz in their articulation of violence is still audible in the feature film, we must simply train ourselves to hear it.

"WAIT A MINUTE, WAIT A MINUTE": JAZZ AND THE INTRUSION OF SPONTANEITY

I have called the operatic leitmotif the large form of the classical Hollywood film score, and will now label the jazz image its small form. This designation is not intended to divide the score into nondiegetic orchestral music and diegetic popular songs, for I have already described how such a simplistic separation would certainly be ill suited to describe how film music works. What I suggest instead is that classical Hollywood scores often speak in a jazz mode, by which I mean that they use "jazziness" as a way to acknowledge the unpredictability of cinema's technological origins, which reveal themselves in a jazz image that may be visual, sonic, or both at once. Although the conversion to sound brought an impression of "liveness" to the screen, it simultaneously eliminated the need for musicians, projectionists, and managers to assist with the construction of the cinematic event, thus making the progression of the narrative appear more inevitable. To study the operation of the jazz image, I will look at two films: *The Jazz Singer* (1927) and *Modern Times* (1936), showing how each adopts the jazz mode in order to make audiences more comfortable with the loss of improvisation at the site of exhibition while at the same time reintroducing the possibility of spontaneity in the recorded text.

I have selected these films in part for the valuable role each plays in the evolution of the classical Hollywood score, and as well for the way each self-consciously carves out its place in the history of film sound. At the same time that it heralds the arrival of the talkies, *The Jazz Singer* is an audition of sorts. Its sparse use of dialogue suggests that the soundtrack, like Jolson's character, is not ready to ignore its heritage. Far from being a complete departure, jazz might be used to signal the cinematic liveness that recorded sound threatened to eliminate. *Modern Times* frames itself as a throwback, a silent film with a recorded score nostalgic for an era without the mediated voice. Yet here too, the innovations produced by the film's sound-image relationship, particularly with regard to its jazz sources, belie its sensibilities. In each case, the jazz image reveals the true intentions of these films, which are far less evident than they first appear.

Even if we are careful to read jazz within the context of the 1930s, understanding it along the lines of popular music, we must be cautious not to call jazz a simple sign that points to a list of traits we might immediately associate with the narrative. For example, it would be naïve to clump together all instances of a single refrain as they appear in films and then generalize about the characters or setting on the basis of their relationship to this song. Such a formulation would assume that the meanings contained in the creation of a particular jazz song persist throughout its history, tainting the bodies that perform it with Hollywood's version of its origins. This would simplify the meaning of jazz and the significance of performance, as well as overlook the development of the films that employ jazz music. The instances of jazz that scholars most often address are diegetic, in which the popularity of the song is usually at least part of the motivation for its appearance. But what if we assume that "jazz" was not a type of song, but a style of performance?

Simon Frith claims that any analysis of a song ought to be based on the performance of its lyrics rather than the words alone, noting how audiences have "misunderstood" the intention of protest songs and incorporated them to serve dominant political goals, thereby changing their meaning.[77] In this vein, it is important to consider the way that the cinema performs jazz in order to determine what exactly "jazz" means. Yet the creation and circulation of jazz prior to its incorporation by the film industry makes it a special category of popular music. Unlike contemporary pop songs, which are usually intimately linked to particular recordings, singers, or bands, jazz is diffused much more extensively throughout the music industry under the banner of the "standard."[78] Jazz standards often have words, yet these frequently remain unknown to listeners, who might be more familiar with an instrumental version. Perhaps most importantly, jazz is a style built on improvisation. Thus it is defined by a mutability unavailable to the typical popular song and recognized by the way a performer organizes clusters of sound.[79] As the film that best articulates the cinematic status of jazz, *The Jazz Singer* (1927) established the model through which Hollywood represented the relationship between jazz and sound technology. Scholars may disagree about whether what Jolson performs is actually jazz,[80] but treating jazz as a mode makes the singer's authenticity irrelevant: it is Jolson's performance of jazziness that matters, not a musicological confirmation of his songs. A brief analysis of the film's legendary "Blue Skies" sequence will demonstrate how its jazz mode contextualizes film sound as a means of cinematic improvisation.

The "Blue Skies" sequence opens in "silence": Jakie Rabinowitz (Jack Robin) enters the family home for the first time since his childhood banishment and inaudibly utters the word "Mama." Hearing her son, Sara turns around and warmly welcomes him home. After much discussion, the two move toward the piano. Jack talks about his prospects on Broadway, saying in a dialogue title: "I'll sing you one of the songs I'm going to try out." Immediately thereafter, we hear a piano introduction followed by Jolson's distinctive voice belting out the tune. He interrupts his own rendition to make excessive promises to his mother about their future, and then continues in a self-proclaimed "jazzy" style until he is finally silenced by the entrance of his father, Cantor Rabinowitz, who angrily shouts "Stop!" thus ending the talking portion of the film. This moment has been mythologized as the death of the silent era, staged within an Oedipal, generational, and ethnic conflict that places the future of entertainment on the shoulders of Americanized youth.[81] Certainly, without jazz it would be difficult to effectively express this clash of cultures. Imagine, for a moment, if the film were titled, *The Opera Singer*. The story might still be capable of staging an

Oedipal scene, but the signifiers of ethnicity, age, and class would be entirely different. The jazz mode classifies progress as youthful and American, and it gives technology the illusion of spontaneity. Accounts of the "Blue Skies" scene famously claim that Jolson improvised this conversation.[82] Yet the sonic characteristics of the scene belie a true impulsiveness; the loving exchange between mother and son is musically accompanied by Jolson, who continues to play the "Blue Skies" bass line on the piano as they speak. Rather than impromptu dialogue, the scene reads as jazz performance, an improvised refrain on a prearranged harmonic structure.

The novelty of this diegetic presentation of jazz asks us to notice the technological capabilities of the Vitaphone. Indeed, one review of *The Jazz Singer* addressed the baring of the device by noting that after Cantor Rabinowitz makes his infamous command, "the Vitaphone withdraws."[83] This connection of Jolson's voice to the instrument of the Vitaphone equates the jazz mode with a technological performance unavailable to the film's other musical styles. *The Jazz Singer*'s score is a combination of "classical," Hebrew, and "jazz" melodies, all of which might be articulated inside and outside of the diegesis. However, only jazz requires extensive signifiers of synchronization. The "classical" music is performed by an unseen orchestra and the Cantor's singing is purely vocal, but Jack's numbers are accompanied by diegetic musical instruments (a piano in the saloon where we first come upon little Jakie, a violin for Jolson's first scene, and a piano for "Blue Skies"). Though this difference reflects the requirements of realism, the presence of these instruments categorizes both the Vitaphone and jazz music as simultaneously spontaneous and "safe," grounded in an industrial structure that can easily adapt to the emergence of a new star. *The Jazz Singer* thus uses jazz to comfort a nervous film industry; like Jack Robin singing to his mother, this is merely a tryout for the film industry's conversion.

The intrusions of jazz in *The Jazz Singer* work to expose the impossibility of musical suture by directing our attention toward another space and an alternate musical history. Yet they do so in a reductionist manner. *The Jazz Singer* presents jazz as a form of minstrelsy that had long ago lost its status as an expression of dominant popular culture. By tying themselves to expressions of technology, these assertions of "jazz" exemplify the sonic variant of the impossible objective gaze while at the same time making Casetti's terminology all the more relevant. For this version of history is not "objective" at all. The "classical" music from *The Jazz Singer* pretends that the compositional practices of the silent era can be simplistically grafted onto synchronous sound recordings. Announcing itself as a function of the cinema's mediation, the jazz image assures us that something has changed. The stodgy characters in these films are but a ruse; pretending that it is possible to stitch the film together again, they stop the flow of jazz, but it is too late, for we have already been exposed to the brutal imagery on which the music relies.

As a consequence of Charlie Chaplin's renowned antagonism toward sound cinema, the musical "interruptions" in *Modern Times* similarly make loud pronouncements about jazz history while reflecting on jazz's incorporation by the cinema. The story finds Chaplin's tramp character working in a factory and suffering a nervous breakdown. He is more satisfied with life in prison—where the chirping birds greet him as he wakes—than he ever had been in the noisy working world—where his every movement was accompanied by a barrage of mechanical sounds. The plot thus mirrors Chaplin's own discomfort with sound technology; an artist who constructed his persona out of the restrictions of the silent film, Chaplin understood that to let the tramp speak would be to hail his own demise. Though *Modern Times* does speak, its voices are almost always heard through some technological device such as a radio or phonograph, or, most imaginatively, an invasive television that allows the company president to appear on a screen to bark commands at his employees, even while they are in the restroom. Despite the obvious critique Chaplin makes of sound technology's effects as reflections of the inhumanization of society as a whole, it is difficult to see this film as merely a lament about the death of silent cinema. It recognizes itself as an anachronistic product, but *Modern Times* makes an aesthetic declaration about the possible uses of the recorded soundtrack that are most evident in its music.

Chaplin worked closely with his arrangers, David Raksin and Edward Powell, who ended up doing much of the composing themselves. Though an amateur violinist who used his violin extensively in his films and, according to anecdote at least, practiced a great deal,[84] Chaplin was unable to transcribe his many musical ideas. Raksin recalled that his daily sessions with Chaplin involved extensive discussions during which the director would sing short melodies and make suggestions for their instrumentation and development.[85] Chaplin also recommended musical sounds by referring to composers. In the story Raksin recounts about the music for *Modern Times*, Chaplin's two inspirations come from jazz and opera:

> Charlie might say, 'A bit of 'Gershwin' might be nice there'...And indeed there is one phrase that makes a very clear genuflection toward one of the themes in 'Rhapsody in Blue.' Another instance would be the tune that later became a pop song called 'Smile.' Here, Charlie said something like, 'What we need here is one of those 'Puccini' melodies. Listen to the result, and you will hear that although the notes are not Puccini's, the style and feeling are.[86]

The way these two melodies are used in the film is important for under-standing the value of opera and jazz for Chaplin, and their potential for sound film in general. The melody later called "Smile," after it was given lyrics in 1954 and recorded by Nat King Cole, constitutes the film's love theme, used to signify the relationship between the tramp and the "gamin," played by his then-wife Paulette Goddard. We first hear the tune after the tramp and gamin escape from the police. Sitting in the front yard of a more economically successful young couple, the two discuss their lack of either home or gainful employment while watching, somewhat wistfully, as their unnamed ideals part ways to begin their day. After this point, the theme returns whenever the two consider their future, culminating in the ending, during which the gamin cries, "What's the use of trying," in a dialogue title whose position in relation to the music matches the placement of the later lyric, "What's the use of crying." Indeed, the potential vocality of Chaplin's tune is enhanced not only by the fact that it served as the source material for this popular song, but also by the way it seems to direct both dialogue and action.

The tramp and gamin are like children, playacting at work and marriage, and they would hardly be believable as a couple at all were it not for the introduction of the song and the connotations that arise between this pair and the tragically bohemian destinies of those that appear in Puccini's operas. The opposition of this homeless and unemployed couple to the giddy homeowners in the scene from *Modern Times* mirrors the stark divi-sion between the poverty of the women in *La bohème* and *Madame Butterfly* and the riches of the princes and emperors in operas such as *Turandot*. By making this connection, hearing Puccini as the motivation for the composi-tion of the theme and its placement in the score, we are able to read "Smile" not just as a product inspired by Chaplin's film but perhaps as an idea that was there lying dormant all along. As such, when Chaplin instructs the gamin to smile and they walk away from the camera toward the distant hills, the "style and feeling" of Puccini and its reference to opera, a genre able to voice itself without technological mediation, suggests the tragedy of this conclusion in spite of its apparent optimism. Facing a world that operates in synchronous sound, what hope could a silent couple have?

The Gershwin motif that Raksin mentions occurs for the first time after Chaplin's release from prison, when he is enlisted to help build a boat. A repeated note in the trumpets recalls a passage from "Rhapsody in Blue," which is then followed by a recurring three-note phrase in the strings, played continuously, but not always on the downbeat, so that it produces a syncopated effect resembling the texture created by the piano in the background of a trumpet solo during an early section of Gershwin's piece.

The jazziness of the moment in the film is emphasized by adding a layer of muted trumpets, using the tenor saxophone in a prominent role, and constructing the melody so that it slides down a half-step and back up again. Thus the citation of Gershwin is not the typical clarinet glissando or even contained within the melody itself; it is established by the combination of the elements that make "Rhapsody" signify as concert jazz. Moreover, the use of this phrase in the score of *Modern Times* persists in relation to another statement that also seems to reference Gershwin's music. The uncomfortable harmonic relationships between a set of brass chords used repeatedly in *Modern Times* sound quite similar to the conclusion of a frantic brass accelerando that takes place prior to the recapitulation of the piano theme in the concluding minute of "Rhapsody." We hear this brief statement in Chaplin's film whenever the narrative mentions labor or puts our hero to work. The insertion of mechanization into the lackadaisical life of the tramp induces fearful discord, which resolves itself in the jazz theme requested by Chaplin.

When these two themes are considered in tandem, we can see that the brass chords express the potential for the destructive capabilities of the jazz image, while the larger tune suggests its power of redemption. Just before Chaplin gets his first job as a boat builder, the brass announcement of danger assures us of his eventual failure. The Gershwinesque sound that follows, then, allows us to appreciate the ensuing chaos according to the regulations of the silent film, a place where Chaplin's nonverbal antics are generically acceptable. The spontaneity of the sound and its whimsical feel strip the "Rhapsody" of its lower register and percussion section, making it seem as if this lighthearted romp has little impact on the narrative, in which Chaplin has just set a large boat adrift to meet its certain demise. The second time we hear the Gershwin reference immediately follows the initial statement of the "Smile" melody and finds Chaplin working as a night watchman at a department store, where he and the gamin tear the place up by eating the food, playing with the toys, and roller skating around an upper floor. Thus the jazz mode in *Modern Times* demonstrates its capacity to upset the intentions of the love theme that would seemingly want to see Chaplin a success, the ideology that values gainful employment over spontaneous play, and the system of labor characteristic of the Hollywood studio system that models itself on efficiency.

The one unmediated presentation of Chaplin's voice in *Modern Times* embodies the delicate balance between the film's impression of spontaneity and its carefully orchestrated score. The tramp has been hired as a singing waiter, a job description that gives him reservations for obvious reasons. As he prepares backstage for his entrance, his fellow waiters sing

"In the Evening by the Moonlight," the minstrel ballad reminiscing about the carefree banjo concerts of plantation days that had been used in the Warner Bros. jazz film featuring Paul Tremaine and His Aristocrats (as well as by countless others in live acts and recordings since its publication in 1880). Rather than show us the performance, the camera takes us backstage, where we see the tramp practicing, making repeated false starts as he forgets the words and seems unable to find his voice.

The inaudibility of Chaplin's pantomime begs us to listen more closely to "In the Evening," a song that is in itself an exercise in forgetting. By misremembering the past in close harmony, the singing waiters strip the song of the jazzy context it had been given by bands such as Tremaine's, deny its relationship to its source material, and reinscribe it within the genre of the barbershop quartet. In the performance that follows, however, Chaplin restores the jazz image that the scene had thus far worked to deny. Bounding onto the floor and doing an exaggerated dance to defer the moment the song might begin, the tramp loses the words that the gamin had written on his cuff and starts to panic. From backstage she shouts in a title: "Sing!! Never Mind the Words." Heeding her instructions, the tramp sings nonsense that sounds an awful lot like French, but whose actual meaning is provided by Chaplin's gestures. Ira S. Jaffe praises the scene's clarity, calling the diegetic audience's appreciation of the music a confirmation of Chaplin's ability to communicate clearly in spite of the inarticulate nature of his speech.[87] However, because of its contrast with the previous song, it seems to me that Chaplin's number works better as a commentary on the multiplicity of meanings that might be produced by the recorded voice, and that deliberately recalls the way that jazz artists use scat or other incoherent sounds to speak about events too painful to put into words.[88] The visual arrangement of Chaplin's act seems to suggest that the physical performance of the lyrics can do little other than confirm their predetermined meaning; the primacy of recorded music for cinematic interpretation has been ensured.

An alternative to this reading has been set up by the deliberate elision of the image of the white waiters singing "In the Evening." Reproducing such blatantly offensive lyrics without showing their source, Chaplin suggests that, regardless of what we see, we would be just as likely to hear the song as a historical relic that tells a story about jazz's origins. Yet by singing nonsense syllables, Chaplin asks us to take apart our assumptions about how language functions in music, noting that the potential vocality of a tune might enable all kinds of meaningful constructions and urging us not to accept synchronization as a substitute for truth. *Modern Times* thus uses the jazz image to critique sound cinema's production of jazz itself, a project that echoes the film's overarching reflection on the technological process of its own production. The possibility for misreading encouraged by Chaplin's gleeful sincerity suggests that the spectator has far more agency that his singing waiter would admit.

We can now see how the significance of opera and jazz in classical Hollywood film music provided an answer to American critics' calls for a jazz-opera. According to Raymond Knapp, works such as Dvořák's *From the New World* (1893), which developed themes originating in the musical sounds of Native and African Americans, prefigured a democratic mythology that was central to the national imagination and that became a strong component of American musical theater after the Second World War.[89] Like the stage musical, the unified ideal of the jazz-opera would first of all aid in the construction of a uniquely American cultural sphere, and second it would exploit the nation's growing musical awareness of jazz through radio, records, and nightclubs and infuse it with the artistic capital of immigrant artists and entrepreneurs. As we have seen, the failure of this project in the 1920s may have had more to do with space than form, though certainly voluble arguments over what shape such a work would take played a role in the unlikelihood of it ever being produced.

During the conversion era, the fantasy of inclusion was conveyed by the availability of a wide variety of short films, yet taken alone each would be more likely understood as an example of segregation. Segregation continued in the classical Hollywood film score's representation of jazz. Even in the feature films of the 1930s and beyond, the jazz mode is conjured primarily by European composers, which may initially give us pause when declaring to what extent the film score might actually represent American feelings about jazz, race, and ethnicity. Knapp calls our attention to a similar practice in stage musicals, where in productions such as *Show Boat* and *Porgy and Bess* "the primary way that blacks are allowed to express themselves is through words written by whites."[90] Yet Knapp provides an important caveat: "we must also acknowledge that more goes into a performance than the words spoken and sung. . . ."[91] Defining the jazz mode as a performance style rather than as a series of attributes expressed on a page of manuscript paper allows us to see how stars such as Charlie Chaplin and Louis Armstrong could use their bodies and voices to alter the meaning of particular songs, and also how technology itself could be understood as a performer, announcing its contribution to the creation of the text. As such, what may have first seemed like an impossible form (an expression of ethnic, racial, and cultural diversity written by a single composer) becomes more feasible as collective practice, where the intentions of the author and the performance of the players collide with a multiplicity of readers, who are all the more capable of creating new interpretations thanks to film technology's assertiveness during the conversion. Moreover, wrapping concerns about literal and musical integration into a form that made extensive use of both opera and jazz shifted the development of the jazz-opera from a sphere fraught with a national inferiority complex to a space where the United States had achieved cultural dominance, and hoped to continue in this vein in part by establishing a national film sound.

Conclusion

Throughout these pages I have argued that opera and jazz played a vital role in both selling the cultural value of sound cinema and molding the contours of classical Hollywood film music. By looking at conversion-era opera and jazz shorts as bold attempts to justify the intrusion of sound, I have shown that producers in the late 1920s and early 1930s were not just standardizing sound technologies; they were solidifying American attitudes toward performance and power. Although they differed from one studio to the next, the representational practices of the conversion era established the ideological lens through which classical Hollywood used opera and jazz thereafter. Warners' variety format tried to raise the reputation of jazz while popularizing opera, thus allowing the styles to mix in the classical Hollywood film score. The effort to smooth class tensions, however, was prevented by the history of jazz, which seeped through the cracks in Warner's mode of address, as well as by the elite standards of opera appreciation, which put pressure on the studio to recontextualize the music.

While opera either fell by the wayside or became increasingly associated with the tenor, films produced during the conversion tended to resituate jazz in the center of the text. For example, the voices in the Paramount shorts were marginalized by the films' style, which restricted their agency to moments when the studios granted them permission to sing. These limitations find their way into film music beyond the period of conversion, where the jazz mode articulates the possibility of technological freedom, but only insofar as such flights of fancy are checked by the security measures of the sound film. Recognizing the jazz mode for what it is allows us to see how race and ethnicity were mobilized to give sound recordings the impression of spontaneity. Although these practices of incorporating opera and jazz were normalized by classical Hollywood, my comparative analyses have demonstrated that the conversion-era studios' depictions of these musical forms had distinct aims. Moreover, these disparities suggest that the uncertainty of the period made room for the creation of the "jazz-opera" in a manner that had remained impracticable on the stage. Whether the musical styles were united in films such as *Yamekraw* or featured in independent shorts shown as part of the same evening program, conversion-era producers asserted that together opera and jazz might make valuable contributions to American cultural production.

I have written this story of the relationship among opera, jazz, and Hollywood cinema as a progression from the short to the feature film. I made this choice because the standardization of sound shifted the locus of musical signification; no longer necessary to promote the value of competing sound technologies, opera and jazz became critical tools in establishing American scoring practices. I do not want to give the impression, however, that short films suddenly became less important in 1932, or that the shorts released thereafter neglected opera and jazz entirely. A great deal of work has yet to be done on Hollywood sound shorts, many of which use opera and jazz either as elements in a larger narrative or in order to feature musical numbers.[1] Indeed, short films continued to reveal the ideological conflicts that had been tucked into the crevices of the classical Hollywood score long after the conversion was complete.[2]

The persistence of opera and jazz in the short films of the 1930s and the resurgence of the concept of the jazz-opera in postwar stage productions such as Kurt Weill's *Street Scene* show us that sound standardization did not entirely ease anxieties about the meaning and function of these musical forms. Of course, Hollywood shorts and American operatic works are not the only genres in need of revisiting with regard to this book's thesis about the cinematic prominence of opera and jazz. The recent glut of attention to opera, popular music, and film is often inclined to differentiate works by period or country of origin. The kinds of connections I have been able to trace between music and technology would be useful in drawing a stylistic comparison between, for example, Ingmar Bergman's televised *The Magic Flute* (1975) and a YouTube video of Beverly Sills singing Mozart's "Queen of the Night" aria, or Edison's and Syberberg's versions of *Parsifal*, produced more than eighty years years apart. Although these texts most certainly do not define "opera" the same way and may have very different ideas about the role of media in the presentation of music, this should not prohibit us from exploring them in relation to one another. It is precisely these differences that reveal the changing significance of opera, jazz, and technologies of sound reproduction. Rather than looking for a simple explanation for opera's influence on the cinema, or singular examples of cinematic techniques on the stage, we might learn something far more valuable from putting individual texts into conversation with one another.

I have written *Sounding American* with these problems in mind, attempting to unify discourses from the general spheres of music and cinema and also those that arise within cultural histories of sound, film musicology, and film theory. Solidifying the connection between film theory and historical events improves our analysis of the past and grounds artistic production in personal and communal experiences. Bringing together technological history and textual analysis is important, not because we should aim to construct a grand unified theory of film sound but because we can understand neither new technologies nor cultural products without grasping their mutual influence. Opera and jazz were able to make such an impact on the development of Hollywood film sound because musical styles are inherently unstable; music's content and cultural significance change as they come into contact with new modes of presentation and preservation. Throughout this book I have aimed to preserve the value of theory by grounding its revelations in the specific conditions of the conversion era. Nevertheless, certain avenues have been left unexplored. Beyond this cursory conclusion, the ultimate effects of conversion-era innovations on the music itself have yet to be studied in detail. Further research remains to be done on how music's appropriation by the cinema transformed the circulation and comprehension of opera and jazz outside of the movie theater. Yet I hope that by examining a concrete historical period through the lens of the short film, I have been able to expand our knowledge of the relationship between music and technology, opera and jazz, and stage and screen.

NOTES

INTRODUCTION

1. This debate is elaborated in detail in MacDonald Smith Moore's *Yankee Blues: Musical Culture and American Identity* (Bloomington: Indiana University Press, 1985).
2. The score for *Don Juan* not only illustrates the point about the ease of reorchestration, it also set the precedent for the typically quick composition of recorded classical Hollywood film scores. The contract for the score was drawn up on May 19, 1926, and promised that the compilers/composers would deliver the final product less than four weeks later, with the stipulation that their fee would cover "our work in arranging the score, plus whatever original composition we deem advisable and necessary." Contract between Edward Bowes, managing director of the Capitol Theater in New York and the Vitaphone Corporation, University of Southern California Warner Bros. Archives (hereafter USCWB).
3. Douglas Gomery, for example, recounts the Warners' early skepticism of talking films because of their continued failure and notes that the Warners planned to concentrate on producing films of musical performances. *The Coming of Sound: A History* (New York: Routledge, 2005), 36–37.
4. Cited in James P. Kraft, *Stage to Studio: Musicians and the Sound Revolution, 1890–1950* (Baltimore: Johns Hopkins University Press, 1996), 56.
5. For an excellent comparison of the technological awareness of viewers during this period to those experiencing the earliest cinematic productions, see Robert Spadoni, *Uncanny Bodies: The Coming of Sound Film and the Origins of the Horror Genre* (Berkeley: University of California Press, 2007).
6. Rick Altman discusses several of these in part VI of *Silent Film Sound* (New York: Columbia University Press, 2004).
7. Steven Shaviro, *The Cinematic Body* (Minneapolis: University of Minnesota Press, 1993), 35.
8. Spadoni, 14–15.
9. Vivian Sobchack, *The Address of the Eye: A Phenomenology of Film Experience* (Princeton: Princeton University Press, 1992), 10.
10. Quoted in Dolores Foster, "Gilbert's Voice Is All Right," *Photoplay*, June 1930: 37.
11. Leonid Sabaneev, "Opera at the Present Day," *Musical Times*, July 1, 1930: 595.
12. Steven Connor, *Dumbstruck: A Cultural History of Ventriloquism* (New York: Oxford University Press, 2000), 401.
13. Jean Mitry, *The Aesthetics and Psychology of the Cinema*, trans. Christopher King (Bloomington: Indiana University Press, 1997), 249.

14. Krin Gabbard, *Jammin' at the Margins: Jazz and the American Cinema* (Chicago: University of Chicago Press, 1996), 8–19.
15. Winthrop Sargeant, *Jazz: Hot and Hybrid* (New York: Dutton, 1946), 52.
16. Lawrence Levine, "The Sacrilization of Culture," in *Highbrow/Lowbrow: The Emergence of Cultural Hierarchy in America* (Cambridge: Harvard University Press, 1988), 83–168.
17. "McCormack Thrills Radio Fans," *New York Sun*, January 2, 1925.
18. Shawn Vancour, "Popularizing the Classics: Radio's Role in the American Music Appreciation Movement, 1922–34," *Media, Culture and Society*, vol. 31, no. 2 (2009): 289–307.
19. See, for example, James Buhler, "Frankfurt School Blues: Rethinking Adorno's Critique of Jazz," in *Apparitions: New Perspectives on Adorno and Twentieth-Century Music*, ed. Berthold Hoeckner (New York: Routledge, 2006), 114.
20. Of course, there is some disagreement about exactly which dates mark the beginning and end of the conversion era. Recorded musical experimentation starts with the Vitaphone sound shorts in 1926 and continues in the multiple jazz shorts released throughout 1932. Charles O'Brien claims that music ceases to be used primarily as a cinematic spectacle in 1933, when Hollywood abandons the extensive exploitation of popular songs in favor of a thoroughly composed score; *Cinema's Conversion to Sound: Technology and Film Style in France and the U.S.* (Bloomington: Indiana University Press, 2005), 29. It is worth noting that this is also the accepted view of most film musicologists, who date the establishment of the recorded score from Max Steiner's composition for *King Kong* in 1933. Thus, when we imagine that meaning might originate with sound rather than image and periodize accordingly, 1926 and 1932 seem the most logical markers of the era.
21. Examples of the former trend are Donald Crafton, *The Talkies: American Cinema's Transition to Sound 1926–1931, in History of the American Cinema*, Vol. 4 (Berkeley: University of California Press, 1997); Douglas Gomery, *The Coming of Sound*; and Scott Eyman, *The Speed of Sound: Hollywood and the Talkie Revolution, 1926–1930* (Baltimore: Johns Hopkins University Press, 1999). Accounts that fall into the latter category are James Lastra, *Sound Technology and the American Cinema: Perception, Representation, Modernity* (New York: Columbia University Press, 2000); and Steve J. Wurtzler, *Electric Sounds: Technological Change and the Rise of Corporate Mass Media* (New York: Columbia University Press, 2007).
22. Included among these are Gabbard, *Jammin' at the Margins*; Michal Grover-Friedlander, *Vocal Apparitions The Attraction of Cinema to Opera* (Princeton: Princeton University Press, 2005); Peter Stanfield, *Body and Soul: Jazz and Blues in American Film, 1927–63* (Urbana: University of Illinois Press, 2005); Jeongwon Joe, *Opera as Soundtrack* (Farnham, Surrey, UK: Ashgate, 2013); and Jeongwon Joe and Rose Theresa, eds., *Between Opera and Cinema* (New York: Routledge, 2002).
23. The invitation was mentioned in the *New York Times*, but denied later by Kahn himself. "Jazz Opera in View for Metropolitan," *New York Times*, November 18, 1924.
24. Although there were reasons to suspect that opera would experience a monumental decline in quality and popularity in the 1920s, Rachel Emily Nussbaum argues that journalists, at least in the German context, overstated the case. *The Kroll Opera and the Politics of Reform in the Weimer Republic*, Dissertation, Cornell University, 2005.

25. William Saunders, "National Opera, Comparatively Considered," *Musical Quarterly*, vol. 13, no. 1 (January 1927): 82.

26. Charles Hiroshi Garrett, *Struggling to Define a Nation: American Music and the Twentieth Century* (Berkeley: University of California Press, 2008).

27. The author of "Chicago Opera Patrons Chase and Kiss Composer" referred to it as "jazz as an operatic motif." *Buffalo Express*, December 27, 1925.

28. Herbert F. Peyser, "Jazz Knocks in Vein at Opera's Door," *Musician* (March 1929). Reprinted in *Jazz in Print (1856–1929): An Anthology of Selected Readings in Jazz History*, ed. Karl Koenig (Hillsdale, NY: Pendragon Press, 2002), 553.

29. Burns Mantle was quoted on the piece in Gerald Martin Bordman, *American Musical Theater: A Chronicle*, 3rd ed. (Oxford: Oxford University Press, 2001), 467.

30. Other reviewers referred to the piece as a "grand opera" or an "operetta." "Gershwin's *Blue Monday* (1922) and the Promise of Success," in *The Gershwin Style: New Looks at the Music of George Gershwin*, ed. Wayne Schneider (New York: Oxford University Press, 1999), 126.

31. *Rhapsody in Blue*, dir. Irving Rapper, Warner Bros. 1945.

32. In a letter to his brother written on February 18, 1923, George Gershwin mentioned an incident where a journalist questioned him about composing such a piece. The letter is reprinted in *The George Gershwin Reader*, ed. Robert Wyatt and John Andrew Johnson (Oxford: Oxford University Press, 2004), 43–44.

33. Moore, *Yankee Blues*, 117.

34. Quoted in "The Descent of Jazz Upon Opera," *Literary Digest*, March 13, 1926. Reprinted in *Jazz in Print (1856–1929)*, 454–55.

35. A.H. "Is Jazz 'The American Soul?'" *Musical America*, November 24, 1923. Reprinted in *Jazz in Print (1856–1929)*, 264.

36. Rick Altman, "Moving Lips: Cinema as Ventriloquism," in "Cinema/Sound," ed. Rick Altman, special issue, *Yale French Studies*, vol. 60, no. 1 (1980): 67–79.

37. Henry Jenkins, '"Shall We Make It for New York or Distribution?' Eddie Cantor, *Whoopee*, and Regional Resistance to the Talkies," *Cinema Journal*, vol. 29, no. 3 (Spring 1990): 32–52.

CHAPTER 1

1. Michael Curtiz, original story "The Clown" or "Pagliacci," 1927, USC Warner Bros. Archives, School of Cinema-Television, University of Southern California (hereafter, USCWB).

2. In identifying these features, Bordwell is comparing the classical Hollywood film score to the opera score, in particular that composed by Richard Wagner. David Bordwell, Janet Staiger, and Kristin Thompson, *The Classical Hollywood Cinema: Film Style and Mode of Production to 1960* (New York: Columbia University Press, 1985), 34.

3. Andrew L. Erdman, *Blue Vaudeville: Sex, Morals and the Mass Marketing of Amusement, 1895-1915* (Jefferson, NC: McFarland, 2004), 51.

4. See Rick Altman, *Silent Film Sound*, for a discussion of this tune and other ragtime hits in nickelodeon sing-alongs, 206–8.

5. Ibid., 362.

6. Tetrazzini's appearances are mentioned in Paul Fryer, *The Opera Singer and the Silent Film* (Jefferson, NC: McFarland, 2005), 132.

7. Jacob Smith, *Vocal Tracks: Performance and Sound Media* (Berkeley: University of California Press, 2008).

8. Mary Ann Doane, "The Voice in the Cinema: The Articulation of Body and Space." "Cinema/Sound." *Yale French Studies*, vol. 60 (1980): 33–50.

9. Sargeant, *Jazz: Hot and Hybrid*, 47–48.

10. Ibid., 48.

11. Boris M. Èjxenbaum, "O. Henry and the Theory of the Short Story," *Readings in Russian Poetics: Formalist and Structuralist Views*, ed. Laislav Matejka and Krystyna Pomorska (Ann Arbor: Michigan Slavic Publications, 1978), 231.

12. Roman Jakobson, "The Dominant," *Readings in Russian Poetics: Formalist and Structuralist Views*: 82.

13. Èjxenbaum, "O. Henry," 231–32.

14. Rick Altman has spoken at length about this trait, particularly in a class titled Film Sound Between the Wars, University of Iowa, 2007.

15. Sobchack, *Address of the Eye*, 178.

16. Bordwell et al., "The Central Producer System: Centralized Management After 1914" and "The Producer-Unit System: Management by Specialization After 1931," in *The Classical Hollywood Cinema*, 128–41, 320–29.

17. See William Shaman, "Operatic Vitaphone Shorts," *ARSC Journal*, vol. 22, no. 1 (Spring 1991): 41.

18. For more on the independent short film production during the conversion to sound, see "The Sound of Custard: Shorts, Travelogues, and Animated Cartoons," in Crafton, *The Talkies*, 381–401.

19. Bordwell et al., *The Classical Hollywood Cinema*, 325.

20. Robert F. Storey, *Pierrot: A Critical History of a Mask* (Princeton: Princeton University Press, 1978), 27–28.

21. Storey, *Pierrot*, 38–39. The law against the spoken word (initially pertaining only to dialogue but later extended to include monologue) did not apply only to the *commedia dell'arte* but to French productions as well, and was intended to discourage performances at fairs and other popular locations in favor of the Opera and the Comédie Française. For more on this distinction, see Robert M. Isherwood, "Popular Musical Entertainment in Eighteenth-Century Paris," *International Review of the Aesthetics and Sociology of Music*, vol. 9, no. 2 (Dec. 1978): 295–310.

22. One reviewer of the composer's half-hour reduction at the Hippodrome in London in 1911 stated that "what is left is the cream of the opera; and it makes its half-hour seem too short." Quoted in Matteo Sansone, "The 'Verismo' of Ruggiero Leoncavallo: A Source Study of 'Pagliacci'," *Music and Letters*, vol. 70, no. 3 (1989): 362.

23. Mordaunt Hall, "Vitaphone Stirs as Talking Movie," *New York Times*, August 7, 1926.

24. "The Vitaphone Makes Its Debut," *Musical Courier*, August 12, 1926.

25. Ruth Russell, "Voice Is Given to Shadows of Silver Screen," *Chicago Daily Tribune*, September 16, 1926.

26. Art Meyer, "Vitaphone Thrills Los Angeles," *Motion Picture Bulletin of California*, October 28, 1926.

27. "Vitaphone at a Glance," *Variety*, Don Juan Special, August 7, 1926.

28. Harry M. Warner, "Future Developments," talk at Harvard University, printed in *The Story of the Films as Told by Leaders of the Industry to the Students of the Graduate School of Business Administration George F. Baker Foundation Harvard University* (Chicago: A. W. Shaw, 1927): 335.

29. Like all good myths, there are variations on this story. Harry Warner insists that Sam called him to witness a twelve-piece orchestra ("Future Developments").

Both versions could well have been true, as Will Hays suggests that two separate demonstrations took place, one for each brother, *See and Hear: A Brief History of Motion Pictures and the Development of Sound*, advisory editor Martin S. Dworkin, *Screen Monographs II* (New York: Arno, 1970).

30. "History of Warner Bros.," Studio Legal Department, no date recorded, but presumed to be drawn up in the late 1940s, USCWB, 13–14.
31. For example, in a promotional brochure for *Don Juan*, Warner Bros. asserted that it offered "even the smallest theatre of the hinterland the musical offerings of the world's greatest theatres." Distributed by Warner Bros. Theatre in Hollywood and KFWB Radio Station, no date, USCWB.
32. "How First Vitaphone Film Was Photographed," *American Cinematographer*, September 1926: 10, 16.
33. Lee De Forest, "The Talking Pictures," *American Cinematographer*, February 1928: 4.
34. Four excellent accounts are Altman, *Silent Film Sound*; Crafton, *The Talkies*; Gomery, *The Coming of Sound*; and Lastra, *Sound Technology and American Cinema*.
35. Bordwell et al., *The Classical Hollywood Cinema*.
36. Gomery, *The Coming of Sound*.
37. J. S. O'Connell, "Advertising the Sound Picture," *Exhibitors Herald World*, July 14, 1928: 31.
38. Dan Roche, "Advertising the Sound Picture," *Exhibitors Herald World*, July 7, 1928: 34.
39. Ibid.
40. These ads appear in 1929 in *Photoplay Magazine*'s February, April, and June issues respectively.
41. These quotations are taken from Paramount ads printed in 1929 in *Photoplay Magazine*'s August and September issues respectively.
42. Wurtzler, *Electric Sounds*.
43. Advertisement for Warner Bros. studio, *The Film Daily 1930 Yearbook*, ed. Maurice D. Kann (New York: Film Daily, 1930), 297.
44. Vitaphone program for *Don Juan*, from B. S. Moss's Colony Theatre, Broadway and 53rd Street. Archived in the USCWB.
45. Warner, "Future Developments," 334.
46. Like *The Jazz Singer* and many other films of the period, *The Singing Fool* was released as both a silent film and a talkie. See Crafton, *The Talkies*, 111, for more on the *Jazz Singer*'s earnings.
47. The Martinelli film in question is Vitaphone catalogue no. 198 from 1926. The other films for which Warner eventually sought permission to use the opera include no. 436 with John Barclay, no. 481 with John Charles Thomas, no. 571 with the Arnaut Bros., no. 785 with Fred Ardath, and no. 791 with Jack White. Letter from E. H. Murphy to Mr. MacDonald, June 27, 1930, USCWB.
48. These troubles are outlined in legal files and correspondence on the Vitaphone short films in the USCWB.
49. Warner Bros. filed an application on July 29, 1929, for the license of seventy-nine entire or partial uses of other musical material, but *Pagliacci* is not among them. File on *The Singing Fool*, USCWB.
50. The story also misidentifies the composer of the opera as Puccini, a fact that was royally mocked when recounted in *Photoplay*, January 1928: 102.
51. Scholars, listeners, and Warner Bros. have used a corporeal analogy to make sense of phonography. Friedrich Kittler famously compares the phonograph to

the brain, an unthinking prosthesis that can preserve the real because it has no understanding of the symbolic; *Gramophone, Film, Typewriter*, trans. Geoffrey Winthrop-Young and Michael Wutz (Stanford: Stanford University Press, 1999). James Lastra outlines how phonography perfected the human experience of listening, while John Durham Peters shows how the phonograph preserves ghostly bodies, and Mark Sandberg talks about the proximity of phonographs and wax effigies that infused life into the ersatz corpses housed in Scandinavian museums. Lastra, *Sound Technology*; John Durham Peters, *Speaking into the Air: A History of the Idea of Communication* (Chicago: University of Chicago Press, 1999), Mark B. Sandberg, *Living Pictures, Missing Persons: Mannequins, Museums, and Modernity* (Princeton: Princeton University Press, 2003). As Mark Katz explains, phonography promised the ability to spread "good music" throughout the United States at an affordable price; *Capturing Sound: How Technology Has Changed Music* (Berkeley: University of California Press, 2004), 48–68. Steve Wurtzler further details the strategies of phonograph manufacturers to conjure up images of opera stars by proposing the machine as an appropriate substitute for Caruso; *Electric Sounds*, 126–32. Phonography was thus figured as a conduit for the legendary singer to enter the typical American home, simultaneously heralding cultural awareness and domesticating a technological monstrosity. When Warner Bros. alluded to the phonograph as a familiar technology on which to base the experience of the Vitaphone, then, it was not without baggage.

52. Wurtzler, *Electric Sounds*, 232.
53. Examples of this would be Victor's tone tests, which compared the recorded voices of stars to their physically present counterparts; Lyman Howe's traveling shows; and the existence of phonograph parlors as destinations of entertainment.
54. In Warner Bros. films such as *The First Auto* (1927), *Noah's Ark* (1928), and *The Singing Fool* (1928), sound is used in an illustrative fashion, but not always narratively. As Wurtzler notes, the employment of sound effects in these early Vitaphone features "performed the possibility of synchronization"; *Electric Sounds*, 246.
55. Ibid., 242.
56. This is not to say that all film exhibition is not in some sense a performance, however; the larger role played by projectionists in the screening of Vitaphone films is worth noting. Emily Thompson's forthcoming book *Sound Effects* will no doubt explore the intensity of projectionists' work, particularly when it comes to sound-on-disc technology.
57. Mae Tinee, "Vitaphone and John Take All the Honors," *Chicago Daily Tribune*, September 19, 1926.
58. Hays, *See and Hear*, 3–4.
59. Ibid., 7.
60. Michael Rogin, *Blackface, White Noise: Jewish Immigrants in the Hollywood Melting Pot* (Berkeley: University of California Press, 1996).
61. Ted Merwin, *In Their Own Image: New York Jews in the Jazz Age* (New Brunswick, NJ: Rutgers University Press, 2006).
62. Joel Dinerstein, "Introduction: Bodies and Machines," *Swinging the Machine: Modernity, Technology, and African American Culture Between the World Wars* (Amherst: University of Massachusetts Press, 2003), 3–28.
63. Krin Gabbard points to this fact in *Jammin' at the Margins*, 14–16, and there quotes Michael Rogin doing the same.
64. Sargeant, *Jazz: Hot and Hybrid*, 173.

65. Gabbard provides an informative debate about the difference between Jolson and Armstrong's rural references and the general association of jazz with the city in *Jammin' at the Margins*, 13–19.
66. Rogin, *Blackface, White Noise*, 147.
67. Curtiz, "The Clown" or "Pagliacci," 40.
68. Ibid., 26–27.
69. According to Evan Eisenberg, Enrico Caruso and Louis Armstrong mark the poles through which phonography traveled to become serious business; *The Recording Angel* (New York: Penguin, 1987), 147–48. Or as Jacob Smith puts it, between *bel canto* and the "rasp," phonography is born, *Vocal Tracks*, 115–62.
70. It seems evident that, even in Curtiz's story, Abie Rachman is written as a Jewish character. Certainly the importance of *The Jazz Singer* on the film's design and the casting of Al Jolson as the central character cannot be denied.
71. *The Singing Fool*, reduced score, cue 77, file on *The Singing Fool*, USCWB.
72. Gomery, *The Coming of Sound*, 95.
73. Concerning *Songs*, the paper complains that the "throatiness" of the Western Electric horns complicates the clarity of Jolson's lines. Review of "*Say It With Songs* with Al Jolson," *Harrison's Reports*, August 17, 1929: 130.
74. On the week of the August release of *Say It With Songs*, Exhibitors Herald-World published an article by L. A. Elmer of Bell Labs that attempted to offset some of these complaints by describing a change-over device designed to overcome the coordination problems often experienced with sound-on-disc projection. "The Problems in Rotating Discs for Recording," August 3, 1929, 46. Even *Photoplay* weighed in on the issue of competing sound systems: in late 1929 the magazine called the process of sound reproduction used by Warners "old fashioned" in comparison to the Fox Grandeur Movietone film. "The Film of the Future," *Photoplay Magazine*, December 1929: 58.
75. This possibility is suggested by Al Cohn in "How Talkies Are Made," *Photoplay Magazine*, April 1929: 28–31, 130.
76. Eric W. Rothenbuhler and John Durham Peters, "Defining Phonography: An Experiment in Theory," *Musical Quarterly*, vol. 81, no. 2 (1997): 245.
77. Dinerstein, *Swinging the Machine*.
78. Quoted in John A. Kouwenhoven, "What's 'American' About America?" In *The Jazz Cadence of American Culture*, ed. Robert G. O'Meally (New York: Columbia University Press, 1998), 127.
79. This advertisement was printed in *Photoplay Magazine*, February 1929.
80. This advertisement was printed in *Photoplay Magazine*, October 1929.
81. Wurtzler, *Electric Sounds*, 129.
82. This advertisement was printed in *Photoplay Magazine*, July 1929.
83. Mordaunt Hall, "Amazing Invention Coupling Sound with Screen Images Stirs Audiences," *New York Times*, August 15, 1926.
84. Ryan Jerving not only establishes a wonderful cultural history of the song, he also convincingly argues for its inclusion as "jazz"; "Jazz Language and Ethnic Novelty," *Modernism/modernity*, vol. 10, no. 2 (2003): 239–68.
85. Letter from W. C. Kyle, Jr., "Music Broadcast from Mouth of Jolson Cutout Is Good Idea," *Exhibitors Herald-World*, February 9, 1929: 48.
86. "Effective Exploitation for 'The Singing Fool'," *Film Daily*, October 14, 1928: 7.
87. Scott E. Brown, *James P. Johnson: A Case of Mistaken Identity* (Metuchen, NJ: Scarecrow Press and the Institute of Jazz Studies, 1986), 184–85.

88. For more on Johnson's life and music, see John Howland, *Ellington Uptown: Duke Ellington, James P. Johnson, and the Birth of Concert Jazz* (Ann Arbor: University of Michigan Press, 2009).

89. Dave Peyto, "The Musical Bunch," *Chicago Defender*, December 10, 1927: 6.

90. Howland, *Ellington Uptown*, 48.

91. Howland does an extensive analysis of the differences between the two versions. Aside from the voices, these mainly amount to cuts, and the relatively simple additions of a "classical" cadenza, a bridge for the train scene, and "honky-tonk riffs." John Howland, "Jazz Rhapsodies in Black and White: James P. Johnson's *Yamekraw*," *American Music* 24.4 (2006): 445–509.

92. Quoted in Howland, *Ellington Uptown*, 91.

93. S. M. Eisenstein, V. I. Pudovkin, and G. V. Alexandrov, "A Statement," in Sergei Eisenstein, *Film Form: Essays in Film Theory*, ed. and trans. Jay Leyda (San Diego: Harcourt, 1977), Appendix A, 257–60.

94. André Bazin, "Theater and Cinema," in *What is Cinema?* Vol. 1, trans. Hugh Gray (Berkeley: University of California Press, 1967), 88–89.

95. Bazin used this idea to describe the adaptations of Jean Cocteau; "Theater and Cinema," 90.

96. Review of *Yamekraw* in *Variety*, April 30, 1930: 17.

97. Howland, *Ellington Uptown*, 97.

98. One summary of the work states: "What emerges is a collage of short themes that seem to be lifted out of context and lose all sense of spontaneity. It's like seeing scenes from a movie in the form of 'previews of coming attractions'." Terry Waldo, *This Is Ragtime* (New York: Hawthorn Books, 1976), 117. Quoted in Brown, *James P. Johnson*, 187.

99. Howland has transcribed this brief aria (though heard the lyrics differently than I have), *Ellington Uptown*, 96.

100. As others, including Howland and Roy Liebman, have noted, Warners was sued over the rights to *Yamekraw*, most likely because it initially failed to include an on-screen credit for Johnson, though studio communication indicates that the lawsuit was over the similarities to the "Scenario and Lyrics of *Road to Yamekraw*" by Michael Hoffmann. File for *Yamekraw* short, USCWB.

101. Klaus Stratemann makes the comparison to the later film in *Duke Ellington: Day by Day and Film by Film* (Copenhagen: Jazz-Media, 1992), 123.

102. Indeed, Gerald Mast suggests that this approach is what made the American musical a success; *Can't Help Singin': The American Musical on Stage and Screen* (New York: Overlook, 1995), 29–30.

103. Hays, *Dawn of Sound*, 17.

CHAPTER 2

1. For a few examples, see "Anna Case Sings; Charms Throng," *Washington Post*, December 11, 1920; "Anna Case Applauded," *New York Times*, October 20, 1921; and "Musical Season Opens," *Washington Post*, October 22, 1921.

2. For examples of critics' responses to Case's performance of German music, see "Miss Anna Case's Recital," *New York Times*, October 12, 1916; and "Miss Anna Case Sings," *New York Times*, December 6, 1922.

3. Indeed, this was how a later cinematic opera star used "Old Folks at Home." Deanna Durbin's performance of the song at a Fourth of July party in *Nice Girl?* (1941) helped to overturn the legacy of her Canadian heritage and challenged the classical origins of her typical musical selections.

4. From the films included therein, the Index at my disposal, owned by Sol Dolgin at the Warner Bros. Pacific Coast Theatres, appears to have been initially issued in 1928. The missing opera shorts, Vitaphone nos. 296, 308, 432, and 542, all feature women (the last of these is Rosa Raisa's duet with Giacomo Rimini). Lewis' short, no. 432, may not have been completed (see William Shaman, "The Operatic Vitaphone Shorts," *ARSC Journal*, vol. 22, no. 1, Spring 1991: 74).

5. For studies of these respective questions, see Paul Fryer, *The Opera Singer and the Silent Film*; Daniel Goldmark, *Tunes for 'Toons: Music and the Hollywood Cartoon* (Berkeley: University of California Press, 2005); and Paul Heyer, "Live from the Met: Digital Broadcast Cinema, Media Theory, and Opera for the Masses," *Canadian Journal of Communication*, vol. 33 (2008): 591–604.

6. Compelling works that attempt such a grand theory include Stanley Cavell, "Opera in (and As) Film," *Cavell on Film*, ed. William Rothman (Albany: State University of New York Press, 2005); and Michal Grover-Friedlander, *Vocal Apparitions*.

7. Theodor Adorno, "The Radio Symphony: An Experiment in Theory," in *Radio Research*, ed. P. F. Lazarsfeld and F. N. Stanton (New York: Duell, Sloan and Pearce, 1941), 110–39.

8. Theodor Adorno, "On the Fetish-Character in Music and the Regression of Listening," in *The Essential Frankfurt School Reader*, ed. Andrew Arato and Eike Gebhardt (New York: Urizen Books, 1978), 270–99.

9. Rick Altman, "General Introduction: Cinema as Event," in *Sound Theory/Sound Practice*, ed. Rick Altman (New York and London: Routledge, 1992), 1–14.

10. This practice is explained in far greater detail in Rick Altman, "Nickelodeon Sound," and "The Campaign to Standardize Sound," in *Silent Film Sound* (New York: Columbia University Press, 2004), 119–288.

11. Lawrence Levine cites many examples of such substitution and addition, notably in the case of Rossini's *Barber of Seville* and other Italian works. He is also careful to state that this is not a situation limited to the United States, and in fact, that Rossini planned his works around these kinds of additions. *Highbrow/Lowbrow: The Emergence of Cultural Hierarchy in America* (Cambridge, MA: Harvard University Press, 1988), 93.

12. Ibid., 90–91.

13. Katherine K. Preston, *Opera on the Road: Traveling Opera Troupes in the United States, 1825–1960* (Urbana and Chicago: University of Illinois Press, 1993).

14. For more on Isham, see Errol Hill and James Vernon Hatch, *A History of African American Theatre*, vol. 18, *Cambridge Studies in American Theatre and Drama* (Cambridge: Cambridge University Press, 2003), 146–48.

15. Levine's term refers to the social, political, and economic means by which certain forms that were once enjoyed by a large portion of the U.S. population came to be understood as belonging to members of a certain class. "The Sacralization of Culture," in *Highbrow/Lowbrow*, 83–168.

16. John Dizikes, *Opera in America: A Cultural History* (New Haven and London: Yale University Press, 1993), 126–38.

17. There were some very vocal English language opera proponents in the nineteenth and early twentieth centuries. The Chautauqua Institution still translates all operas performed there into English. Historically, however, "translations" of operas were often rather less-than-literal. Levine understands such popularization to indicate that nineteenth-century Americans did not regard the operatic text as a completed work; rather, it was malleable for the particular performance situation. The first example Levine locates is the 1790s song "Away with

Melancholy," adapted from an aria from Mozart's *Magic Flute*, 96. One can find such mutations in American film and theater as well: Alexander Borodin's music forms the basis of Vincente Minnelli's *Kismet* (1955), from which is drawn the popular song "Stranger in Paradise," and there are many other examples to be found in the films produced by Joe Pasternak for MGM.

18. For a good overview of the history of the American orchestra, see Richard Crawford, *America's Musical Life: A History* (New York: Norton, 2001).

19. Levine, *Highbrow/Lowbrow*, 220.

20. Dizikes, *Opera in America*, 215–16.

21. Jacques Attali, *Noise: The Political Economy of Music*, trans. Brian Massumi (Minneapolis: University of Minnesota Press, 1985).

22. Levine, Highbrow/Lowbrow, 146.

23. Levine, "Order, Hierarchy, and Culture," in *Highbrow/Lowbrow*, 169–242. Representative work on this subject from the field of film studies includes Robert Sklar, *Movie Made America: A Cultural History of American Movies* (New York: Vintage, 1976); *American Movie Audiences: From the Turn of the Century to the Early Sound Era*, ed. Melvyn Stokes and Richard Maltby (London: BFI, 1999); and *American Cinema's Transitional Era*, ed. Charles Keil and Shelly Stamp (Berkeley: University of California Press, 2004).

24. Jonathan Crary, *Suspensions of Perception: Attention, Spectacle, and Modern Culture* (Cambridge: MIT Press, 1999), 248–54.

25. Rick Altman, "Film Sound: All of It," *Iris*, vol. 27 (Spring 1999): 36. Altman further connects the shift of attention from fellow members of the aristocracy to the stage with the elimination of the amateur and the rise of the virtuoso.

26. Levine, *Highbrow/Lowbrow*, 177–200. Levine comments that some conductors even tried to do away with applause altogether, wishing to create an atmosphere of reverence not unlike that found in a church.

27. Rick Altman notes that what accompanists actually produced was a simplistic version of Wagner's leitmotivic composition in which a theme, usually a known piece, was produced with variations, but rarely blended with others or used to the level of depth and development as happens in Wagnerian operas. *Silent Film Sound*, 372–79; and "Early Film Themes: Roxy, Adorno, and the Problem of Cultural Capital," in *Beyond the Soundtrack: Representing Music in Cinema*, ed. Daniel Goldmark, Lawrence Kramer, and Richard Leppert (Berkeley: University of California Press, 2007), 205–24.

28. There are four major sources in which to find a directory of opera shorts from this period. The first is the Vitaphone Release Index, a document produced for exhibitors that categorizes the films by genre. It is, however, incomplete, as some films were taken out of circulation, and therefore it cannot tell us exactly how many opera films the studio produced, but just how many were available in a given year. Roy Liebman's *Vitaphone Films: A Catalogue of the Features and Shorts* does not differentiate the films by genre but instead lists all features, shorts, and trailers by their assigned studio number (Jefferson, NC: McFarland, 2003). To determine the operatic status of a given short from this list, one must decide if the composer, star, or scene ought to qualify. Edwin M. Bradley's book on Hollywood sound shorts, on the other hand, divides the films by studio and identifies a category of "opera and operatic stars" for each production company. According to Bradley, Warner Bros. created fifty-one opera shorts during the 1926–1931 period; however, the author does not provide any criteria for including films in this group, other than to note that classification is a difficult process; *The First*

Hollywood Sound Shorts, 1926–1931 (Jefferson, NC: McFarland, 2005), 136. In his examination of the Vitaphone opera films, William Shaman identifies sixty-four such films; "The Operatic Vitaphone Shorts," *ARSC Journal*, vol. 22, no. 1 (Spring 1991): 35–94. My list does not just add one to his but combines the catalogues on the basis of my own definition.

29. Under the heading "Miscellaneous Vitaphone Shorts of Related Interest," Shaman also briefly mentions two films shot at the Warner Bros. Burbank studio and featuring Allan Prior and Joseph Diskay, respectively the "Famous Australian" and "Hungarian" tenor. I see no reason, on the basis of repertoire or vocal quality, not to include both in the count. Prior's short includes an aria from *Rigoletto* and Diskay sings Cadman's art song "At Dawning." There were other films that highlighted the ethnicity of the singers *without* including opera, however. For example, "Song of the Volga Boatman" featured four Russian singers, but the catalogue does not name them, and the Vitaphone Release Index calls their song "weird." Vitaphone Release no. 178.

30. In light of this fuzziness, we could create an alternate list that includes among the "opera shorts" those films that poke fun at the opera. These films respond to the Vitaphone's mission of bringing high culture to the masses by making it easier for audiences to enjoy the opera alongside more traditional vaudevillian fare. John Barclay, Willie and Eugene Howard (the husband and wife team "The Naggers"), and Coscia and Verdi all perform mock versions of famous arias or imitate renowned divas. Since Warner Bros. often had to go through the arduous process of gaining the rights to perform these operatic bits, in the eyes of the publisher "opera" was "opera," whether played straight or used for comedic effect. However, it is difficult to tell in which films such comedic treatments might appear, assess how much of the film is taken up with such shenanigans, or analyze the qualities of the voice. For this reason I have left them out of the total count.

31. Vitaphone Release no. 746.

32. *Metro Movietone Revue #4*, for example, has both Regan and Washington, along with the Ponce Sisters performing jazz, Miss Ella Shields dancing a hornpipe, and M. C. Jack Pepper playing the ukulele (MGM, 1930).

33. Bradley, *The First Hollywood Sound Shorts, 1926–1931*.

34. Martinelli's 1931 releases, for example, frame his face in a medium close-up during an aria's most exciting moments or cut away during orchestral interludes, returning not to the establishing shot but to detail parts of the set.

35. Paul Heyer attributes these patterns to televisual influence but acknowledges that the history of the music video may also play a role. Vitaphone opera shorts would arguably be included under this category "Live from the Met," 597.

36. These acts are listed in Bradley, *The First Hollywood Sound Shorts: 1926–1931*. Richard Koszarski notes that Shipa was the studio's sole classical musician, *Hollywood on the Hudson: Film and Television in New York from Griffith to Sarnoff* (New Brunswick, NJ: Rutgers University Press, 2008), 202.

37. Shaman, however, notes that the soundtracks for two of the Titta Ruffo films were released on LP in 1959. "Operatic Vitaphone Shorts," 49. Part of Shipa's 1929 "Una furtive lagrima" short appears to have been included in a documentary and is available online: http://www.youtube.com/watch?v=4LgQw_AYddg.

38. Koszarski notes that at least one of Paramount's "single act" films, a 1929 short starring Ruth Etting, was also filmed in a single shot. *Hollywood on the Hudson*, 202.

39. Charles Wolfe suggests that this transformation was a slow process that began as early as 1927. "On the Track of the Vitaphone Short," in *Dawn of Sound*, ed. Mary Bandy (New York: Museum of Modern Art, 1989), 39.

40. It should be noted that there are more appearances of operatic melodies than those in what I am calling "opera shorts." For example, Vitaphone no. 571, *The Arnaut Bros. "The Famous Loving Birds,"* is full of popular tunes and therefore not qualified to be found on my list, but it does contain sixteen bars of *Pagliacci*, a fact that caused Warners a great deal of legal trouble.

41. There may be a third recording of *Il Trovatore* by Rosa Raisa, though it is uncertain what she sang with Giacomo Rimini in Vitaphone no. 542, 1927. The two did indeed perform a duet from the opera in an earlier short, no. 524, released that same year.

42. William Shaman lays out the historical evidence for such a position by noting problems with the assignment of Vitaphone serial numbers (for example, why films premiering in the same month in 1927 should be assigned such wholly distinct identifiers, one less than 1000 and the other greater than 2100); "The Operatic Vitaphone Shorts," 43. However, this issue was addressed by Roy Liebman's 2003 catalogue dividing releases by production location, demonstrating that those films with serial numbers greater than 2100 were shot at Vitaphone's Burbank studio. At least nine of the shorts included on my list fall into this category, all released in late 1927 and early 1928 and likely shot when the Manhattan location was under construction.

43. Production records for Vitaphone shorts recovered at USWB, labeled "The Vitaphone Corporation: Eastern Production Studio" for release numbers 899–900 (September 9–10, 1929), 916 (October 7, 1929), 932 (October 4, 1929), 944 (November 29, 1929), 953 (December 16, 1929), and 974 (January 27, 1930).

44. Shaman does make space for this alternative on the basis of an acknowledgment of an artistic progression. "The Operatic Vitaphone Shorts," 43.

45. Alda filmed another short, no. 943, in November 1929 at the Brooklyn location; it featured a convent and nuns in costume.

46. These notes refer to Vitaphone Releases nos. 517, 509–10, and 552 respectively.

47. Letter from the Secretary of the Vitaphone Corporation to Mr. Ernest Henkel dated February 10, 1928, USCWB. The letter states Warners' intent to produce three Martinelli shorts by January 1929, six more by January 1930, and a final eight by May 1931.

48. Wolfe, "Vitaphone Shorts and *The Jazz Singer*," 60.

49. Laura Mulvey, "Visual Pleasure and Narrative Cinema," *Screen*, vol. 16, no. 3 (1975): 6–18.

50. See Kaja Silverman, "Lost Objects and Mistaken Subjects: A Prologue," in *The Acoustic Mirror: The Female Voice in Psychoanalysis and Cinema* (Bloomington: Indiana University Press, 1988), 1–41.

51. Listed in Bradley, *First Hollywood Sound Shorts*, 148.

52. Susan McClary, *Feminine Endings: Music, Gender, and Sexuality* (Minneapolis: University of Minnesota Press, 1991), 93.

53. As far as I am aware, this is the only Technicolor opera short produced during the period. Mezzo-soprano Alice Gentle sang the Habanera from *Carmen*; Vitaphone Release no. 3336, 1930.

54. W. J. Henderson, "*When a Man Loves* to Music," *New York Sun*, February 5, 1927, quoted in Richard Koszarski, "On the Record: Seeing and Hearing the Vitaphone,"

in *The Dawn of Sound*, ed. Mary Lea Bandy (New York: Museum of Modern Art, 1989), 18.

55. Quoted in Richard Barrios, *A Song in the Dark: The Birth of the Musical Film* (Oxford: Oxford University Press, 1995), 30.

56. Letter from George E. Quigley to Jack Warner dated June 5, 1928, file on Madam Ernestine Schumann-Heink, USCWB.

57. Schumann-Heink received $3,500 for a short that was over seven minutes in length, Martinelli was paid $5,000, and Hackett $2,500. Contract for Madam Ernestine Schumann-Heink dated September 28, 1926, USCWB. Martinelli's figures come from his earliest contract located in the files of the same archive, and Hackett's are found in Liebman's *Vitaphone Films*, 44–45.

58. Deanna Durbin became a cinematic opera star in her own right, though the MGM Schumann-Heink film that would feature her was never made.

59. Catherine Clément, *Opera: Or, The Undoing of Women* (Minneapolis: University of Minnesota Press, 1988).

60. Grover-Friedlander, *Vocal Apparitions*.

61. Clément, *Opera*, 26.

62. This is a reference to Linda Williams's discussion of the impossibility of representing the female orgasm in *Hard Core: Power, Pleasure, and the "Frenzy of the Visible"* (Berkeley: University of California Press, 1989); and it also references Wayne Koestenbaum's discussion of the throat as a vocal/sexual zone in *The Queen's Throat*.

63. This claim is, of course, based on the shorts available for viewing. Two of those I have not been able to see feature Reinald Werrenrath in a series of concert songs, experience with which indicates they are unlikely to be awarded much cutting. Anna Case's *Swanee River* is probably shot in a style not unlike that of her first film, since its production number indicates it was likely filmed at the same time, and Mary Lewis's number would logically follow similarly, seeing as it includes a number of additional players. Schumann-Heink's performances remain a mystery; although the setting is a concert stage, records indicate that she had both a pianist and a violinist for her accompaniment, which may have increased the shot rate.

64. Silverman makes this point with regard to the normative procedures of classical Hollywood cinema in *The Acoustic Mirror*.

65. Angus Heriot, *The Castrati in Opera* (New York: De Capo Press, 1975), 31.

66. Jennifer Jones, "Sounds Romantic: The Castrato and English Poetics Around 1800," *Opera and Romanticism*, Romantic Circles, Praxis Series, ed. Orrin N. C. Wang (University of Maryland): http://www.rc.umd.edu/praxis/opera/jones/jones.html, 9.

67. Charles Burney, *An Eighteenth-Century Musical Tour in France and Italy*, ed. Percy A. Scholes (London: Oxford University Press, 1950), 15. Quoted in Enid Rhodes Peschel and Richard E. Peschel, "Medicine and Music: The Castrati in Opera," *Opera Quarterly*, vol. 4, no. 4 (1986): 25.

68. An example of such remarks made about the "natural" abilities of women in comparison to those of the castrato can be found in Pietro Francesco Tosi's 1742 *Observations on the Florid Song* as quoted in Heriot, *The Castrati in Opera*, 30.

69. John Potter demonstrates how tenors received training from castrati throughout the eighteenth century, in "The tenor-castrato connection, 1760–1860," *Early Music*, vol. 35, no. 1 (2006): 100.

70. Naomi André, *Voicing Gender: Castrati, Travesti, and the Second Woman in Early-Nineteenth-Century Italian Opera* (Bloomington and Indianapolis: Indiana University Press, 2006), 89.

71. Jones, "Sounds Romantic," 12.

72. Susan J. Leonardi and Rebecca A. Pope, *The Diva's Mouth: Body, Voice, Prima Donna Politics* (New Brunswick, NJ: Rutgers University Press, 1996), 42.

73. See Leonardi and Pope, "Pieces and Breeches," in *The Diva's Mouth*, 24–47.

74. Kann's review from *Film Daily*, August 8, 1926, is quoted in Crafton, *The Talkies*, 77.

75. Mordaunt Hall, "Vitaphone Stirs as Talking Movie," *New York Times*, August 7, 1926.

76. Balzac's 1830 novella "Sarrassine" is reprinted in Roland Barthes, *S/Z: An Essay* (New York: Macmillan, 1975), 229–30.

77. Kann's review from *Film Daily*, August 8, 1926: 3 is quoted in Crafton, *The Talkies*, 77.

78. Mary Ann Smart, *Mimomania: Music and Gesture in Nineteenth-Century Opera* (Berkeley: University of California Press, 2004), 4–5.

79. Vitaphone Release no. 974.

80. Thomas Doherty, for example, describes the extreme class differences expressed by MGM and Warner Bros. during the Great Depression. It is difficult to find evidence of this distinction in opera films, however, perhaps because the genre is itself atypical of the production of either studio. *Pre-Code Hollywood: Sex, Immorality, and Insurrection in American Cinema 1930–1934* (New York: Columbia University Press, 1999), 53–58.

81. Feuer, *The Hollywood Musical*, 2nd ed. (Bloomington: Indiana University Press, 1993), 53.

82. Sobchack, *Address of the Eye*, 178.

83. Quote reprinted in Bradley, *The First Hollywood Sound Shorts, 1926–1931*, 213.

84. *Variety* comment reprinted in Bradley, *The First Hollywood Sound Shorts, 1926–1931*, 213.

85. Catherine Clément, "Through Voices, History," in *Siren Songs: Representations of Gender and Sexuality in Opera*, ed. Mary Ann Smart (Princeton and Oxford: Princeton University Press, 2000), 17–28.

86. Peter G. Davis describes how Giulio Gatti-Casazza would sell an American opera to the board of directors by noting that Tibbett would be able to appear in it. *The American Opera Singer: The Lives and Adventures of America's Great Singers in Opera & Concert from 1825 to the Present* (New York: Anchor, 1997), 313.

87. One should be quick to acknowledge that the analyses in both Mulvey's article and Bordwell, Thompson, and Staiger's book *Classical Hollywood Cinema* are based on feature films.

88. Vitaphone Release no. 552, 1927.

89. Richard Dyer, *Stars*, new ed. (London: BFI, 1998), 17.

90. Vitaphone Release no. 1174.

91. Vitaphone Release no. 1213.

CHAPTER 3

1. The film itself no longer exists, but the dialogue is available in the script collection at the Wisconsin Historical Society, Madison, Wisconsin (hereafter, WHS), Vitaphone 8.3 D, Box 7.

2. This reference from Adorno's "Oxforder Nachträge" was brought to my attention by James Buhler. It is discussed in Harry Cooper, "On Über Jazz': Replaying Adorno with the Grain," *October*, vol. 75 (Winter 1996): 107.

3. Ibid. "Tear into rags" is Cooper's translation of Adorno's use of the word *zerfetzen* in relation to his criticism of ragtime.
4. Theodor Adorno, "On Jazz," in *Essays on Music*, ed. Richard Leppert (Berkeley: University of California Press, 2002).
5. Eric Lott, *Love and Theft: Blackface Minstrelsy and the American Working Class* (New York: Oxford University Press, 1993), 151. The connection of castration, Adorno, and Lott has been noted by both James M. Harding and Richard Leppert.
6. Alice Maurice, "'Cinema at Its Source': Synchronizing Race and Sound in the Early Talkies," *Camera Obscura*, vol. 49 (2002): 31–71.
7. Paul Gilroy, *The Black Atlantic: Modernity and Double Consciousness* (London: Verso, 1993), 101.
8. Adorno, "On the Fetish-Character in Music," 277.
9. Nathaniel Mackey, *Bedouin Hornbook* (Lexington: University of Kentucky, 1986). Quoted and discussed in Brent Hayes Edwards, "Louis Armstrong and the Syntax of Scat," *Critical Inquiry*, vol. 28 (Spring 2002): 624–25.
10. Mackey, *Bedouin Hornbook*, 159–60.
11. Ibid., 160.
12. Ibid., 20.
13. Sobchack, *Address of the Eye*, 168.
14. The absorbance of the cinematic experience central to apparatus theory is one of the major strains of film theory that Vivian Sobchack is critiquing in her phenomenological approach. See, for example, *Address of the Eye*, 178–80.
15. Gabbard cites Michael Rogin, against whom he establishes his more inclusive definition in *Jammin' at the Margins*, 14–17.
16. Some of this work includes David Butler, *Jazz Noir: Listening to Music from Phantom Lady to The Last Seduction* (Westport: Praeger, 2002); Dinerstein, *Swinging the Machine* (2003); Krin Gabbard, *Jammin' at the Margins*, and the collection of essays in Gabbard's twin anthologies *Representing Jazz* (Durham: Duke University Press, 1995) and *Jazz Among the Discourses* (Durham: Duke University Press, 1995); and Peter Stanfield, *Body and Soul*.
17. Gilbert Seldes, "The Dæmonic in the American Theatre," *The American Stage: Writing on Theater from Washington Irving to Tony Kushner*, ed. Laurence Senelick (New York: Penguin, 2010), 335.
18. Henry Pleasants, *The Great American Popular Singers* (New York: Simon and Schuster, 1974), 51–52.
19. Ibid., 53. The critic was Patterson James, and the piece was written in December 1921.
20. Krin Gabbard, "Al Jolson: The Man Who Changed the Movies Forever," in *Idols of Modernity: Movie Stars of the 1920s*, ed. Patrice Petro (New Brunswick, NJ: Rutgers University Press, 2009), 202–26.
21. Seldes, "Dæmonic," 338.
22. See the Warner Bros. Pressbooks for *The Singing Fool* or *Say It with Songs* for stories that discuss Jolson's past and its similarities with the plot of *The Jazz Singer*, 1928 and 1929 respectively.
23. Pleasants, *Great American Popular Singers*, 57.
24. "Jolson and Mike in (Accord?) [word blotted out] in "Say It with Songs," Warner Bros. Pressbook for *Say It with Songs* (1929): 4. Henry Pleasants points out, however, that Jolson hated the microphone and was reluctant to appear on the air, where he could not interact with a crowd; *Great American Popular Singers*, 61.
25. James Buhler pointed out to me that even the jazziness of "Red Red Robin" is somewhat weak.

26. *Blossom Seeley and Bennie Fields, with the Music Boxes Chas. Bourne and Phil Ellis*, Vitaphone Release no. 548, 1928.

27. The chandelier is particularly prominent in *Gus Arnheim and His Ambassadors*, Vitaphone Release no. 2585, 1928; and *Paul Tremaine and His Aristocrats*, Vitaphone Release no. 742, 1929.

28. Lynne Kirby, *Parallel Tracks: The Railroad and Silent Cinema* (Durham: Duke University Press, 1997).

29. Ibid., chapter 4, "National Identity in the Train Film," 189–240.

30. *Grove Music Online*, s.v. "Banjo" (by Jay Scott Odell and Robert B. Winans), http://www.oxfordmusiconline.com/public/ (accessed November 12, 2008).

31. Interestingly, the banjoist returns to illustrate this point in grand fashion in a post-conversion 1936 Warner Bros. jazz short titled *Harry Reser and His Eskimos*. One such "Eskimo," dressed in furs and boots, plays his banjo atop an enormous beer bottle housed in an ice cave. Not only does the film literally freeze jazz, it does so about as far north of New Orleans as it is possible for humans to travel, while the bottle is so unwieldy as to prove no temptation to intoxication.

32. Reisman's orchestra was the house dance band of the Hotel Brunswick in Boston and the Waldorf Astoria in New York. William A. Studwell and Mark Baldin, *The Big Band Reader: Songs Favored by Swing Era Orchestras and Other Popular Ensembles* (Binghamton: Haworth Press, 2000), 199.

33. The African American as shadow was a common association that was made literal in Ted Lewis's song "Me and My Shadow" in *Here Comes the Band* (1935), in a scene where a black actor mimics the white musician's actions. The song was staged similarly with Frank Sinatra and Sammy Davis, Jr., much later, on *The Frank Sinatra Show*, season 1, episode 16, 1958, though they reversed the roles as part of the number.

34. Paul Young, *The Cinema Dreams Its Rivals: Media Fantasy Films from Radio to the Internet* (Minneapolis: University of Minnesota Press, 2006), 87.

35. Pamela Robertson Wojcik, "The Girl and the Phonograph; or the Vamp and the Machine Revisited," in *Soundtrack Available: Essays on Film and Popular Music*, ed. Pamela Robertson Wojcik and Arthur Knight (Durham: Duke University Press, 2001), 433–54.

36. Michael Rogin describes how sound cinema may have ended the application of blackface for actors in dramatic works, but it also restored interest in the comedic use of burnt cork. *Blackface, White Noise*, 166–67.

37. Corin Willis, "Blackface Minstrelsy and Jazz Signification in Hollywood's Early Sound Era," in *Thriving on a Riff: Jazz and Blues Influences in African American Literature and Film*, ed. Graham Lock and David Murray (New York: Oxford University Press, 2009), 40–64.

38. From an interview with Richard Hadlock, quoted in Joshua Berrett, "Louis Armstrong and Opera," *Musical Quarterly* 76.2 (1992): 236.

39. Richard Koszarski points out that Paramount was focused on comedic short films and did not really invest in black-cast musical shorts until 1932, *Hollywood on the Hudson*, 205. George Dewey Washington's *Ol' King Cotton* (1930) is a notable exception.

40. Donald Bogle, *Toms, Coons, Mulattoes, Mammies, and Bucks: An Interpretive History of Blacks in American Film* (New York: Continuum, 1992), 8.

41. Krin Gabbard, "Signifyin(g) the Phallus: *Mo' Better Blues* and Representations of the Jazz Trumpet," in *Representing Jazz*, 104–30.

42. The term is elaborated much more eloquently to form the foundation of Gates's literary criticism. Henry Louis Gates, Jr., *The Signifying Monkey: A Theory of Afro-American Literary Criticism* (New York and Oxford: Oxford University Press, 1988).

43. Ibid., 58.

44. Gabbard, "Signifyin(g) the Phallus."

45. Edwards, "Louis Armstrong and the Syntax of Scat," 618–20.

46. For more on the relationship between conversion-era sound films and vaudevillian aesthetics, particularly with regard to a Paramount short film, see Michael Slowik, "'The Plasterers' and Early Sound Cinema Aesthetics," *Music, Sound, and the Moving Image*, vol. 4, no. 1 (July 2010): 55–75. Also useful is Henry Jenkins, *What Made Pistachio Nuts? Early Sound Comedy and the Vaudeville Aesthetic* (New York: Columbia University Press, 1992).

47. Critics such as Joseph McBride discuss the possibility of Fetchit Signifyin(g) on the stereotype of the lazy black male by using his performance to expose the ridiculousness of white impressions of blackness. "Stepin Fetchit Talks Back," *Film Quarterly*, vol. 24, no. 4 (Summer, 1971): 20–26.

48. McCracken, "Real Men Don't Sing Ballads," 112–18.

49. Young, *The Cinema Dreams its Rivals*, 143.

50. Ibid., 144.

51. This comment is of course in reference to Adorno's essays "On the Fetish-Character in Music" and "The Radio Symphony: An Experiment in Theory," *Radio Research*, ed. P. F. Lazarsfeld and F. N. Stanton (New York: Duell, Sloan and Pearce, 1941), 110–39.

52. Full-page advertisement for five MGM features, *Photoplay*, July 1929, 135.

53. "M-G-M Signs Big Array of Movietone Talent—30 B'way Stars on Roster," *Film Daily*, September 8, 1928: 1.

54. MGM published its shorts release schedule in a full-page ad for the Joan Crawford vehicle *Our Dancing Daughters*, in *Film Daily*, September 26, 1928: 3.

55. "Twenty-Six One-Reelers, All with Sound, Are Announced for Release Immediately," ad insert in *Film Daily*, September 29, 1928: 5.

56. These numbers are according to Bradley, *The First Hollywood Sound Shorts: 1926–1931*, 209–11.

57. Stanfield, *Body and Soul*, 5–6.

58. Robert C. Allen, *Horrible Prettiness: Burlesque and American Culture* (Chapel Hill: University of North Carolina Press, 1991), 78.

59. Ibid., 102–7. Allen distinguishes between this variety and a more theatrical mode that did not necessarily have to include the presentation of women's bodies.

60. Ibid., 124.

61. Siegfried Kracauer, *The Mass Ornament: Weimar Essays*, trans. Thomas Y. Levin (Cambridge, MA: Harvard University Press, 1995), 75–79.

62. The dialogue from *Operator's Opera* is found in the script collection at WHS, Vitaphone 8.3 D, Box 6.

CHAPTER 4

1. These adjectives are references to the titles of Laurence E. MacDonald's *The Invisible Art of Film Music: A Comprehensive History* (New York: Ardsley House, 1998) and Claudia Gorbman's *Unheard Melodies: Narrative Film Music* (Bloomington: Indiana University Press, 1987). Although many of these publications can be found in my bibliography, examples of the historical and interview work in the 1990s

is located in the MacDonald text, as well as in Royal S. Brown, *Overtones and Undertones: Reading Film Music* (Berkeley: University of California Press, 1994), and Kathryn Kalinak, *Settling the Score: Music and the Classical Hollywood Film*.

2. In 1929, the trade journal *Harrison's Reports* was one such source for the concern with the differences in musical quality.
3. Spadoni, *Uncanny Bodies*.
4. Examples of such organizations and publications that existed in the 1920s are the American Relay Radio League, *Phonograph Monthly Review, Popular Mechanics, Radio Broadcast,* the Radio Club of America, *Radio Digest,* and *Wireless Age.* There were, of course, many more.
5. Rick Altman describes the compromises that led to the standardization of Hollywood sound in "Sound Space," *Sound Theory/Sound Practice,* 46–64.
6. Charles O'Brien details the major differences between American and French soundtracks in *Cinema's Conversion to Sound.*
7. Katherine Spring, "Pop Go the Warner Bros., et al.: Marketing Film Songs during the Coming of Sound," *Cinema Journal,* vol. 48, no. 1 (Fall 2008): 72.
8. For more on the use of songs in Warners cartoons, see Scott Curtis, "The Sound of Early Warner Bros. Cartoons," *Sound Theory/Sound Practice,* 191–203.
9. Ulf Lindberg, "Popular Modernism? The 'urban' style of interwar Tin Pan Alley," *Popular Music,* vol. 22, no. 3 (2003): 285.
10. See Daniel Goldmark, "Creating Desire on Tin Pan Alley," *Music Quarterly,* vol. 90, no. 2 (2007): 197–229. Goldmark references the work of Larry Hamberlin on this topic, particularly Hamberlin's dissertation from Brandeis in 2004.
11. Reebee Garofalo, "From Music Publishing to MP3: Music and Industry in the Twentieth Century," *American Music,* vol. 17, no. 3 (Fall 1999): 322.
12. Arthur Jones, as told to Louise Howard and Jeron Criswell, *How to Crash Tin-Pan Alley: The Authoritative Handbook for a Successful Song Writing Career* (New York: Howard and Criswell, 1939), 18.
13. Philip Furia, *The Poets of Tin Pan Alley: A History of America's Great Lyricists* (New York: Oxford University Press, 1990). Referenced in Ulf Lindberg, "Popular Modernism?" 287.
14. Mark Garrett Cooper, *Love Rules: Silent Hollywood and the Rise of the Managerial Class* (Minneapolis: University of Minnesota Press, 2003).
15. Garofalo, "From Music Publishing to MP3," 323.
16. Spring, "Pop Go the Warner Bros," 68, 82.
17. Scott D. Paulin, "Richard Wagner," 59.
18. In a private communication, James Buhler called my attention to the fact that Wagner's leitmotifs were primarily instrumental and pointed me in the direction of Paulin's essay, August 2011.
19. Paulin, "Richard Wagner," 68–69.
20. For more on New Deal musical productions, see Kenneth J. Bindas, *All This Music Belongs to the Nation: The WPA's Federal Music Project and American Society* (Knoxville: University of Tennessee Press, 1996).
21. Bordwell, Thompson, and Staiger, *The Classical Hollywood Cinema,* 3.
22. Gorbman, *Unheard Melodies,* 70.
23. Caryl Flinn, *Strains of Utopia: Gender, Nostalgia, and Hollywood Film Music* (Princeton: Princeton University Press, 1992), 14.
24. Flinn, *Strains of Utopia,* 32–34.
25. Ibid., "The New Romanticism," in *Strains of Utopia,* 13–50.
26. Gorbman, *Unheard Melodies,* 15.

27. Theodor Adorno and Hanns Eisler, *Composing for the Films* (Oxford: Oxford University Press, 1947), 32.
28. Gorbman, Flinn, and Kalinak all present accounts of Adorno and Eisler's arguments in the publications cited above.
29. Adorno and Eisler, *Composing for the Films*, 136.
30. Ibid., 137.
31. Scott Paulin brings up Adorno and Eisler's attention to heterogeneity, claiming that the two wanted film music to announce its disunity and acknowledge the falseness of the image's supposed continuity; "Richard Wagner," 73.
32. Flinn, *Strains of Utopia*, 39.
33. Adorno and Eisler, *Composing for the Films*, 5–6.
34. Flinn, *Strains of Utopia*, 13–50.
35. Many film musicologists proceed from its institutional and stylistic Classicism to identify a flawed, but fundamental, Romanticism at the core of the Hollywood score. For example, Annette Davidson shows how discussions of the standardization of the means of production are connected to claims about the normative functions of film music most frequently located in Romantic practices; in her *Hollywood Theory, Non-Hollywood Practice: Cinema Soundtracks in the 1980s and 1990s* (Aldershot, England: Ashgate, 2004). On the other hand, by *ignoring* the historical specificity of "classical" music, Royal S. Brown gives perhaps the most persuasive account of its cinematic effects. Instead of connecting the Classical or Romantic periods to Hollywood film style, Brown considers the current connotations of these terms, associating classical music with a highbrow orchestral performance considered complex in relation to its popular contemporaries. Yet even Brown's revision could lend itself to a Romantic infatuation with the composer. Those who appreciate the highbrow artifact pride themselves on recognizing its author. See Brown, *Overtones and Undertones*.
36. Gorbman, *Unheard Melodies*, 73.
37. Although this is a persistent problem, two strong examples include Kent Jones's statement that Jean-Luc Godard's *Breathless* (1960) "feels like a free-jazz improvisation" and Michel Chion's likening of John Ford's *The Informer* (1935) to a "spoken opera." The first reference is found in an essay, "*Hiroshima Mon Amour:* Time Indefinite," written by Jones for the 2003 Criterion DVD release of *Hiroshima Mon Amour* (1959), http://www.criterion.com/current/posts/291, while the second is located in *Audio-Vision: Sound on Screen* (New York: Columbia University Press, 1994), 52.
38. One example of this narrative can be found in Kalinak's *Settling the Score*, which traces the changes from silent accompaniments to sound scores through the limits of technology. After it had overcome the constraints of single-track recording, Hollywood used Max Steiner to institute the standard procedures of composition, which closely resembled the habits of the silents; 66–78. Daniel Goldmark's chapter in *Tunes for 'Toons* on Carl Stalling draws a similar parallel between silent accompaniment and cartoon music. Michael Slowik's book *After the Silents: Hollywood Film Music in the Early Sound Era, 1926–1934* (forthcoming, New York: Columbia University Press, 2014), will analyze the scores of films released prior to *King Kong* to draw attention to the new uses of sound in Hollywood films of the early 1930s.
39. Gorbman, *Unheard Melodies*, 33–36.
40. Altman, *Silent Film Sound*; see in particular chapters 11 and 13.
41. Steiner's work habits on *The Informer* are described by Kalinak in *Settling the Score*, 114–15.

42. Two such texts are Kalinak's *Settling the Score* and Chion's *Audio-Vision*, 49–54.
43. This list was found in a file on scores from Warner Bros. and First National Pictures at USCWB.
44. This cue sheet also comes from a file on scores from Warner Bros. and First National Pictures at USCWB.
45. The list for this score can be found in a file on scores from Warner Bros. and First National Pictures at USCWB.
46. Chion, *The Voice in Cinema*, 3.
47. These films form types that are then analyzed as such in Chion's *The Voice in Cinema*.
48. Ben Winters, "The Non-Diegetic Fallacy: Film, Music, and Narrative Space," *Music and Letters*, vol. 91, no. 2 (2010): 224–44.
49. Daniel Dayan, "The Tutor-Code of Classical Cinema," *Film Quarterly*, vol. 28, no. 1 (1974): 27.
50. Gorbman, *Unheard Melodies*, 40.
51. I am talking, of course, about a phenomenology of film. See Sobchack, *The Address of the Eye*.
52. Ibid., 186.
53. Dayan, "Tutor-Code," 30.
54. William Rothman, "Against 'The System of Suture,'" *Film Quarterly*, vol. 29, no. 1 (1975), 45–50. Reprinted in *Film Theory and Criticism*, 7th ed., ed. Leo Braudy and Marshall Cohen (New York and Oxford: Oxford University Press, 2009), 118–24.
55. Dayan, "Tutor-Code," 31.
56. Francesco Casetti, *Inside the Gaze: The Fiction Film and Its Spectator*, trans. Nell Andrew with Charles O'Brien (Bloomington: Indiana University Press, 1998), 49.
57. See Sobchack, *Address of the Eye*, 191–203.
58. For an account of all these lyrical examples, see Altman, *Silent Film Sound*.
59. I would argue that it is not the strangeness of nondiegetic music but the existence of its potential for revelation that makes the band in the middle of the desert funny in Mel Brooks's *Blazing Saddles* (1974).
60. Sergei Eisenstein, "From Lectures on Music and Colour in *Ivan the Terrible* (1947)," in *The Eisenstein Reader*, ed. Richard Taylor, trans. Richard Taylor and William Powell (London: BFI, 1998), 171–72.
61. Kalinak describes Raksin's method in "'Not Exactly Classical, But Sweet:' *Laura*: New Directions," in *Settling the Score*, 159–83.
62. These are characteristics mentioned by Rick Altman in "Musical Practices," in *Silent Film Sound*, 367–92.
63. With reference to Max Steiner, this is the title of Kalinak's fifth chapter, in *Settling the Score*, 113–34.
64. Altman, *Silent Film Sound*, 375.
65. Interestingly, this is the impression of Don José given by Bess Meredyth's film treatment. Meredyth describes José as a "stern, hawk-faced man" who inspires "fear and uneasiness in his wife." As he arranges to catch his wife in the act, Meredyth describes him as "brooding, in his eyes a strange mixture of suffering and hatred." "Don Juan," story by Bess Meredyth, file on *Don Juan*, USCWB.
66. Casetti, "The Place of the Spectator," in *Inside the Gaze*, 45–83.
67. The possibility for reading the gaze not merely as the experience of being "*looked at* from all sides" (emphasis mine) but also as being heard in three dimensions is available in the original Lacan, *The Four Fundamental Concepts of Psychoanalysis*,

The Seminar of Jacques Lacan, Book XI, ed. Jacques-Alain Miller, trans. Alan Sheridan (New York: Norton, 1981), 72.

68. Indeed, Robert Spadoni would say that most conversion-era sound films belong to this category thanks to their production of "medium-sensitive viewers"; *Uncanny Bodies*.

69. Casetti, *Inside the Gaze*, 63. These four positions are outlined in a section titled "The Geography of the Spectator."

70. Ibid., 19.

71. Indeed, these melodies, like those discussed by Altman, are largely drawn from other sources. The 375-page score was "arranged" by William Axt, Major Edward Bowes, and David Mendoza, who were paid a total of $3,500 for their labors. It included pieces by Axt, Mouton, Lalo, and Fosse, among others. File on *Don Juan*, USCWB.

72. Silverman points out that the spaces closed off by the text are not entirely consistent with those in which we see the characters. Over-the-shoulder shots tend to dominate the shot/reverse shot structure, giving us a glimpse at each character even as we are asking to occupy their space, *The Subject of Semiotics* (New York: Oxford University Press, 1983), 202.

73. Sobchack, *Address of the Eye*, 178.

74. See in particular the section titled "Opera vs. Jazz: The Theme of Popular vs. Elite Art" in Jane Feuer's *The Hollywood Musical*, 2nd ed. (Bloomington: Indiana University Press, 1993), 54–57.

75. Chion, *Audio-Vision*, 91.

76. Lacan tells the story of the sardine can in *The Four Fundamental Concepts of Psychoanalysis*.

77. Simon Frith, *Performing Rites: On the Value of Popular Music* (Cambridge: Harvard University Press, 1998), 158–67. Frith gives the example of Ronald Reagan's attempt to usurp Bruce Springsteen's "Born in the USA" for his 1984 presidential campaign.

78. I am grateful to Corey Creekmur for this insight. When we were discussing *American Idol* in 2007, Creekmur noted that the hopefuls often perform a particular singer's version of a song rather than imaging the song as available for reinterpretation. The existence of jazz "standards" demonstrates that jazz often operates differently.

79. As I explained in Chapter 3, this recognition is culturally determined. "Jazziness" to a 1920s ear may be different from "jazziness" today.

80. Michael Rogin notoriously claims that the film has no jazz, but Krin Gabbard shows how the identification of "jazzy" characteristics in the era's music extended to Jolson's performances and fell under the heading of "jazz" to the contemporary ear. The argument between the two scholars is presented in Gabbard, *Jammin' at the Margins*, 14–15.

81. Rogin provides the most detailed articulation of this claim in *Blackface, White Noise*, 73–120.

82. This is an extraordinarily popular rumor that circulates about the film. One example of this claim can be found in Betty Richardson, "Al Jolson," in *The Guide to U.S. Popular Culture*, ed. Ray B. Browne and Pat Browne (New York: Popular Press, 2001), 444–45.

83. Robert Sherwood, "The Jazz Singer," *Life*, October 27, 1927: 24. Quoted in Rogin, *Blackface, White Noise*, 83.

84. Ariane Todes, "Charlie Chaplin," *Strad*, vol. 119, no. 1424 (December, 2008), 22–28.

85. David Raksin, "'Music Composed by Charles Chaplin': Auteur or Collaborateur?" *Journal of the University Film Association*, vol. 31, no. 1 (Winter 1979): 47–50.

86. Ibid., 50.

87. Ira S. Jaffe, "'Fighting Words:' *City Lights, Modern Times*, and *The Great Dictator*," *Journal of the University Film Association*, vol. 31, no. 1 (Winter 1979): 23–32.

88. See Nathaniel Mackey's *Bedouin Hornbook* for an elaboration of this concept.

89. Raymond Knapp, *The American Musical and the Formation of National Identity* (Princeton: Princeton University Press, 2005), 119–20.

90. Ibid., 190.

91. Ibid.

CONCLUSION

1. In addition to prominent examples such as *Operator's Opera* (1933), the 1930s welcomed a number of Warner Bros. shorts explicitly devoted to swing music. Among them were *Hotel a la Swing* (dir. Roy Mack, 1937), *Prisoner of Swing* (dir. Roy Mack, 1939), *Public Jitterbug #1* (dir. Joseph Henabery, 1939), *Sophomore Swing* (dir. Roy Mack, 1938), *Swing for Sale* (dir. Joseph Henabery, 1936), and *Swing Styles* (dir. Lloyd French, 1939).

2. *A Swing Opera* (dir. Roy Mack, 1939) is one such example. The story is lifted virtually intact from Michael Balfe's 1843 opera *Bohemian Girl*, which details a love affair between Thaddeus, an exiled Polish aristocrat, and Arline, an Austrian noblewoman stolen in her youth and raised by a band of gypsies. The film maintains the general structure of the operatic work, but it inserts jazzy melodies and humorous references to swing music throughout, thus corresponding to my identification of opera and jazz as the large and small forms of the score respectively. The adaptation transforms *Bohemian Girl* into a comedy in part by intensifying the ethnic, racial, and class-based tensions of the original work. Arline, an heiress disguised as a "bohemian girl," is played by Tess Gardella, an actress also known as "Aunt Jemima," a notorious blackface performer. The jazz records popular in the gypsy camp are contrasted to the classical music of the Austrian nobility, heightening the difference between the ethnic origins of the lovers and that of the gypsies. The script for this film is located at the WHS, "A Swing Opera," 8.3 Vitaphone D, Box 8.

BIBLIOGRAPHY

Articles originally printed in newspapers and magazines such as the *New York Times,* *Time,* and *Photoplay* appear only in the endnotes.

ARCHIVAL SOURCES
Motion Picture, Broadcasting, and Recorded Sound Division, Library of Congress, Washington, D.C.
USC Warner Bros. Archives, School of Cinema-Television, University of Southern California, Los Angeles (abbreviated to USCWB).
UCLA Film and Television Archive, Los Angeles.
Wisconsin Center for Film and Theater Research, Wisconsin Historical Society, Madison (abbreviated to WHS).

BOOKS AND ARTICLES
Abbate, Carolyn. *Unsung Voices: Opera and Musical Narrative in the Nineteenth Century.* Princeton: Princeton University Press, 1991.

Abel, Sam. *Opera in the Flesh: Sexuality in Operatic Performance.* Boulder: Westview Press, 1996.

Adams, John. "Giovanni Martinelli and the Joy of Singing, 1885–1969." In *Atti Del II Congresso internazionale di studi verdiani,* 593–99. Parma, Istituto di studi verdiani, 1971.

Adorno, Theodor. *"The Curves of the Needle."* Translated by Thomas Y. Levin. *October* 55 (Winter 1990): 48–55.

Adorno, Theodor. *"The Form of the Phonograph."* Translated by Thomas Y. Levin. *October* 55 (Winter 1990): 56–61.

Adorno, Theodor. *In Search of Wagner.* Translated by Rodney Livingstone. London: NLB, 1981.

Adorno, Theodor. "On the Fetish-Character in Music and the Regression of Listening." In *The Essential Frankfurt School Reader,* edited by Andrew Arato and Eike Gebhardt, 270–99. New York: Urizen Books, 1978.

Adorno, Theodor. "On Jazz." In *Essays on Music,* edited by Richard Leppert, 470–95. Berkeley: University of California Press, 2002

Adorno, Theodor. "Perennial Fashion—Jazz." In *Prisms.* Translated by Samuel and Shierry Weber. Cambridge: MIT Press, 1994.

Adorno, Theodor. "The Radio Symphony: An Experiment in Theory." In *Radio Research,* edited by P. F. Lazarsfeld and F. N. Stanton, 110–39. New York: Duell, Sloan and Pearce, 1941.

Adorno, Theodor, and Hanns Eisler. *Composing for the Films.* Oxford: Oxford University Press, 1947.

Adorno, Theodor, and Max Horkheimer. *Dialectic of Enlightenment.* Translated by John Cumming. New York: Seabury Press, 1972.

Alexander, Michael. *Jazz Age Jews.* Princeton: Princeton University Press, 2001.

Allen, Robert C. *Horrible Prettiness: Burlesque and American Culture.* Chapel Hill: University of North Carolina Press, 1991.

Altman, Rick. *The American Film Musical.* Bloomington: Indiana University Press, 1987.

Altman, Rick. "Cinema and Popular Song: The Lost Tradition." In *Soundtrack Available: Essays on Film and Popular Music,* edited by Pamela Robertson Wojcik and Arthur Knight, 19–30. Durham: Duke University Press, 2001.

Altman, Rick. "Deep Focus Sound: *Citizen Kane* and the Radio Aesthetic." *Quarterly Review of Film and Video* 15, no. 3 (1994): 1–33.

Altman, Rick. "Early Film Themes: Roxy, Adorno, and the Problem of Cultural Capital." In *Beyond the Soundtrack: Representing Music in Cinema,* edited by Daniel Goldmark, Lawrence Kramer, and Richard Leppert, 205–24. Berkeley: University of California Press, 2007.

Altman, Rick. *Film/Genre.* London: BFI, 1999.

Altman, Rick. "Film Sound: All of It." *Iris* 27 (Spring 1999): 31–48.

Altman, Rick. "Moving Lips: Cinema as Ventriloquism." *Yale French Studies* 60, no. 1 (1980): 67–79.

Altman, Rick. *Silent Film Sound.* New York: Columbia University Press, 2004.

Altman, Rick. "Sound Space." In *Sound Theory/Sound Practice,* edited by Rick Altman, 46–64. New York: Routledge, 1992.

Altman, Rick, ed. *Sound Theory/Sound Practice.* New York: Routledge, 1992.

Altman, Rick. "The Technology of the Voice" (Part I). *Iris* 3, no.1 (1985): 3–20.

André, Naomi. *Voicing Gender: Castrati, Travesti, and the Second Woman in Early-Nineteenth-Century Italian Opera.* Bloomington: Indiana University Press, 2006.

Attali, Jacques. *Noise: The Political Economy of Music.* Translated by Brian Massumi. Minneapolis: University of Minnesota Press, 1985.

August, Gary Joel. "In Defense of Canned Music." *Musical Quarterly* 17, no. 1 (January 1931): 142.

Ayres, Harry Morgan, and W. Cabell Greet. "American Speech Records at Columbia University." *American Speech* 5, no. 5 (June 1930): 333–58.

Balázs, Béla. *Theory of the Film: Character and Growth of a New Art.* New York: Arno, 1972.

Balio, Tino. *Grand Design: Hollywood as a Modern Business Enterprise, 1930–1939.* Vol. 5, *History of the American Cinema.* Berkeley: University of California Press, 1993.

Bandy, Mary Lea, ed. *The Dawn of Sound.* New York: Museum of Modern Art, 1989.

Barlow, William. *Voice Over: The Making of Black Radio.* Philadelphia: Temple University Press, 1999.

Barrios, Richard. *A Song in the Dark: The Birth of the Musical Film.* Oxford: Oxford University Press, 1995.

Barthes, Roland. "Diderot, Brecht, Eisenstein." In *Image, Music, Text,* edited and translated by Stephen Heath, 69–78. New York: Hill and Wang, 1977.

Barthes, Roland. "The Grain of the Voice." In *Image, Music, Text,* 179–89.

Barthes, Roland. "Musica Practica." In *Image, Music, Text,* 149–54.

Barthes, Roland. *S/Z: An Essay.* Translated by Richard Miller. New York: Hill and Wang, 1974.

Barthes, Roland. "The Third Meaning." In *Image, Music, Text,* 52–68.

Baudry, Jean-Louis. "The Apparatus: Metaphychological Approaches to the Impression of Reality in the Cinema." *Communications* 23 (1975): 206–23.

Baudry, Jean-Louis. "Ideological Effects of the Basic Cinematographic Apparatus." *Cinéthique* 7–8 (1970): 1–8.

Bazin, André. *What Is Cinema?* vol 1. Translated by Hugh Gray. Berkeley: University of California Press, 1967.

Belton, John. *Widescreen Cinema*. Cambridge, MA: Harvard University Press, 1992.

Benjamin, Walter. "Unpacking My Library." In *Walter Benjamin: Selected Writings, 1931–1934*. Vol. 2, part 2, edited by Michael W. Jennings, Howard Eiland, and Gary Smith, 486–93. Cambridge, MA, and London: Belknap Press, 1999.

Benjamin, Walter. "Work of Art in the Age of Mechanical Reproduction." In *Illuminations*, edited by Hannah Arendt and translated by Harry Zohn, 217–52. New York: Schocken, 1969.

Bergstrom, Janet. "Murnau, Movietone and Mussolini." *Film History* 17 (2005): 187–204.

Berrett, Joshua. "Louis Armstrong and Opera." *Musical Quarterly* 76, no. 2 (1992): 216–41.

Bindas, Kenneth J. *All This Music Belongs to the Nation: The WPA's Federal Music Project and American Society*. Knoxville: University of Tennessee Press, 1996.

Blum, Daniel. *A Pictorial Treasury of Opera in America*. New York: Greenberg, 1954.

Bogle, Donald. *Toms, Coons, Mulattoes, Mammies, and Bucks: An Interpretive History of Blacks in American Film*. New York: Continuum, 1992.

Bonitzer, Pascal. "The Silences of the Voice." In *Narrative, Apparatus, Ideology*, edited by Philip Rosen, 319–34. New York: Columbia University Press, 1986.

Bordman, Gerald Martin. *American Musical Theater: A Chronicle, 3rd ed.* Oxford: Oxford University Press, 2001.

Bordwell, David, Janet Staiger, and Kristin Thompson. *The Classical Hollywood Cinema: Film Style and Mode of Production to 1960*. New York: Columbia University Press, 1985.

Borges, Jorge Luis. Review of *Street Scene*. *Sur* 5 (Summer 1932). Translated by Gloria Waldman, and Ronald Christ and reprinted in *October* 15 (Winter 1980): 6–7.

Bradley, Edwin M. *The First Hollywood Sound Shorts, 1926–1931*. Jefferson, NC: McFarland, 2005.

Brooks, Tim. *Lost Sounds: Blacks and the Birth of the Recording Industry, 1890–1919*. Urbana: University of Illinois Press, 2004.

Brown, Royal S. *Overtones and Undertones: Reading Film Music*. Berkeley: University of California Press, 1994.

Brown, Scott E. *James P. Johnson: A Case of Mistaken Identity*. Metuchen, NJ: Scarecrow Press and Institute of Jazz Studies, 1986.

Buhler, James. "Frankfurt School Blues: Rethinking Adorno's Critique of Jazz." In *Apparitions: New Perspectives on Adorno and Twentieth-Century Music*, edited by Berthold Hoeckner, 103–30. New York: Routledge, 2006.

Butler, David. *Jazz Noir: Listening to Music from Phantom Lady to The Last Seduction*. Westport: Praeger, 2002.

Butte, George. "Suture and the Narration of Subjectivity in Film." *Poetics Today* 29, no. 2 (Summer 2008): 277–308.

Cabarga, Leslie. *The Fleischer Story*. New York: Da Capo Press, 1988.

Carey, James. "Technology and Ideology: The Case of the Telegraph." In *Communications as Culture: Essays on Media and Society*. New York: Routledge, 1992.

Caruso, Enrico. *How to Sing*. London: John Church, 1913.

Caruso, Enrico, Jr., and Andrew Farkas. *Enrico Caruso: My Father and My Family*. Portland, OR: Amadeus Press, 1990.

Casetti, Francesco. *Inside the Gaze: The Fiction Film and Its Spectator*. Translated by Nell Andrew with Charles O'Brien. Bloomington: Indiana University Press, 1998.

Cass, John L. "The Illusion of Sound and Pictures." *Journal of the Society of Motion Picture Engineers* 14 (1930): 323–26.

Cassidy, Donna M. "Jazz Representations and Early Twentieth-Century American Culture: Race, Ethnicity, and National Identity." In *Music and Modern Art*, edited by James Leggio. 203–26. New York: Routledge, 2002.

Cavell, Stanley. "Opera in (and As) Film." In *Cavell on Film*, edited by William Rothman. Albany: State University of New York Press, 2005.

Cavell, Stanley. "Ugly Duckling, Funny Butterfly: Bette Davis and *Now Voyager*." *Critical Inquiry* 16, no. 2 (1990): 213–47.

Chion, Michel. *Audio-Vision: Sound on Screen*. Translated by Claudia Gorbman. New York: Columbia University Press, 1994.

Chion, Michel. *The Voice in Cinema*. Translated by Claudia Gorbman. New York: Columbia University Press, 1999.

Citron, Marcia J. *Opera on Screen*. New Haven: Yale University Press, 2000.

Clément, Catherine. *Opera, or the Undoing of Women*. Translated by Betsy Wing. Minneapolis: University of Minnesota Press, 1988.

Clément, Catherine. "Through Voices, History." In *Siren Songs: Representations of Gender and Sexuality in Opera*, edited by Mary Ann Smart, 17–28. Princeton: Princeton University Press, 2000.

Connor, Steven. *Dumbstruck: A Cultural History of Ventriloquism*. New York: Oxford University Press, 2000.

Cooper, Harry. "On 'Über Jazz': Replaying Adorno with the Grain." *October* 75 (Winter 1996): 100–33.

Cooper, Mark Garrett. *Love Rules: Silent Hollywood and the Rise of the Managerial Class*. Minneapolis: University of Minnesota Press, 2003.

Copeland, Aaron. *Our New Music: Leading Composers in Europe and America*. New York: McGraw-Hill, 1941.

Cowan, Ruth Schwartz. *A Social History of American Technology*. New York: Oxford University Press, 1997.

Crafton, Donald. *The Talkies: American Cinema's Transition to Sound 1926–1931*. In *History of the American Cinema*, Vol. 4. Berkeley: University of California Press, 1997.

Crary, Jonathan. *Suspensions of Perception: Attention, Spectacle, and Modern Culture*. Cambridge, MA, and London: MIT Press, 1999.

Crawford, Richard. *America's Musical Life: A History*. New York: Norton, 2001.

Cripps, Thomas. *Slow Fade to Black: The Negro in American Film, 1900–1942*. New York: Oxford University Press, 1977.

Curtis, Scott. "The Sound of Early Warner Bros. Cartoons." In *Sound Theory/Sound Practice*, edited by Rick Altman, 191–203. New York: Routledge, 1992.

Curtiz, Michael. "The Clown" or "Pagliacci." Warner Bros. Story Dept. file on *The Singing Fool*. USCWB, undated but determined to be 1927.

Davidson, Annette. *Hollywood Theory, Non-Hollywood Practice: Cinema Soundtracks in the 1980s and 1990s*. Aldershot, England: Ashgate, 2004.

Davis, Angela. "I Used to Be Your Sweet Mama: Ideology, Sexuality, and Domesticity." *Blues Legacies and Black Feminism: Gertrude "Ma" Rainey, Bessie Smith, and Billie Holiday*. New York: Vintage, 1999.

Davis, Peter G. *The American Opera Singer: The Lives and Adventures of America's Great Singers in Opera & Concert from 1825 to the Present*. New York: Anchor, 1997.

Dayan, Daniel. "The Tutor-Code of Classical Cinema." *Film Quarterly* 28, no. 1 (1974): 22–31.

De Forest, Lee. "The Talking Pictures." *American Cinematographer*. February 1928: 4.

Deleuze, Gilles, and Félix Guattari. *A Thousand Plateaus: Capitalism and Schizophrenia*. Translated by Brian Massumi. Minneapolis: University of Minnesota Press, 1987.

Delson, Susan B. *Dudley Murphy: Hollywood Wild Card*. Minneapolis: University of Minnesota Press, 2006.

Dickstein, Morris. *Dancing in the Dark: A Cultural History of the Depression*. New York: Norton, 2009.

Dizikes, John. *Opera in America: A Cultural History*. New Haven: Yale University Press, 1993.

Dinerstein, Joel. *Swinging the Machine: Modernity, Technology, and African American Culture Between the World Wars*. Amherst: University of Massachusetts Press, 2003.

Doane, Mary Ann. "The Voice in the Cinema: The Articulation of Body and Space." "Cinema/Sound." *Yale French Studies* 60 (1980): 33–50.

Doherty, Thomas. *Pre-Code Hollywood: Sex, Immorality, and Insurrection in American Cinema 1930–1934*. New York: Columbia University Press, 1999.

Dolar, Mladen. "The Object Voice." In *Gaze and Voice as Love Objects*, edited by Renata Salecl and Slovoj Zizek, 7–31. Durham: Duke University Press, 1996.

Douglas, Susan. *Listening In: Radio and the American Imagination*. New York: Random House, 1999.

Dreher, Carl. "Stage Technique in the Talkies." *American Cinematographer* 10, no. 9 (December 1929): 2–26.

Dryden, Konrad. *Leoncavallo: Life and Works*. Lanham, MD: Scarecrow Press, 2007.

Du Maurier, George. *Trilby*. New York: Dover, 1994.

Dupree, Mary Herron. "'Jazz', the Critics, and American Art Music in the 1920s." *American Music* 4, no. 3 (Autumn, 1986): 287–301.

Durgnat, Raymond, and Scott Simmon. *King Vidor, American*. Berkeley: University of California Press, 1988.

Dyer, Richard. *Stars*, new ed. London: BFI, 1998.

Edelman, Lee. *Homographesis: Essays in Gay Literary and Cultural Theory*. New York and London: Routledge, 1994.

Edwards, Brent Hayes. "The Literary Ellington." In *Uptown Conversation: The New Jazz Studies*, edited by Robert G. O'Meally, Brent Hayes Edwards, and Farah Jasmine Griffin, 326–56. New York: Columbia University Press, 2004.

Edwards, Brent Hayes. "Louis Armstrong and the Syntax of Scat." *Critical Inquiry* 28 (Spring 2002): 618–49.

Einstein, Alfred. *Music in the Romantic Era*. New York: Norton, 1947.

Eisenberg, Evan. *The Recording Angel*. New York: Penguin, 1987.

Eisenstein, Sergei. *Film Form: Essays in Film Theory*, edited and translated by Jay Leyda. San Diego: Harcourt, 1977.

Eisenstein, Sergei. "From Lectures on Music and Colour in *Ivan the Terrible* (1947)." In *The Eisenstein Reader*, edited by Richard Taylor, translated by Richard Taylor and William Powell, 167–86. London: BFI, 1998.

Èjxenbaum, Boris M. "O. Henry and the Theory of the Short Story." In *Readings in Russian Poetics: Formalist and Structuralist Views*, edited by Laislav Matejka and Krystyna Pomorska, 227–70. Ann Arbor: Michigan Slavic Publications, 1978.

Ellington, Duke. "The Duke Steps Out." In *Rhythm* (1931). Reprinted in *The Duke Ellington Reader*, edited by Mark Tucker, 46–50. New York: Oxford University Press, 1993.

Ellis, John. *Visible Fictions: Cinema, Television, Video*. Rev. ed. New York: Routledge, 1992.

Eyman, Scott. *The Speed of Sound: Hollywood and the Talkie Revolution, 1926–1930*. Baltimore: Johns Hopkins University Press, 1999.

Fawkes, Richard. *Opera on Film*. London: Duckworth, 2000.

Feuer, Jane. *The Hollywood Musical*. 2nd ed. Bloomington: Indiana University Press, 1993.

Fleeger, Jennifer. "How to Say Things with Songs: Al Jolson, Vitaphone Technology, and the Rhetoric of Warner Bros. in 1929." *Quarterly Review of Film and Video* 27, no. 1 (2010): 27–43.

Fleeger, Jennifer. "Projecting an Aria, Singing the Cinema: In Search of a Shared Vocabulary for Opera and Film Studies." *Music, Sound, and the Moving Image* 2:2 (2009): 15–19

Fleischer, Richard. *Out of the Inkwell: Max Fleischer and the Animation Revolution*. Lexington: University Press of Kentucky, 2005.

Flinn, Caryl. *Strains of Utopia: Gender, Nostalgia, and Hollywood Film Music*. Princeton: Princeton University Press, 1992.

Franklin, Peter. "Movies as Opera (Behind the Great Divide)." In *A Night in at the Opera: Media Representations of Opera*, edited by Jeremy Tambling, 79–112. London: Libbey, 1994.

Fraser, Nancy. "Rethinking the Public Sphere: A Contribution to the Critique of Actually Existing Democracy." In *Habermas and the Public Sphere*, edited by Craig Calhoun, 109–42. Cambridge, MA: MIT Press, 1992.

Friedman, Lester D. "Celluloid Palimpsests: An Overview of Ethnicity and the American Film." In *Unspeakable Images: Ethnicity and the American Cinema*, edited by Lester D. Friedman, 11–38. Urbana: University of Illinois Press, 1991.

Freud, Sigmund. "Splitting of the Ego" (1938). In *Collected Papers*, Vol. 5. Edited by James Strachey, 372–75. London: Hogarth Press, 1952.

Frith, Simon. *Performing Rites: On the Value of Popular Music*. Cambridge, MA: Harvard University Press, 1998.

Fryer, Paul. *The Opera Singer and the Silent Film*. Jefferson, NC: McFarland, 2005.

Furia, Philip. *The Poets of Tin Pan Alley: A History of America's Great Lyricists*. New York: Oxford University Press, 1990.

Gabbard, Krin. "Al Jolson: The Man Who Changed the Movies Forever." In *Idols of Modernity: Movie Stars of the 1920s*, edited by Patrice Petro, 202–26. New Brunswick, NJ: Rutgers University Press, 2009.

Gabbard, Krin. *Black Magic: White Hollywood and African American Culture*. New Brunswick, NJ: Rutgers University Press, 2004.

Gabbard, Krin. *Jammin' at the Margins: Jazz and the American Cinema*. Chicago: University of Chicago Press, 1996.

Gabbard, Krin. ed. *Jazz Among the Discourses*. Durham: Duke University Pres, 1995.

Gabbard, Krin. ed. *Representing Jazz*. Durham: Duke University Press, 1995.

Gabbard, Krin. "Signifyin(g) the Phallus: *Mo' Better Blues* and Representations of the Jazz Trumpet." *Representing Jazz*, 104–30.

Garofalo, Reebee. "From Music Publishing to MP3: Music and Industry in the Twentieth Century." *American Music* 17, no. 3 (Fall 1999): 318–53.

Garrett, Charles Hiroshi. *Struggling to Define a Nation: American Music and the Twentieth Century*. Berkeley: University of California Press, 2008.

Gates, Henry Louis, Jr. *The Signifying Monkey: A Theory of Afro-American Literary Criticism*. New York: Oxford University Press, 1988.

Gershwin, George. "Our New National Anthem." *Theatre Magazine* (August 1925). Reprinted in *The George Gershwin Reader*, edited by Robert Wyatt and John Andrew, 89–90. Johnson. Oxford: Oxford University Press, 2004.

Gilman, Todd S. "The Italian (Castrato) in London." In *The Work of Opera: Genre, Nationhood, and Sexual Difference*, edited by Richard Dellamora and Daniel Fischlin. 49–72. New York: Columbia University Press, 1997.

Gilroy, Paul. *The Black Atlantic: Modernity and Double Consciousness*. London: Verso, 1993.

Gitelman, Lisa. "How Users Define New Media: A History of the Amusement Phonograph." In *Rethinking Media Change: The Aesthetics of Transition*, edited by David Thorburn, Henry Jenkins, and Brad Seawell, 61–80. Cambridge, MA: MIT Press, 2003.

Gitelman, Lisa. *Scripts, Grooves, and Writing Machines: Representing Technology in the Edison Era*. Stanford: Stanford University Press, 1999.

Goldmark, Daniel. "Creating Desire on Tin Pan Alley." *Music Quarterly* 90, no. 2 (2007): 197–229.

Goldmark, Daniel. *Tunes for 'Toons: Music and the Hollywood Cartoon*. Berkeley: University of California Press, 2005.

Gomery, Douglas. *The Coming of Sound: A History*. New York: Routledge, 2005.

Gomery, Douglas. *The Hollywood Studio System: A History*. London: BFI, 2005.

Gorbman, Claudia. *Unheard Melodies: Narrative Film Music*. Bloomington: Indiana University Press, 1987.

Grant, Barry Keith. "'Jungle Nights in Harlem': Jazz, Ideology and the Animated Cartoon." *University of Hartford Studies in Literature* 21, no. 3 (1989): 3–12.

Green, I. W., and J. P. Maxfield. "Public Address Systems." *Transactions of the American Institute of Electrical Engineering* 42 (1923): 64–75.

Greenfeld, Howard S. *Caruso: An Illustrated Life*. London: Collins and Brown, 1991.

Grover-Friedlander, Michal. *Vocal Apparitions: The Attraction of Cinema to Opera*. Princeton: Princeton University Press, 2005.

Gunning, Tom. "The Cinema of Attractions: Early Film, Its Spectator and the Avant-Garde." In *Early Cinema: Space, Frame, Narrative*, edited by Thomas Elsaesser, 56–62. London: BFI, 1990.

Habermas, Jürgen. *The Structural Transformation of the Public Sphere: An Inquiry into a Category of Bourgeois Society*. Cambridge, MA: MIT Press, 1991.

Hall, Leonard. "The Reaction of the Public to Motion Pictures with Sound." *Transactions of the Society of Motion Picture Engineers* 12, no. 35 (1928): 603–13.

Hansen, Miriam. *Babel and Babylon: Spectatorship in American Silent Film*. Cambridge, MA: Harvard University Press, 1991.

Harding, James. M. "Adorno, Ellison, and the Critique of Jazz." *Cultural Critique* 31 (1995): 129–58.

Hays, Will. *See and Hear: A Brief History of Motion Pictures and the Development of Sound*. Advisory editor Martin S. Dworkin. *Screen Monographs II*. New York: Arno, 1970.

Heriot, Angus. *The Castrati in Opera*. New York: De Capo Press, 1975.

Heyer, Paul. "Live from the Met: Digital Broadcast Cinema, Media Theory, and Opera for the Masses." *Canadian Journal of Communication* 33 (2008): 591–604.

Hill, Errol, and James Vernon Hatch. *A History of African American Theatre*. Vol. 18, *Cambridge Studies in American Theatre and Drama*. Cambridge: Cambridge University Press, 2003.

Hilmes, Michele. *Hollywood and Broadcasting: From Radio to Cable*. Urbana: University of Illinois Press, 1990.

Hilmes, Michele. *Radio Voices: American Broadcasting, 1922–1952*. Minneapolis: University of Minnesota Press, 1997.

"History of Warner Bros." Studio Legal Department. No date recorded, but presumed to be drawn up in the late 1940s. USCWB.

Horowitz, Joseph. *Classical Music in America: A History of Its Rise and Fall*. New York: Norton, 2005.

Howland, John. *Ellington Uptown: Duke Ellington, James P. Johnson, and the Birth of Concert Jazz*. Ann Arbor: University of Michigan Press, 2009.

Howland, John. "Jazz Rhapsodies in Black and White: James P. Johnson's *Yamekraw*." *American Music* 24, no. 4 (2006): 445–509.

Hughes, Langston. *Hollywood Mammy*. Alexandria, VA: Alexander Street Press, 2005.

Isherwood, Robert M. "Popular Musical Entertainment in Eighteenth-Century Paris." *International Review of the Aesthetics and Sociology of Music* 9, no. 2 (December 1978): 295–310.

Isaacson, Charles D. "A New Musical Outlook—And the War." *Musical Quarterly* 6, no. 1 (January 1920): 3.

Jaffe, Ira S. "'Fighting Words': *City Lights, Modern Times*, and *The Great Dictator*." *Journal of the University Film Association* 31, no. 1 (Winter 1979): 23–32.

Jakobson, Roman. "The Dominant." In *Readings in Russian Poetics: Formalist and Structuralist Views*, edited by Laislav Matejka and Krystyna Pomorska, 82–87. Ann Arbor: Michigan Slavic Publications, 1978.

Jefferson, Miles M. "The Negro on Broadway, 1946–1947." *Phylon* 8, no. 2 (1947): 146–59.

Jenkins, Henry. "'Shall We Make It for New York or Distribution?' Eddie Cantor, *Whoopee*, and Regional Resistance to the Talkies." *Cinema Journal* 29, no. 3 (Spring 1990): 32–52.

Jenkins, Henry. *What Made Pistachio Nuts? Early Sound Comedy and the Vaudeville Aesthetic*. New York: Columbia University Press, 1992.

Jerving, Ryan. "Jazz Language and Ethnic Novelty." *Modernism/modernity* 10, no. 2 (2003): 239–68.

Joe, Jeongwon. *Opera as Soundtrack*. Farnham, Surrey, UK: Ashgate, 2013.

Joe, Jeongwon. "*Opera on Film, Film in Opera: Postmodern Implications of the Cinematic Influence on Opera*." Dissertation. Evanston: Northwestern University, 1998.

Joe, Jeongwon, and Rose Theresa, eds. *Between Opera and Cinema*. New York: Routledge, 2002.

Johnson, John Andrew. "Gershwin's *Blue Monday* (1922) and the Promise of Success." In *The Gershwin Style: New Looks at the Music of George Gershwin*, edited by Wayne Schneider, 111–44. New York: Oxford University Press, 1999.

Jones, Arthur, Louise Howard, and Jeron Criswell. *How to Crash Tin-Pan Alley: The Authoritative Handbook for a Successful Song Writing Career*. New York: Howard and Criswell, 1939.

Jones, Jennifer. "Sounds Romantic: The Castrato and English Poetics Around 1800." *Romanticism and Opera*. Romantic Circles Praxis Series, 2005. http://www.rc.umd.edu/praxis/opera/jones/jones.html.

Jones, Kent. "*Hiroshima Mon Amour*: Time Indefinite." Essay for the DVD release of *Hiroshima Mon Amour*. Criterion Collection, 2003. www.criterion.com/current/posts/291.

Kahn, Douglas. *Noise, Water, Meat: A History of Sound in the Arts*. Cambridge, MA: MIT Press, 1999.

Kalinak, Kathryn. *Settling the Score: Music and the Classical Hollywood Film*. Madison: University of Wisconsin Press, 1992.

Kassabian, Anahid. *Hearing Film: Tracking Identifications in Contemporary Hollywood Film Music*. New York: Routledge, 2001.

Katz, Mark. *Capturing Sound: How Technology Has Changed Music*. Berkeley: University of California Press, 2004.

Keil, Charles. *Urban Blues*. Chicago: University of Chicago Press, 1966.

Keil, Charles, and Shelly Stamp, eds. *American Cinema's Transitional Era*. Berkeley: University of California Press, 2004.

King, Thomas A. "The Castrato's Castration." *SEL* 46, no. 3 (Summer 2006): 563–83.

Kirby, Lynne. *Parallel Tracks: The Railroad and Silent Cinema*. Durham: Duke University Press, 1997.

Kirk, Elise K. *American Opera*. Urbana: University of Illinois Press, 2001.

Kittler, Friedrich A. *Gramophone, Film, Typewriter*. Translated by Geoffrey Winthrop-Young and Michael Wutz. Stanford: Stanford University Press, 1999.

Knapp, Raymond. *The American Musical and the Formation of National Identity*. Princeton: Princeton University Press, 2005.

Knee, Adam. "Class Swings: Music, Race, and Social Mobility in *Broken Strings*." In *Soundtrack Available: Essays on Film and Popular Music*, edited by Pamela Robertson Wojcik and Arthur Knight, 269–94. Durham: Duke University Press, 2001.

Koenig, Karl, ed. *Jazz in Print (1856–1929): An Anthology of Selected Readings in Jazz History*. Hillsdale, NY: Pendragon Press, 2002.

Koestenbaum, Wayne. *The Queen's Throat: Opera, Homosexuality, and the Mystery of Desire*. New York: Poseidon Press, 1993.

Koszarski, Richard. *An Evening's Entertainment: The Age of the Silent Feature Picture, 1915–1928*. Vol. 3, *History of the American Cinema*, edited by Charles Harpole. New York: Scribner, 1997.

Koszarski, Richard. *Hollywood on the Hudson: Film and Television in New York From Griffith to Sarnoff*. Piscataway, NJ: Rutgers University Press, 2008.

Koszarski, Richard. "On the Record: Seeing and Hearing the Vitaphone." In *The Dawn of Sound*, edited by Mary Lea Bandy, 15–21. New York: Museum of Modern Art, 1989.

Kouwenhoven, John A. "What's 'American' About America?" In *The Jazz Cadence of American Culture*, edited by Robert G. O'Meally, 123-136. New York: Columbia University Press, 1998.

Kowalke, Kim H. "Kurt Weill, Modernism, and Popular Culture: *Offentlichkeit als Stil*." *Modernism/Modernity* 2, no. 1 (1995): 27–69.

Kracauer, Siegfried. *The Mass Ornament: Weimar Essays*. Translated by Thomas Y. Levin. Cambridge, MA: Harvard University Press, 1995.

Kracauer, Siegfried. "Opera on the Screen." *Film Culture* 1, no. 2 (1955): 19–21.

Kraft, James P. *Stage to Studio: Musicians and the Sound Revolution, 1890–1950*. Baltimore: Johns Hopkins University Press, 1996.

Krenek, Ernst. *Jonny spielt auf*, CD booklet with libretto. Translated by Gery Bramall. London: Decca Records, 1993.

Lacan, Jacques. *The Four Fundamental Concepts of Psychoanalysis. The Seminar of Jacques Lacan XI*, edited by Jacques-Alain Miller and translated by Alan Sheridan. New York: Norton, 1981.

Lanza, Joseph. *Elevator Music: A Surreal History of Muzak, Easy-Listening, and Other Moodsong*. New York: St. Martin's Press, 1994.

Lastra, James. *Sound Technology and the American Cinema: Perception, Representation, Modernity.* New York: Columbia University Press, 2000.

Lawrence, Amy. *Echo and Narcissus: Women's Voices in Classical Hollywood Cinema.* Berkeley: University of California Press, 1991.

Lehman, Christopher P. *The Colored Cartoon: Black Representation in American Animated Short Films, 1907–1954.* Amherst: University of Massachusetts Press, 2007.

Leonard, Neil. "The Jazzman's Verbal Usage." *Black American Literature Forum* 20, no. 1/2 (Spring–Summer, 1986): 151–60.

Leonardi, Susan J., and Rebecca A. Pope. *The Diva's Mouth: Body, Voice, Prima Donna Politics.* New Brunswick, NJ: Rutgers University Press, 1996.

Leoncavallo, Ruggiero. *Libretto for Pagliacci.* New York: Metropolitan Opera Record Club, 1958.

Leoncavallo, Ruggiero. *Pagliacci: Drama in Two Acts* (full score). New York: Dover, 1992.

Levine, Lawrence W. *Highbrow/Lowbrow: The Emergence of Cultural Hierarchy in America.* Cambridge, MA, and London: Harvard University Press, 1988.

Levinson, André. "The Nature of the Cinema." *Theatre Arts Monthly* 13, no. 9 (September 1929): 684–93.

Liebman, Roy. *Vitaphone Films: A Catalogue of the Features and Shorts.* Jefferson, NC: McFarland, 2003.

Lichtenwanger, William, ed. *Oscar Sonneck and American Music.* Urbana: University of Illinois Press, 1983.

Lindberg, Ulf. "Popular Modernism? The 'Urban' Style of Interwar Tin Pan Alley." *Popular Music* 22, no. 3 (2003): 283–98.

Lindenberger, Herbert. "Why (What? How? If?) Opera Studies?" In *Operatic Migrations: Transforming Works and Crossing Boundaries,* edited by Roberta Montemorra Marvin and Downing A. Thomas, 253–64. Aldershot, England: Ashgate, 2006.

Lindvall, Terry, and Ben Fraser. "Darker Shades of Animation: African-American Images in the Warner Bros. Cartoon." In *Reading the Rabbit: Explorations in Warner Bros. Animation,* edited by Kevin S. Sandler, 121–36. New Brunswick, NJ: Rutgers University Press, 1998.

London, Kurt. *Film Music: A Summary of the Characteristic Features of Its History, Aesthetics, Technique, and Possible Development.* London: Faber & Faber, 1936.

Lott, Eric. *Love and Theft: Blackface Minstrelsy and the American Working Class.* New York: Oxford University Press, 1993.

Mabie, Janet. "Interview with Duke Ellington." *Christian Science Monitor,* 1930. Reprinted in *The Duke Ellington Reader,* edited by Mark Tucker, 42–43. New York: Oxford University Press, 1993.

MacDonald, Laurence E. *The Invisible Art of Film Music: A Comprehensive History.* New York: Ardsley House, 1998.

Mackey, Nathaniel. *Bedouin Hornbook.* Lexington: University Press of Kentucky, 1986.

Maher, Michael J. *John Charles Thomas: Beloved Baritone of American Opera and Popular Music.* Jefferson, NC: McFarland, 2006.

Malsky, Matthew. "Sounds of the City: Alfred Newman's "Street Scene" and Urban Modernity." In *Lowering the Boom: Critical Studies in Film Sound,* edited by Jay Beck and Tony Grajeda, 105–22. Urbana: University of Illinois Press, 2008.

Mannoni, Octave. "Je sais bien... mais quand même: La Croyance." *Les Temps Modernes* 212 (1964): 1262–86.

Marks, Martin Miller. *Music and the Silent Film: Contexts and Case Studies, 1895–1924.* New York: Oxford University Press, 1997.

Mast, Gerald. *Can't Help Singin': The American Musical on Stage and Screen*. Woodstock, NY: Overlook Press, 1987.

Maurice, Alice. "'Cinema at Its Source'": Synchronizing Race and Sound in the Early Talkies." *Camera Obscura* 49 (2002): 31–71.

McBride, Joseph. "Stepin Fetchit Talks Back," *Film Quarterly* 24, no. 4 (Summer, 1971): 20–26.

McClary, Susan. *Feminine Endings: Music, Gender, and Sexuality*. Minneapolis: University of Minnesota Press, 1991.

McClary, Susan. *Georges Bizet: Carmen*. Cambridge: Cambridge University Press, 1992.

McCracken, Alison. "Real Men Don't Sing…: Crooning and American Culture 1928–1933." Dissertation. Iowa City: University of Iowa, 2000.

McCracken, Alison. "Real Men Don't Sing Ballads: The Radio Crooner in Hollywood 1929–1933." In *Soundtrack Available: Essays on Film and Popular Music*, edited by Pamela Robertson Wojcik and Arthur Knight, 105–33. Durham: Duke University Press, 2001.

Mera, Miguel, and David Burnand, eds. *European Film Music*. Hampshire: Ashgate, 2006.

Meredyth, Bess. "Don Juan." File on *Don Juan*. USCWB.

Merwin, Ted. *In Their Own Image: New York Jews in Jazz Age Popular Culture*. New Brunswick, NJ: Rutgers University Press, 2006.

Mitry, Jean. *The Aesthetics and Psychology of the Cinema*. Translated by Christopher King. Bloomington: Indiana University Press, 1997.

Moore, MacDonald Smith. *Yankee Blues: Musical Culture and American Identity*. Bloomington: Indiana University Press, 1985.

Mulvey, Laura. "Visual Pleasure and Narrative Cinema." *Screen* 16, no. 3 (1975): 6–18.

Nattiez, Jean-Jacques. *Music and Discourse: Toward a Semiology of Music*. Translated by Carolyn Abbate. Princeton: Princeton University Press, 1990.

Neumeyer, David, and James Buhler. "Analytical and Interpretive Approaches to Film Music (1): Analysing the Music." In *Film Music: Critical Approaches*, edited by K. J. Donnelly, 16–38. New York: Continuum, 2001.

Nietzsche, Friedrich. *The Birth of Tragedy*. Translated by Walter Kaufmann. New York: Vintage, 1967.

Nussbaum, Rachael Emily. *The Kroll Opera and the Politics of Reform in the Weimer Republic*. Dissertation, Cornell University, 2005.

O'Brien, Charles. *Cinema's Conversion to Sound: Technology and Film Style in France and the U.S.* Bloomington: Indiana University Press, 2005.

"Operator's Opera." Script Collection. WHS.

Osgood, Henry O. *So This Is Jazz*. New York: Little, Brown, 1926.

Ottenberg, June C. *Opera Odyssey: Toward a History of Opera in Nineteenth-Century America*. Westport, CT: Greenwood, 1994.

Paulin, Scott D. "Richard Wanger and the Fantasy of Cinematic Unity: The Idea of the *Gesamtkunstwerk* in the History and Theory of Film Music." In *Music and Cinema*, edited by James Buhler, Caryl Flinn, and David Neumeyer, 58–84. Hanover, NH: Wesleyan University Press, 2000.

Peschel, Enid Rhodes, and Richard E. Peschel. "Medicine and Music: The Castrati in Opera." *Opera Quarterly* 4, No. 4 (1986): 21–38.

Peters, John Durham. *Speaking into the Air: A History of the Idea of Communication*. Chicago: University of Chicago Press, 1999.

Pleasants, Henry. *The Great American Popular Singers*. New York: Simon and Schuster, 1974.

Potter, John. "The tenor-castrato connection, 1760–1860." *Early Music* 35, no. 1 (2006): 100.

Preston, Katherine K. *Opera on the Road: Traveling Opera Troupes in the United States, 1825–1960*. Urbana: University of Illinois Press, 1993.

Proust, Marcel. *Swann's Way*. Translated by Lydia Davis. Vol. 1, *In Search of Lost Time*. New York: Viking Press, 2003.

Pupin, Michael I. "No Closer Approach to Resurrection Has Ever Been Made by Science." Original Warner Bros. Vitaphone Souvenir Program Book. Reproduced with *The Jazz Singer* 80th Anniversary Edition DVD. Warner Bros. Pictures, 2007.

Rabinovitz, Lauren. *For the Love of Pleasure: Women, Movies, and Culture in Turn-of-the-Century Chicago*. New Brunswick, NJ: Rutgers University Press, 1998.

Raksin, David. " 'Music Composed by Charles Chaplin': Auteur or Collaborateur?" *Journal of the University Film Association* 31, no. 1 (1979): 47–50.

Richardson, Betty. "Al Jolson." In *The Guide to U.S. Popular Culture*, edited by Ray B. Browne and Pat Browne, 444–45. New York: Popular Press, 2001.

Rice, Elmer. *Street Scene*. In *Elmer Rice: Three Plays*. New York: Hill and Wang, 1965.

Rogin, Michael. *Blackface, White Noise: Jewish Immigrants in the Hollywood Melting Pot*. Berkeley: University of California Press, 1996.

Rosar, William H. "The Dies Irae in Citizen Kane: Musical Hermeneutics Applied to Film Music." In *Film Music: Critical Approaches*, edited by K. J. Donnelly, 103–16. New York: Continuum, 2001.

Ross, Alex. *The Rest Is Noise: Listening to the Twentieth Century*. New York: Picador, 2007.

Rosselli, John. *Singers of Italian Opera: The History of a Profession*. Cambridge: Cambridge University Press, 1992.

Rothenbuhler, Eric W., and John Durham Peters. "Defining Phonography: An Experiment in Theory." *Musical Quarterly* 81, no. 2 (1997): 242–64.

Rothman, William. "Against 'The System of Suture'." *Film Quarterly* 29, no. 1 (1975), 45–50.

Roy, William G. " 'Race Records' and 'Hillbilly Music': Institutional Origins of Racial Categories in the American Commercial Recording Industry." *Poetics* 32 (2004): 265–79.

Sabaneev, Leonid. "Opera and Cinema." *Musical Times* (January 1940): 9–11.

Sandberg, Mark B. *Living Pictures, Missing Persons: Mannequins, Museums, and Modernity*. Princeton: Princeton University Press, 2003.

Sansone, Matteo. "The 'Verismo' of Ruggiero Leoncavallo: A Source Study of 'Pagliacci'." *Music and Letters* 70, no. 3 (1989): 342–62.

Sargeant, Winthrop. *Jazz: Hot and Hybrid*. New York: Dutton, 1946.

Saunders, William. "National Opera, Comparatively Considered." *Musical Quarterly* 13, no. 1 (January 1927): 82.

"Sax Appeal." Script Collection. WHS.

Schatz, Thomas. *The Genius of the System: Hollywood Filmmaking in the Studio Era*. New York: Holt, 1988.

Schroeder, David. *Cinema's Illusions, Opera's Allure: The Operatic Impulse in Film*. New York: Continuum, 2002.

Schuller, Gunther. *Early Jazz: Its Roots and Musical Development*. New York: Oxford University Press, 1968.

Secrist, John. *Caruso: His Life in Pictures*. New York: Studio Publications, 1957.

Seldes, Gilbert. "The Dæmonic in the American Theatre." In *The American Stage: Writing on Theater from Washington Irving to Tony Kushner*, edited by Laurence Senelick. New York: Penguin, 2010.

Seldes, Gilbert. "Position of Jazz in American Musical Development." *Arts and Decoration* (April 1924). Reprinted in *Jazz in Print (1856–1929): An Anthology of Selected Readings in Jazz History*, edited by Karl Koenig, 303–4. Hillsdale, NJ: Pendragon Press, 2002.

Shaman, William. "The Operatic Vitaphone Shorts." *ARSC Journal* 22, no.1 (Spring 1991): 35–94.

Shaviro, Steven. *The Cinematic Body*. Minneapolis: University of Minnesota Press, 1993.

Shohat, Ella. "Ethnicities-in-Relation: Toward a Multicultural Reading of American Cinema." In *Unspeakable Images: Ethnicity and the American Cinema*, edited by Lester D. Friedman, 215–50. Urbana: University of Illinois Press, 1991.

Silverman, Kaja. *The Acoustic Mirror: The Female Voice in Psychoanalysis and Cinema*. Bloomington: Indiana University Press, 1988.

Silverman, Kaja. *The Subject of Semiotics*. New York: Oxford University Press, 1983.

Singer, Ben. *Melodrama and Modernity: Early Sensational Cinema and Its Contexts*. New York: Columbia University Press, 2001.

Sjogren, Britta. *Into the Vortex: Female Voice and Paradox in Film*. Urbana: University of Illinois Press, 2006.

Sklar, Robert. *Movie Made America: A Cultural History of American Movies*. New York: Vintage, 1976.

Slowik, Michael. *After the Silents: Hollywood Film Music in the Early Sound Era, 1926–1934*. New York: Columbia University Press, 2014, forthcoming.

Slowik, Michael. "'The Plasterers' and Early Sound Cinema Aesthetics." *Music, Sound, and the Moving Image* 4, no. 1 (July 2010): 55–75.

Smart, Mary Ann. *Mimomania: Music and Gesture in Nineteenth-Century Opera*. Berkeley: University of California Press, 2004.

Smith, Jacob. "Tearing Speech to Pieces: Voice Technologies of the 1940s." Annual Conference for the Society for Cinema and Media Studies, Loews Hotel, Philadelphia, March7, 2008.

Smith, Jacob. *Vocal Tracks: Performance and Sound Media*. Berkeley: University of California Press, 2008.

Smith, Jeff. *The Sounds of Commerce: Marketing Popular Film Music*. New York: Columbia University Press, 1998.

Sobchack, Vivian. *The Address of the Eye: A Phenomenology of Film Experience*. Princeton: Princeton University Press, 1992.

Sonneck, O. G. "The American Composer and the American Music Publisher." *Musical Quarterly* 9, no. 1 (January 1923): 122–44.

Sonneck, O. G. "An American School of Composition: Do We Want and Need It?" *Papers and Proceedings of the Music Teachers' National Association*, Minneapolis, December 1927. In *Oscar Sonneck and American Music*, edited by William Lichtenwanger, 158–66. Urbana: University of Illinois Press, 1983.

"Sound Recording and Reproducing." *Bell Lab Record* 1, no. 3 (November 1925): 95–101.

Spadoni, Robert. *Uncanny Bodies: The Coming of Sound Film and the Origins of the Horror Genre*. Berkeley: University of California Press, 2007.

Spring, Katherine. "Pop Go the Warner Bros., et al.: Marketing Film Songs During the Coming of Sound." *Cinema Journal* 48, no. 1 (Fall 2008): 68–89.

Squier, Susan Merrill, ed. *Communities of the Air: Radio Century, Radio Culture*. Durham: Duke University Press, 2003.

Stanfield, Peter. *Body and Soul: Jazz and Blues in American Film, 1927–63*. Urbana: University of Illinois Press, 2005.

Steane, J. B. *Voices: Singers and Critics*. Portland, OR: Amadeus Press, 1992.

Steigman, B. M. "The Great American Opera." *Music & Letters* 6, no. 4 (October 1925): 359–67.

Steinberg, John C. "Fundamentals of Speech, Hearing and Music." *Bell Laboratory Record* 7, no. 3 (November 1928): 75–80.

Sterne, Jonathan. *The Audible Past: Cultural Origins of Sound Reproduction.* Durham: Duke University Press, 2003.

Stewart, Jacqueline Najuma. *Migrating to the Movies: Cinema and Black Urban Modernity.* Berkeley: University of California Press, 2005.

Stilwell, Robynn J. "Sound and Empathy: Subjectivity, Gender and the Cinematic Soundscape." In *Film Music: Critical Approaches*, edited by K. J. Donnelly, 167–87. New York: Continuum, 2001.

Stokes, Melvyn, and Richard Maltby, eds. *American Movie Audiences: From the Turn of the Century to the Early Sound Era.* London: BFI, 1999.

Storey, Robert F. *Pierrot: A Critical History of a Mask.* Princeton: Princeton University Press, 1978.

Stratemann, Klaus. *Duke Ellington: Day by Day and Film by Film.* Copenhagen: Jazz-Media, 1992.

Studwell, William A., and Mark Baldin. *The Big Band Reader: Songs Favored by Swing Era Orchestras and Other Popular Ensembles.* Binghamton, NY: Haworth Press, 2000.

"A Swing Opera." Script Collection. WHS.

Tambling, Jeremy. "Introduction: Opera in the Distraction Culture." *A Night in at the Opera: Media Representations of Opera*, edited by Jeremy Tambling, 1–24. London: Libbey, 1994.

Tambling, Jeremy. *Opera and the Culture of Fascism.* Oxford: Clarendon Press, 1996.

Tambling, Jeremy. *Opera, Ideology and Film.* Manchester: Manchester University Press, 1987.

Taubman, Howard. "On Hearing Pagliacci." *Libretto for Pagliacci.* Ruggiero Leoncavallo. New York: Metropolitan Opera Record Club, 1958.

Taylor, Timothy D. *Strange Sounds: Music, Technology & Culture.* New York: Routledge, 2001.

Thompson, Emily. *The Soundscape of Modernity.* Cambridge: Cambridge University Press, 2000.

Thompson, Kristin. *Exporting Entertainment: America in the World Film Market.* Tonbridge: BFI, 1985.

Thompson, Randall. "The Contemporary Scene in American Music." *Musical Quarterly* 18, no. 1 (January 1932): 9–17.

Thomson, Virgil. "Jazz." *Mercury*, August 1924. Reprinted in *Jazz in Print (1856–1929): An Anthology of Selected Readings in Jazz History*, edited by Karl Koenig, 342–43. Hillsdale, NJ: Pendragon Press, 2002.

Tichi, Cecilia. *Shifting Gears: Technology, Literature, Culture in Modernist America.* Chapel Hill: University of North Carolina Press, 1987.

Titze, Ingo. *Principles of Voice Production.* Englewood Cliffs, NJ: Prentice Hall, 1994.

Todes, Ariane. "Charlie Chaplin." *Strad*, December 2008: 22–28.

Trumpbour, John. *Selling Hollywood to the World: U.S. and European Struggles for Mastery of the Global Film Industry, 1920–1950.* Cambridge: Cambridge University Press, 2002.

Vancour, Shawn. "Popularizing the Classics: Radio's Role in the American Music Appreciation Movement, 1922–34." *Media, Culture and Society* 31, no. 2 (2009): 289–307.

"The Vitaphone Tells Tales of Itself." *Bell Laboratories Record* 3, no. 4 (December 1926): 126–28.

Waldo, Terry. *This Is Ragtime*. New York: Hawthorn Books, 1976.

Richard Watts, Jr. "All Talking." *Theatre Arts Monthly* 13, no. 9 (September 1929): 702–10.

Warner, Harry M. "Future Developments." Talk at Harvard University. In *The Story of the Films as Told by Leaders of the Industry to the Students of the Graduate School of Business Administration George F. Baker Foundation Harvard University*, edited by Joseph P. Kennedy, 319–35. Chicago: A. W. Shaw, 1927.

Warner Bros. Pressbook for *The Better Ole*, 1926.

Warner Bros. Pressbook for *Say It with Songs*, 1929.

Warner Bros. Pressbook for *The Singing Fool*, 1928.

Weiner, Marc A. "Why Does Hollywood Like Opera?" In *Between Opera and Cinema*, edited by Jeongwon Joe and Rose Theresa, 75–91. New York and London: Routledge, 2002.

Weisenfeld, Judith. "'Truths That Liberate the Soul': Eva Jessye and the Politics of Religious Performance." In *Women and Religion in the African Diaspora: Knowledge, Power, and Performance*, edited by R. Marie Griffith and Barbara Dianne Savage, 222–44. Baltimore: Johns Hopkins University Press, 2006.

West, William D. "Canio-Pagliacco and Petrouchka: Two Contrasting Images of Pierrot." In *Fools and Jesters in Literature, Art, and History: A Bio-Bibliographical Sourcebook*, edited by Vicki K. Janik, 120–26. Westport, CT: Greenwood Press, 1998.

Williams, Linda. *Hard Core: Power, Pleasure, and the "Frenzy of the Visible."* Berkeley: University of California Press, 1989.

Willis, Corin. "Blackface Minstrelsy and Jazz Signification in Hollywood's Early Sound Era." In *Thriving on a Riff: Jazz and Blues Influences in African American Literature and Film*, edited by Graham Lock and David Murray, 40–64. New York: Oxford University Press, 2009.

Winnington-Ingram, R. P. *Mode in Ancient Greek Music*. Cambridge: Cambridge University Press, 1936.

Winters, Ben. "The Non-Diegetic Fallacy: Film, Music, and Narrative Space." *Music and Letters* 91, no. 2 (2010): 224–44.

Wojcik, Pamela Robertson. "The Girl and the Phonograph; or the Vamp and the Machine Revisited." In *Soundtrack Available: Essays on Film and Popular Music*, edited by Pamela Robertson Wojcik and Arthur Knight, 433–54. Durham: Duke University Press, 2001.

Wolfe, Charles. "Vitaphone Shorts and *The Jazz Singer*." *Wide Angle* 2, no. 3 (July 1990): 58–78.

Wurtzler, Steve J. *Electric Sounds: Technological Change and the Rise of Corporate Mass Media*. New York: Columbia University Press, 2007.

Wyatt, Robert, and John Andrew Johnson, eds. *The George Gershwin Reader*. Oxford: Oxford University Press, 2004.

Young, Paul. *The Cinema Dreams Its Rivals: Media Fantasy Films from Radio to the Internet*. Minneapolis: University of Minnesota Press, 2006.

Zizek, Slavoj. *Enjoy Your Symptom!* New York: Routledge, 2008.

FILMOGRAPHY

VITAPHONE OPERA SHORTS (1926–1932, DIRECTORS UNCREDITED, WITH CATALOGUE NUMBERS)

Allan Prior, "Famous Australian Tenor." 1927? No. 2106

Alice Gentle. 1930. No. 3336

Anna Case in "La Fiesta." 1926. No. 294

Anna Case in "Swanee River" with Roy Smeck and the Dixie Jubilee Singers. 1926. No. 296

Beniamino Gigli. 1927. No. 414

Beniamino Gigli. 1927. No. 498

Beniamino Gigli and Giuseppe De Luca, Metropolitan Opera Stars. 1927. No. 518

Beniamino Gigli, Tenor of the Metropolitan Opera. 1927. No. 517

Caro Nome, with Marion Talley. 1926. No. 308

Céleste Aïda, with Giovanni Martinelli. 1926. No. 204

Charles Hackett. 1926. No. 392

Charles Hackett. 1927. No. 552

Charles Hackett. 1929. No. 916

Charles Hackett in "Faust," Assisted by Chase Borromeo. 1929. No. 899–900

Charles Hackett, Leading Tenor of Chicago Civic Opera. 1929. No. 890

Charles Hackett, Leading Tenor of Chicago Civic Opera. 1928. No. 2379

Charles Hackett with Rosa Bow in Excerpts from Romeo and Juliet. 1931. No. 1143

Chief Caupolican, "Indian Baritone." 1928? No. 2598

Eleanor Painter, the Lyric Soprano. 1929. No. 746

Ernestine Schumann-Heink. 1927. No. 568

G. Martinelli in "Gypsy Caravan." 1931. No. 1245

G. Martinelli in "The Prison Scene" from Faust. 1930. No. 974

G. Martinelli in "The Ship's Concert." 1931. No. 1162

G. Martinelli in the Temple Scene from Aïda. 1930. No. 1024

G. Martinelli in "The Troubadour." 1931. No. 1226

G. Martinelli Singing Arias from Verdi's Il Trovatore. 1929. No. 944

G. Martinelli Singing "Celeste Aïda" by Verdi. 1929. No. 953

G. Martinelli Singing "Come Back to Sorrento" and "Nina." 1931. No. 1213

G. Martinelli Singing "Love's Garden of Roses" and "Because." 1930. No. 1174

Giovanni Martinelli. 1927. No. 474

Giovanni Martinelli. 1927. No. 510

Giovanni Martinelli, Assisted by D'Angelo. 1927. No. 509

Giovanni Martinelli, Assisted by Livia Marracci. 1929. No. 932

Giuseppe De Luca. 1927. No. 488

Guido Ciccolini and Eric Zardo. 1929. No. 870

Hope Hampton in the Fourth Act of Manon. 1929. No. 740

In a Blacksmith Shop. J Delos Jewkes and Soloists. 1927? No. 2177

Jeanne Gordon "Celebrated Mezzo Soprano." 1929. No. 808

John Barclay "Tallest Baritone in the World." 1927. No. 436

John Barclay "Tallest Baritone in the World." 1927. No. 437

John Charles Thomas, Outstanding American Baritone. 1927. No. 493

John Charles Thomas, Outstanding American Baritone. 1927. No. 495

John Charles Thomas "Renowned Stage and Concert Artist." 1927. No. 481

Joseph Diskay, "The Hungarian Tenor." 1927? No. 2122

Josef Kallini. 1929. No. 893

Josef Kallini, Foremost Tenor of Manhattan Opera House. 1929. No. 892

Joseph Regan, Irish Tenor. 1928? No. 2628

Madame Alda in "Ave Maria" by Verdi. 1929. No. 943

Madame Ernestine Schumann-Heink. 1926. No. 379

Madame Ernestine Schumann-Heink. 1926. No. 380

Madame Frances Alda. 1929. No. 805

Madame Frances Alda and the Vitaphone Symphony. 1927. No. 451

Madame Rosa Raisa, "Soprano for the Chicago Civic Opera." 1928. No. 2545

Madame Rosa Raisa, "Soprano for the Chicago Civic Opera." 1928. No. 2546

Marie Vero. 1929. No. 911

Marion Talley and Beniamino Gigli. 1927. No. 499

Mary Lewis. 1927. No. 432

Mary Lewis in "Way Down South." 1926. No. 383

Pascale Amato," Operatic Baritone" in Neapolitan Romance. 1927. No. 2254

Quartet from Rigoletto. 1927. No. 415

Reinald Werrenrath Concert Baritone. 1926. No. 361

Reinald Werrenrath Concert Baritone. 1926. No. 365

Rosa Raisa and Giacomo Rimini. 1927. No. 524

Rosa Raisa and Giacomo Rimini. 1927. No. 542

Vesti la giubba, with Giovanni Martinelli. 1926. No. 198

OTHER SHORT FILMS

The Audition. Roy Mack. Warner Bros. 1932.

Ben Polack and His Orchestra. Joseph Henabery. Warner Bros. 1934.

Black and Tan. Dudley Murphy. RKO. 1929.

Blossom Seeley and Bennie Fields. Director uncredited. Warner Bros. 1926.

Cab Calloway's Hi-Di-Ho. Fred Waller. Paramount. 1933.

Devil's Cabaret. Nick Grinde. MGM. 1930.

Faust. Director uncredited. Official Films. 1929.

Harlem Mania. Director uncredited. Warner Bros. 1929.

Harry Reser and His Eskimos. Roy Mack. Warner Bros. 1936.

Hotel a la Swing. Roy Mack Warner Bros. 1937.

Isham Jones and His Orchestra. Roy Mack. Warner Bros. 1933.

Jammin' the Blues. Gjon Mili. Warner Bros. 1944.

Jazzmania Quintette. Director uncredited. Warner Bros. 1928.

Joseph Regan. Director uncredited. MGM. 1928.

Leo Reisman and His Hotel Brunswick Orchestra in Rhythms. Director uncredited. Warner Bros. 1929.

Ol' King Cotton. Roy Cozine. Paramount. 1930.

Opera Versus Jazz. Lee de Forest. De Forest Phonofilm. 1923.
Operator's Opera. Director uncredited. Warner Bros. 1933.
Over the Counter. Jack Cummings. MGM. 1932.
Marion Harris. Director uncredited. MGM. 1928.
Metro Movietone Revue II. Nick Grinde. MGM. 1929.
Metro Movietone Revue IV. Nick Grinde. MGM. 1930.
Musical Doctor. Ray Cozine. Paramount. 1932.
Parsifal. Edwin S. Porter. Edison. 1904.
Paul Tremaine and His Aristocrats. Director uncredited. Warner Bros. 1929.
Pie Pie Blackbird. Roy Mack. Warner Bros. 1932.
A Plantation Act. Philip Roscoe. Warner Bros. 1926.
The Ponce Sisters. Director uncredited. MGM. 1928.
Prisoner of Swing. Roy Mack. Warner Bros. 1938.
Public Jitterbug #1. Joseph Henabery. Warner Bros. 1939.
Red Nichols and His Five Pennies. Joseph Henabery. Warner Bros. 1935.
Rhapsody in Black and Blue. Aubrey Scotto. Paramount. 1932.
Sax Appeal. Director uncredited. Warner Bros. 1931.
Sing, Bing, Sing. Babe Stafford. Paramount. 1933.
Sophomore Swing. Roy Mack. Warner Bros. 1938.
St. Louis Blues. Dudley Murphy. RKO. 1929.
Swing for Sale. Joseph Henabery. Warner Bros. 1936.
A Swing Opera. Roy Mack. Warner Bros. 1939.
Swing Styles. Lloyd French. Warner Bros. 1939.
Symphony in Black: A Rhapsody of Negro Life. Fred Waller. Paramount. 1935.
Walt Roesner and the Capitolians. Director uncredited. MGM. 1928.
What Price Jazz. Sam Baerwitz. MGM. 1934.
Wild People. Ray McCarey. MGM. 1932.
Yamekraw. Murray Roth. Warner Bros. 1930.

A SHORT LIST OF RELEVANT FEATURES
Broken Strings. Bernard B. Ray. Goldport, L. C. Borden. 1940.
Cabin in the Sky. Vincente Minnelli. MGM. 1943.
The Desert Song. Roy Del Ruth. Warner Bros. 1929.
Don Juan. Alan Crosland. Warner Bros. 1926.
Elevator to the Gallows (Ascenseur pour l'échafaud). Louis Malle. Lux. 1958.
The First Auto. Roy Del Ruth. Warner Bros. 1926.
Hallelujah! King Vidor. MGM. 1929.
Here Comes the Band. Paul Sloane. MGM. 1935.
I Sing for You Alone. Mario Bonnard. Caesar Film. 1932.
In Old Arizona. Irving Cummings. Fox. 1928.
The Informer. John Ford. RKO. 1935.
Ivan the Terrible. Sergei Eisenstein. Alma Ata. 1947.
The Jazz Singer. Alan Crosland. Warner Bros. 1927.
King Kong. Merian C. Cooper and Ernest B. Schoedsack. RKO. 1933.
King of Jazz. John Murray Anderson. Universal. 1930.
A Lady's Morals. Sidney Franklin. MGM. 1930.
Laura. Otto Preminger. Twentieth-Century Fox. 1944.
Love and the Devil. Alexander Korda. Warner Bros. 1929.
The Magic Flute. Ingmar Bergman. Sveriges Television. 1975.
Modern Times. Charlie Chaplin. United Artists. 1936.

Moonstruck. Norman Jewison. MGM. 1987.

My Man. Archie May. Warner Bros. 1928.

Nice Girl? William A. Seiter. Universal. 1941.

Night at the Opera. Sam Wood. MGM. 1935.

Noah's Ark. Michael Curtiz. Warner Bros. 1928.

One Night of Love. Victor Schertzinger. Columbia. 1934.

Parsifal. Hans-Jürgen Syberberg. Gaumont, TMS Film. 1982.

The Prodigal. Harry A. Pollard. MGM. 1931.

The Public Enemy. William A. Wellman. Warner Bros. 1931.

Rhapsody in Blue. Irving Rapper. Warner Bros. 1945.

Say It with Songs. Lloyd Bacon. Warner Bros. 1929.

The Singing Fool. Lloyd Bacon. Warner Bros. 1928.

Singing in the Rain. Gene Kelly and Stanley Donen. MGM. 1952.

Speakeasy. Benjamin Stoloff. Fox. 1929.

Street Scene. King Vidor. United Artists. 1931.

Sunrise. F. W. Murnau. Fox. 1927.

Suspiria. Dario Argento. Seta Spettacoli. 1977.

Svengali. Archie Mayo. Warner Bros. 1931.

The Terror. Roy Del Ruth. Warner Bros. 1928.

The Testament of Dr. Mabuse. Fritz Lang. Rota-Film. 1932.

The Third Man. Carol Reed. London, British Lion. 1949.

Thru Different Eyes. John G. Blystone. Fox. 1929.

INDEX

"f" indicates material in figures. "n" indicates material in endnotes.

American film musical formula, 82
American identity, 15, 17, 32, 35, 95
American Idol, 181n78
American music in 20th century, 10, 125
American theater in 19th century, 119
Anderson, John Murray, 10
André, Naomi, 72
animation, 56. *See also* cartoons
"anti-anti-essentialism," 92–93, 106
apparatus theory, 137, 175n14
"April Showers," 97
Ardath, Fred, 165n47
Armstrong, Louis, 93–95, 107–111, 133, 155, 167n65, 167n69
Arnaut Brothers, 33, 165n47, 172n40
arranger, 50, 123, 128–129, 151
ASCAP public performance licenses, 124
assimilation
    blackface and, 35
    cinema as force of, 24, 34
    jazz-opera and, 10, 32
    narrative, in Jolson's films, 55
    Vitaphone and, 38
    Warner Bros. opera short films and, 32
"At Dawning," 171n29
Attali, Jacques, 60
Audition, The, 103–104
"Away with Melancholy," 169–170n17
Axt, William, 181n71

Baker, Graham, 18
Balfe, Michael, 182n2
Balzac, Honoré de, 76–77, 174n76
banjo, 12, 101–102, 176n31
Barber of Seville, 83, 169n11
Barclay, John, 165n47, 171n30
baritones, 83, 95
Barnum, P. T., 59
Barrymore, John, 144
bass voice, 72
Bayreuth Theater, 62
Bazin, André, 46, 168n95
"Beat of My Heart," 104
Bell Labs, 28, 167n74
"Beloved," 65
Ben Pollack and His Orchestra, 104
Benson, Yvonne, 81, 82
Bergman, Ingmar, *Magic Flute*, 46, 55, 158
Berkeley, Busby, 117

Berlin, Irving, 9, 20, 63, 116, 124
Betty Boop, 111
Between the Acts at the Opera, 96
Billboard, 97
Bizet, Georges, *Carmen*, 63, 133, 135, 172n53
Black and Tan, 13, 50
blackface
    assimilation and, 35
    burlesque and, 118–119
    in comedies vs. dramas, 176n36
    co-presence with African Americans, 107
    in Curtiz's "The Clown" story, 18
    Gardella's use of, 182n2
    recordings and, 106
    in Warner Bros. jazz films, 92, 97–98, 102, 106–107, 118–119
Blake, Eubie, 105
Blazing Saddles, 180n59
Blue Monday, 2, 12, 163n30, 163n32
blues, 21, 124
"Blue Skies," 149–150
Bogle, Donald, 108
Bohemian Girl, 182n2
Bonelli, Richard, 64, 84
Bordwell, David, 19, 29, 128, 130, 163n2
Bori, Lucrezia, 8
"Born in the USA," 181n77
Borodin, Alexander, 170n17
Boston, 20, 60, 176n32
Bowes, Edward, 161n2, 181n71
Bradley, Edwin, 63, 170n28
Brahms, Johannes, 112
Breathless, 179n37
Broadway, 2, 10, 12, 41, 114
Brown, Royal S., 177–178n1, 179n35
Buhler, James, 122, 135, 175n25, 178n18
burlesque, 58, 118–119, 177n59

Cabinet of Dr. Caligari, The, 47
Cadman, Charles Wakefield, 85, 171n29
cakewalks, 19, 58
"Call of the Nile," 67, 85
capitalism, 13, 56, 92, 115, 119–121
Carmen, 63, 133, 135, 172n53
"Caro nome," 70–73, 76–80
cartoons, 124, 178n8, 179n38. *See also* animation

Caruso, Enrico, 8, 26, 27,
     166n51, 167n69
Case, Anna
     cinematography of short films of, 76
     in Edison Tone Tests, 53
     editing of short films of, 89
     German operas and, 53, 168n2
     "La Fiesta," 71
     Martinelli and, 55, 89
     Swanee River, 28, 53–54, 173n63
     in Vitaphone's premiere film, 27, 53
Casetti, Francesco, 138, 143–144, 146,
     150, 180–181nn67–69
castration, 68–69, 73, 92, 94, 175n5
castrato
     African American voices and, 94
     tenors and, 173n69
     Warner Bros. opera shorts and, 16,
          71–78, 80, 102
     women's vocal performances and,
          90, 173n68
Catholic Church, 72, 77
Cavalleria rusticana, 27
censorship, 40, 57–58, 125–126
"Chanson Indoue," 85–86. *See also* "Song
     of India"
Chaplin, Charlie, 151–155
Chautauqua Institution, 169n17
Chicago
     Chicago Symphony Orchestra, 60
     Civic Opera, 11, 62
     Cook's *Uncle Tom's Cabin* and, 11
     Don Juan's premiere in, 34
Chicago Daily Tribune, 27, 34
Chicago Defender, 44
Chion, Michel, 122, 136, 146,
     179n37, 180n47
"cinema as event" approach, 57
"classical" music, 128, 135, 150,
     179n35, 182n2
Clément, Catherine, 71, 83
Cocteau, Jean, 168n95
Cohn, Al, 167n75
Cole, Nat King, 152
Columbia Records, 33
comedy short films, 60, 66, 115, 176n39
"Come Hot It Up with Me," 117–118
commedia dell'arte, 26, 164n21
composers, Gorbman's tenets for,
     132–133

conductors, 62, 128, 170n26
Connor, Steven, 5
continuity editing, 46, 82
contrapuntal soundtracks, 45
conversion era, 162n20
Cook, William Marion, 11
Cooper, Mark Garrett, 125
copyright, 33, 124–125, 129,
     165nn47–49, 172n40
Coscia, Phil, 171n30
Crafton, Donald, 40, 77
Crary, Jonathan, 61
Crawford, Joan, 177n54
Creekmur, Corey, 181n78
Crosby, Bing, 23
cue sheets, 3
culture
     "jazziness" and, 181n79
     jazz-opera and, 155
     jazz short films and, 60, 95
     opera short films and, 60, 83
     recordings and, 60, 155
     "sacralization of," 59, 169n15
     technological change and, 125
     trains on film and, 100
Curtiz, Michael, 18–19, 32–34, 37–39

D'Angelo, Louis, 81
Davidson, Annette, 179n35
Davis, Miles, 133
Davis, Peter G., 174n86
Davis, Sammy, Jr., 176n33
Dayan, Daniel, 137, 138, 145
Deep River, 2, 11–12
De Forest, Lee
     musicians hired by, 3
     on opera short films, 29
     short films by, 1–2, 17, 63
     sound system of (*see* Phonofilm)
     on sound technology, 1
De Luca, Giuseppe, 83
Desert Song, The, 30, 41
Devil's Cabaret, The, 116–120
Diamond Disk Phonograph, 53
Dinerstein, Joel, 36, 40
Diskay, Joseph, 171n29
distribution rights, 25
Dixie Jubilee Singers, 28, 53–54
Dizikes, John, 59, 60
Doane, Mary Ann, 21

identity and, 19
immigration and, 10
integration and, 10
Kahn's request for, 9–10
origins of, 38
in post-WWII stage productions, 158
in short films, 158
on stage, 10–12, 147, 158
jazz short films
African American performers in,
104–107
approaches to, 25
blackface characters in, 92, 97–98,
102, 106–107, 118–119
commercialism and, 119
co-presence in, 107
on creation of jazz, 95
culture and, 60, 95
editing of, 94, 99, 102
of Ellington, 13
Jolson in, 96–98, 106–107
by MGM, 16, 95, 96, 115–120
mise-en-scène in, 102
music in, 22
narratives in, 94, 96, 98, 100, 102
nature footage in, 102, 104
by Paramount, 16, 95–96, 107–114,
119, 157, 176n39
sets and scenery for, 98
song context in, 100–103
style and values in, 16
superimpositions in, 103f, 104
symbols in, 94, 100
trains in, 99–100
by Warner Bros., 16, 92, 95–107,
118–119
Jazz Singer, The
advertising/marketing of, 40
Casetti's gazes and, 150
dialogue in, 148
immigrants and, 36
improvisation in, 150
jazz images in, 148, 150–151
jazz mode in, 148–150
music in, 95
pressbooks on, 175n22
reviews of, 150
score for sound version of, 150
silent and sound versions of, 165n46
The Singing Fool and, 167n70

"talkies" and release of, 3
jazz standards, 149, 181n78
Jenkins, Henry, 15
Jerving, Ryan, 167n84
Jews, 35, 62–63, 150, 167n70
Johnson, James P., 22, 43–51, 168n88,
168n91, 168n98
Johnson-Reed Act, 10
Jolson, Al
African Americans and, 37, 92, 97
blackface character of, 35–39, 42, 92,
97–98, 102, 106, 118–119
Curtiz's "The Clown" story and,
18, 167n70
Gabbard on, 97, 167n65
identity and, 32, 37
improvisation by, 34, 97
The Jazz Singer (see Jazz Singer, The)
"jazzy" characteristics of, 36,
149, 181n80
Mammy, 42
Martinelli and, 54–55, 95
in minstrel shows, 36, 96, 106
one-man stage shows of, 96–97
phonograph and, 42–43
Plantation Act, A, 35, 96–98, 107
pressbooks on, 175n22
radio and, 175n24
recordings of, 97, 175n24
Seldes on, 96–97
The Singing Fool, 32–39
transition to films, 97
Vallee and, 112
Vitaphone and, 35–36, 42–43,
95–98, 150
Yamekraw and, 45, 47
"Yes, We have No Bananas," 42
Jones, Jennifer, 72
Jones, Kent, 179n37
Jonny spielt auf, 12, 38
Joplin, Scott, 11

Kahn, Otto, 9–10, 123, 124, 162n23
Kalinak, Kathryn, 122, 129, 141,
179n28, 179n38, 179n41,
180n42, 180n61
Kallini, Josef, 67
Katz, Mark, 166n51
"Keep a Little Song Handy," 111
Keith, Benjamin Franklin, 20

sound effects, 33–34, 141, 143, 166n54
sound-on-disc systems. *See* Vitaphone
sound-on-film systems
   early experiments with, 34
   editing of, 40
   as industry standard, 110, 121, 124
   Movietone, 4, 20, 29–34, 110, 167n74
   Phonofilm, 4, 29, 33–34
   phonograph and, 22
   photography and, 33
   Photophone, 4, 20, 33, 34
   reality and, 110
   unity in, 34
   Vitaphone and, 20, 22, 32–34
   Warner Bros. conversion to, 48
sound systems
   African Americans and, 92
   censorship and, 125–126
   installation of, 15
   jazz and, 27–28
   sound-on-disc (*see* Vitaphone)
   sound-on-film (*see* sound-on-film
      systems)
   studio identity and, 29
   uncanny effect of, 5
   unlicensed, 40
soundtracks
   ability to record, 139–140
   American vs. French, 178n6
   ASCAP public performance licenses
      and, 124
   contrapuntal, 45
   female and male voices in, 68–69
   Movietone, musicians for, 4, 65
   recordings and, 127
   silent film accompaniments and,
      134–136, 140–141, 147
Soviet filmmakers, 45
Spadoni, Robert, 5, 124, 161n5, 181n68
Speakeasy, 31
Spring, Katherine, 124
Springsteen, Bruce, 181n77
Staiger, Janet, 25, 29, 128, 130
Stalling, Carl, 179n38
Stanfield, Peter, 118
"Star Spangled Banner, The," 62
Steiner, Max
   classical training of, 126
   compositional tenets of scores and,
      132–133

The Informer score by, 135, 179n41
King Kong score by, 131, 162n20
   Romanticism of, 16
   standard procedures for composition
      by, 179n38
Storey, Robert F., 26
Stradivarius instruments, 93
"Stranger in Paradise," 170n17
Stratemann, Klaus, 168n101
Strauss, Richard, 141, 144
Street Scene, 158
striptease, 118
Stroh-Violin, 105–106
Strothotte, Maurice Arnold, 11
"Summertime" (Gershwin), 12
Suspiria, 136
suture, cinematic, 137, 138, 150
Svengali, 139
Swanee River (film), 28, 53–54, 173n63
"Swanee River" (song), 28, 100. *See also*
   "Old Folks at Home"
Swing for Sale, 182n1
swing music, 182n1
Swing Opera, A, 182n2
Swing Styles, 182n1
Syberberg, Hans-Jürgen, *Parsifal*, 46
symphony
   audience behavior at, 62, 170nn25–26
   characteristics of, 56
   film scores and, 131
   in nineteenth century, 16
   performances of full, 60
   radio broadcasts of, 56
   themes in, 142, 155
Symphony in Black, 50

Tallest Baritone in the World, 165n47
Talley, Marion
   background of, 77
   "Caro nome," 70–73, 76–80
   De Forest on, 29
   editing of short films of, 71, 76,
      78–80, 89
   frame grab from "Caro nome," 79f, 80f
   reviews on short films of, 27,
      70, 72, 77
   Vitaphone Release Index on
      films of, 54
Tannhäuser, 99
Tchaikovsky, Pyotr, 89, 135

historical context of, 3–4
image and soundtracks with, 8, 45
Italian operas and, 60–62, 66, 70,
    76–80, 90, 102
Jolson and, 35–36, 42–43, 95–98, 150
Martinelli and, 76–77, 86
vs. Movietone, 20, 34, 167n74
"musical" logo for, 30
vs. Phonofilm, 34
phonograph and, 4, 16, 22, 31–33, 38,
    40–41, 106, 165–166n51
vs. Photophone, 34
premiere of, 3, 53, 162n20
projectionists and, 166n56
publicity for, 31, 40–41
recordings and, 16, 35
reviews on, 34, 39–40
scientific descriptions of, 35
serial number assignments
    for, 172n42
shelf life of, 39
Stroh-Violin and, 105–106
synchronization of, 39, 106, 166n54
Talley and, 77–78
transcription onto disc, 8–9
unity with, 100
Variety on, 27
weight of, 39
Vitaphone Corporation
Bowes contract with, 161n2
Brooklyn studio, 64, 67, 172n45
Burbank studio, 172n42
copyright and, 33,
    165nn47–49, 172n40
on Martinelli's film production
    schedule, 172n47
opera short films by, 63
production records for, 67, 172n43
Vitaphone Release Index, 45, 54, 56–57,
    169n4, 170n28, 171n29
Vitaphone Symphony Orchestra, 24
vocal performances
advertising/marketing of, 6
baritones, 83, 95
bass, 72
class and, 59
in conversion from silent films, 6
cultural coding of, 109
in opera short films, 62–63
presentation of, 9

preservation of, 9
selection of, 9
in short films, 3
soprano (*see* sopranos)
sound systems and, 4–6, 23–24
tenor (*see* tenors)
unifying abilities of, 136
wordless, 93–94, 154
von Flotow, Friedrich, *Martha*, 66,
    70, 87

Wagner, Richard
on audience behavior at operas, 61
Bayreuth Theater design by, 61–62
compositional practices of, 127, 128
leitmotif of, 127, 139,
    170n27, 178n18
satirical shorts on operas of, 66
scores and, 62, 66, 123, 126–128,
    131, 163n2
Tannhäuser, 99
Waldorf Astoria, 176n32
Waller, Fats, 44
Warner, Harry, 27, 32, 34, 164–165n29
Warner, Jack, 70
Warner, Sam, 28, 164–165n29
Warner Bros.
advertising/marketing for, 56
educational mission of, 49, 121, 126
Heller and, 24–25
Mack's team at, 24
music publishing industry and,
    22, 124
silent-to-talking film conversion at,
    3–4, 161n3
style and values in films of,
    23, 174n80
variety format of, 157
Victor Red Seal recording artists
    and, 31
Vitaphone (*see* Vitaphone)
Warner Bros. jazz short films, 16, 92,
    95–107, 118–119
Warner Bros. opera short films
advertising/marketing of, 56
baritones in, 83
castrato and, 16, 71–78, 80, 102
cinematography of, 47, 68
compositions for, 22, 60, 66
duets/trios, 80–81